Transference Neurosis
and
Transference Psychosis

Transference Neurosis
and
Transference Psychosis

Toward Basic Unity

Margaret I. Little
MRCS, LRCP, MRCPsych

NEW YORK • JASON ARONSON • LONDON

ISBN: 0-87668-421-5

Library of Congress Catalog Number 80-66925

Manufactured in the United States of America

In gratitude to all those who, whether living in the here and now or in memory, enabled me to become whatever I really am, and to write this book.

CLASSICAL PSYCHOANALYSIS AND ITS APPLICATIONS

A Series of Books
Edited by Robert Langs, M.D.

CONTENTS

FOREWORD

by Robert Langs, M.D.

The wish for lasting relevance must surely attend the efforts of virtually all psychoanalytic writers. Few in the field, however, have been able to produce a body of work that remains as relevant today as when it appeared ten, twenty, even thirty years ago. Still, there is a quality to the growth of psychoanalysis which leaves room for this, largely because of a certain conservatism in the average analyst or therapist and the slowness with which new ideas ae assimilated.

The work of Margaret Little has achieved this kind of lasting importance. The reader of her papers will come to appreciate the remarkable powers of clinical observation that this analytic writer brings to her work with patients. And yet beyond this gift lies an ability to arrive at strikingly unique and painfully perceptive conceptualizations which are both distinctive and eminently useful.

Such is the genius of this clinician that her earlier papers on countertransference and on borderline and psychotic patients remain filled with insights still awaiting the recognition they deserve. Margaret Little's writings, the earliest written some thirty years ago, are certain to provide the reader fresh understanding, both of himself and of his therapeutic technique.

The pioneering qualities of Margaret Little's work is evident from the table of contents of this volume. At a time when analysts were, as she herself states, phobic about countertransference, Little was able to probe this aspect of the therapeutic interaction with a creative attitude still rarely found in analytic writers. A sense of the deep and unconscious interplay between patient and analyst, and of the patient's sensitivity and perceptiveness regarding the analyst's countertransferences, led her to formulations that are remarkable even today. Her clinical acumen may perhaps best be represented by her discovery that at times, unconsciously and yet very accurately, the patient will offer the erring analyst interpretations that can help him correct the situation. Her realization that as the analyst is a living mirror for his patient, so the patient is a living mirror for his analyst, has helped open the way to many recent researches into the therapeutic interaction. Her papers on this subject provide not only a program for present-day research, but a guide to modern therapeutic and analytic practice.

As for her other main area of interest—the paranoid, borderline, psychotic patient—at a time when psychoanalysis was for the most part restricting its efforts to the so-called neurotic patient, Little was boldly engaged in the psychoanalysis of these more severely disordered patients. Mindful of the dangers and difficulties such work holds for both patient and analyst, she nevertheless forged ahead with firm determination to develop effective techniques and an essential understanding as to how best to engaged these patients in an insightful analytic experience.

Margaret Little made experiments, discarded those which failed her, and wrote of her efforts. She debated such issues as physical contact with these patients, and the means by which an analyst can work usefully with the psychotic part of their personalities. She explored issues of basic unity and symbiosis, and carefully detailed the type of difficult transference responses seen with these patients. In writing of these subjects, she is candid, full of ideas, and deeply human.

It is consistent, then, that Margaret Little has chosen to complete this volume with poems and commentaries which reflect her personal experiences as both an individual and a psychoanalyst; it is in her nature to do the unusual that all may learn and grow. It gives me personally a special sense of satisfaction to have been in some small way helpful in bringing the work of this warm, delightful, and gifted psychoanalyst to a broader audience. Most readers are likely to feel that they have met and experienced a very special person, as I have, having been privileged to meet her and to engage her in dialogue. Psychoanalysis needs more writers of this kind, writers who will put down ideas today that will still be fresh and alive in the twenty-first century.

INTRODUCTION

by Alfred Flarsheim, M.D.

Advances in psychoanalytic psychotherapy have made us aware of the importance of the earliest individual developmental steps to later character formation, both healthy and pathological, and of the deep roots of certain clinical syndromes. Consequently, deep treatment, often longer than was earlier thought necessary, is called for if really profound changes are to be brought about. The work of Dr. Margaret Little is in the forefront of these advances.

Dr. Little covers a broad range of subject matter in her writings, with special attention to two areas. Her writings show us an unusual depth of perception and understanding, and this may be one of the reasons for my finding that however often I read one of her papers, I always learn something new each time. The areas to which I refer are, of course, those of "basic unity" and "delusional transference and countertransference." The concept of "basic unity" provides a coherence to Dr. Little's creative contribution. It is her study of the effects of the underlying most primitive preambivalent, preobject relationship, predifferentiation, "totally homogeneous" stage that is unique, and is most valuable in Dr. Little's contribution to all the areas she has studied.

At the stage of development characterized by what Dr. Little calls "basic unity," there is complete homogeneity of psychic structure. This is the same stage that Freud referred to as the stage of autoerotism, and it precedes the development of narcissism.

In one of Freud's last major works, "An Outline of Psychoanalysis," he stressed the preeminent importance of early experience for later development. The earlier an environmental factor acts upon the developing individual, the more profound will be its effect on subsequent development.

Goetz (1975) tells us that already in 1904 Freud was familiar with a primitive state that "transcends all contradictions," and in many of his papers he considered earliest development (Freud 1914, 1926, 1931, 1939). On the other hand, in much of his work, Freud "took early infant care for granted, but created an environment that could provide for infantile needs in the analytic setting, without needing to make them explicit" (Winnicott 1958, pp. 284–285). Klein (1932, 1945) studied primitive mental mechanisms but attributed ego boundaries with self-object differentiation to earliest infancy. Winnicott introduced the systematic study of a stage before self-object differentiation and before psychosomatic integration. Dr. Little has consistently and systematically investigated the adult derivatives of the earliest developmental stage before such terms as symbiosis are appropriate, and the significance of these derivatives for psychoanalytic treatment. Here she has gone very far in applying the principle of genetic or developmental continuity to psychoanalytic formulations about the origins of mental health and mental illness. Her paper "On Basic Unity" (1960) expresses ideas central to all her work which are developed in various directions in other papers. In her earliest papers (e.g. 1945), Dr. Little's formulations and interpretations are classical and oedipal, but gradually in later papers we see her reaching deeper levels. In 1951 ("Countertransference and the Patient's Response to It") the basic unity idea is anticipated when Dr. Little points out that there are no clear boundaries between ego, id, and superego in the transference regression and that the emotional reactions of the analyst and the analysand, the transference and the countertransference, are inseparable. In 1957 she stresses the equation between objects which precedes a symbolic relationship between them and results in a delusional transference.

The way in which Dr. Little's orientation derives from the depths of her personality is illustrated by a revealing passage in her paper "'R'—the Analyst's Total Response to His Patient's Needs" (1957). She says that before she began her formal psychoanalytic training, she had been aware of the need for flexibility of technique and for adapting it to the varying needs of the individual patient. Then during her formal training she "tried to discard what I already had in favor of a more classical or less unorthodox technique, and (therefore) failed with a number of patients whom I still feel I would and should have been able to treat successfully." Then as she gradually regained her own individuality, she became increasingly able to respect and adapt to her patients.

In the same paper (1957) Dr. Little points out that transference interpretations were not useful in the early part of the treatment because the woman patient absolutely equated the analyst with her own archaic parental imagos. Countertransference interpretations consisting of the analyst's speaking of her own feelings toward her were equally ineffective. This all began to change when Dr. Little allowed herself to express her own immediate feeling reactions to the woman's behavior. This freedom led to the patient becoming aware of the differentiation between her feelings and the analyst's, and thus of her own separate identity. By 1958 the concept of basic unity was virtually complete ("On Delusional Transference [Transference Psychosis]") and then in 1960, the term *basic unity* was the title of her famous paper on this subject.

Dr. Little says (for example in her paper on self-analysis) that if we really are to understand our patient's deepest anxieties, we must accept the reality of our own corresponding anxieties and we must accept repeated experiences of breakdown and reintegration rather than expecting never to experience breakdown. Such experiences are often opportunities for increased personal capacity to deal with inner and outer reality.

I have attended psychoanalytic meetings at which discussants have seemed to be frightened by Dr. Little's freedom in sharing with the audience her awareness of her own emotional functioning, including not only her secondary-process constructs but also primary-process experiences. Certainly the experiencing of depressed moods must have contributed to her motivation to such relentless pursuit of understanding of herself, and of her patients. Further, as her poems illustrate, Dr. Little has what Dr. Winnicott called the *capacity* to bear and to work through depression, along with a very unusual capacity to include and reveal her own inner personal experiences, and to harness these in the service of the analysis of those patients fortunate enough to be under her care. As well as patients, of course, many students and colleagues have benefited from her teaching and example. She is very generous in her acknowledgment of her indebtedness to the writings of others, but we must not let this obscure our perception of her originality and creativity. This book will make Dr. Little's invaluable contributions available to a wider public than has been able to benefit from them in the past.

PREFACE

This is not a tidy book; it is not for those who like to have papers grouped neatly according to topic, and it is not a "text-book".

It is, in fact, a record of the development of my psychoanalytic work, of my ideas, and of my technique, particularly in dealing with psychotic anxiety, whether in "borderline psychotic" patients, or in "psychoneurotics." The emphasis is on the theme of development.

Such development is apt to be untidy; one has only to remember the look of a fledgling chicken or the antics of adolescence to know this.

It has led to the inclusion of some more personal elements than are usually thought suitable for a serious book concerned with psychoanalysis. But they are relevant, for they throw light on my concomitant personal development from being a "false self," through quite a serious mental illness, to at least a relative degree of "mental health," "maturity," and "integration." It is on this experience that any real understanding that I have of the anxieties and difficulties of others is founded.

It represents something of my own "total response" to life.

ACKNOWLEDGMENTS

Permission to quote copyright material is gratefully acknowledged to the following:

The editor of the *International Journal of Psycho-Analysis* for my papers "Counter-Transference and the Patient's Response to It," "'R'—The Analyst's Total Response to His Patient's Needs," "On Delusional Transference (Transference Psychosis)," "On Basic Unity: (Primary Total Undifferentiatedness)," and "Transference in Border-line States."

The editor of the *British Journal of Medical Psychology* for my contribution to a symposium on countertransference.

The editor of *Tipta Yenilikler,* Istanbul, for "Who Is an Alcoholic?"

Jason Aronson Inc., New York, for clinical material appearing in chapter 15 of *Tactics and Techniques in Psychoanalytic Therapy,* written with Dr. Alfred Flarsheim and there entitled "Early Mothering Care and Borderline Psychotic States"; "The Journey from Sickness to Health: Illness, Convalescence and Recovery," from the Festschrift in Honor of Dr. Paula Heimann; and "Notes on Ibsen's Peer Gynt," from the *International Journal of Psychoanalytic Psychotherapy.*

Penguin Books Ltd., Harmondsworth, Middlesex, for the passage from August Strindberg: Samlade Skrifter vol. 22, ed. J. Landquist, 1914, translated by James McFarlane, in Henrik Ibsen, ed. James McFarlane, Penguin Critical Anthologies, p. 109, lines 6–16.

Mr. Norman Ginsbury, and his agents, International Copyright Bureau Ltd., London, and Messrs. Hammond, Hammond, and Co. Ltd. London, for sundry words and phrases from his translation of Ibsen's *Peer Gynt*.

I am deeply indebted to all those authors to whose works I have referred, to the many others whose ideas have lodged with me unconsciously and stimulated mine, and to colleagues and friends who have made helpful and valuable suggestions.

Unfortunately I am an inveterate snippeter and have not been able to trace the exact source in every case. I apologize sincerely for all my omissions and inaccuracies and hope they may be forgiven!

To all those who have helped me in many other ways, I give my grateful thanks, especially to the late Drs. C. V. Ramana and Alfred Flarsheim, who have encouraged me and have read, checked, and copied papers for me; to my editor, Dr. Robert Langs, and to my publisher, Dr. Jason Aronson. Also to those who have patiently typed from my atrocious handwriting and dealt with my manifold changes and corrections: Mrs. Mary Walford, Mrs. Pamela Redwood, and, in particular, Mrs. Joyce Coles.

PART I

TRANSFERENCE NEUROSIS AND TRANSFERENCE PSYCHOSIS

1

THE WANDERER:
NOTES ON A PARANOID PATIENT

This chapter is an account of a patient who came complaining of severe depression. Although depression was her presenting symptom, a strong paranoid element was soon revealed which made me doubtful for some time as to the possibility of carrying out analysis with her. There was also a somatic element of considerable interest, but I do not understand this well enough to be able to discuss it at all fully in relation to the psychopathology.

These are the main points of interest, but it may be that I also chose this patient as my subject because it is possible to see in high relief in such a person the significance of certain tendencies and any modifications which are made.

GENERAL PICTURE OF THE ANALYSIS

Miss Theresa Cutter was recommended to me by a mutual friend, in the autumn of 1941. She was a tall, gaunt, bony woman, with dark hair, rather fierce blue eyes, and a very deep voice. She had previously had some treatment over a period of about eighteen months from a man who was analytically inclined and had considerable knowledge of analysis, but was not actually a psychoanalyst, and she would have gone to him again when she felt the need of further help but he was not available.

She traveled up twice a week from the country to see me until the following summer (1942), when she broke off the treatment. She came again in January 1943 and again broke off in the summer, and it was not until I saw her again a few times in January 1944, after her mother's death, that I decided that analysis was really possible. We started again in October 1944, four times a week, and continued until March 1948, with two more breaks. I will return later to the details of these.

During the early sessions a sadomasochistic element was very much in evidence. If she had had her way, every session would have been forced to take on the appearance of a rape. If I asked a question, or even by silence showed that I expected her to talk, I was attacking her violently; any interpretation was an insult, while the greatest cruelty was inflicted on her by my sitting there while she cried, which she did throughout most of every hour at the beginning.

The repetition compulsion shows markedly in her acting out, in the interruptions in the analysis, and in her suicidal impulses.

Two subjects appeared in the material as almost completely unapproachable, love and money; and these together with the themes of "visitors" or "lodgers," and "knowing" or "telling" provided the greater part of the pattern, recurring and interweaving.

Some modifications of technique were unavoidable from the beginning. I did not press her to use the couch. Her former therapist had insisted on it; this had intensified her anxiety to such a pitch that she became quite unable to talk, and the incessant crying was her self-defense, as I realized only later.

Our having a mutual friend tended to increase the "social" relationship and made some difficulty at first, until she understood that she could safely speak to me of the friend, Philippa, and her family. This also gave her an excuse for expecting from me things that she would not have expected perhaps from another analyst. For instance she brought me some honey, and finding it accepted she brought more, this time with the obvious idea that I would buy it, which I did; to her it was a gift for which I gave something in return, rather than a sale and purchase.

She wanted me to do things for her. Would I buy her some elastic that she needed for her work? She had seen some in a shop near me and couldn't get it at home. Would I treat her physically? would I give a prescription for sleeping tablets? and finally, on her coming back to London after the first break in the analysis, arriving late and in a thick fog, could she come to me for the night? When I said "Yes, if you can't get in anywhere else," she decided never to ask me for anything again.

HISTORY

Miss Cutter was forty-five when she first came to me. She was the middle one of a large family which had remained closely united, with a strong family tradition: "All the Cutters do this," or "No Cutter would ever behave like that." The name Cutter (a pseudonym, related to her real name) was important. It related to her father's work in the clothing trade, to her own work, and her marked interest in clothes. She expressed great resentment at the "familiarity" if anyone addressed her by her first name or any nickname or abbreviation. I never did.

The sons had all stayed at home with their mother until they married. Theresa had broken away as a result of her first "analysis" (incidentally thereby ending it); two of her sisters were still living at home—Daisy, four years older, and Sally, four years younger than she. Theresa was not on good terms with her mother and seldom went home; when she did go, her visits were difficult and aroused a lot of anxiety. The details of the rest of the family were obscure, and it was months before I even knew how many of them there were; one brother's name I only heard for the first time after three years, and one sister's name was never known to me. I gathered eventually that her father lived until she was grown up and that she nursed him in his last illness. The eldest brother died while serving in the 1914–1918 war, an older sister had died of tuberculosis, and another was epileptic and died when Theresa was fourteen. The next child to Theresa, two years younger, was a much wanted boy, Tom, and the youngest of all, Jim, was eight years younger.

Her mother was a very dominating and forceful woman with rigid standards of right and wrong, whose judgment or commands no one dared to question. She died after a long and progressive illness, probably a senile dementia. My patient's picture of her is of someone wholly unloving, utterly implacable, and terribly unjust. "I'll never believe, if I go on with analysis all my life, that she ever loved me." "She said I never got anything by my own merits, only by luck. It wasn't my fault, I was never given any opportunity or fitted for any work, and if I hadn't gone out and found myself a job I'd have been the family drudge still as I'd been for years; nothing but a drudge. It's not only *I* who know that; other people have said it too, that she treated me differently from all the others. A friend who was with me once when she was, and who didn't know the others, said to me 'Who's your sister Sally and why is she different from the rest? Is she the youngest? She's the favorite, isn't she?' And another time, 'Well, *you* aren't the favorite with your mother, are you?'" But then she went on to tell me how they had always teased Daisy by saying that her name wasn't really Cutter, but Brown, and later on there came memories of times when she, Theresa, had been chosen from among them all for some special treat, such as a visit to the zoo.

Her father was the family's skeleton in the cupboard; he drank heavily and got into debt, and there was constant anxiety lest he should lose his job and leave the family destitute. But his doings had to be hidden from the world; no one must know about him, whatever happened.

Theresa was breast-fed for a few days only; she developed rickets badly, with marked bossing of the forehead and spinal curvature, and she did not walk till she was three years old. Her mother blamed herself for not feeding her properly. She was supposed to be "stupid," and whereas all the others went to private secondary schools and two of her sisters went to college, she went to a state school, left it at fourteen, and was apprenticed as a dressmaker. She hated this—she had to work (she said) eleven and a half hours a day. Her sisters despised her, and Daisy "cut" her in the street one day when she was with some companions from the workroom, while Daisy was with her college friends.

She remembered "having convulsions" with rage in childhood and getting ill in order to get attention, but she was never able to let herself enjoy it and always got up again too soon, making it seem that her mother forced her to.

Her brothers teased her, broke her doll, and laughed at her when she cried. This particular episode came back to her again and again whenever she expressed aggression, whether verbally or by crying. "Dr. X. (her former therapist) seemed pleased that I had 'got the aggression out,' as if he were laughing at me," and I too came to stand for the mocking but beloved elder brother.

Her first hour with me brought this to her vividly. She had been that very day to visit the firm for which she had worked until she left home and had there had news of the only young man for whom she had felt an attraction which she believed was returned. Their friendship had ended when she was told that he had said something disparaging about her, and she had only discovered too late that this was not true. Now she heard that he had been killed in action, blown to pieces, and as she sat weeping for his loss she thought that I was laughing.

She was unhappy at her dressmaking and gave it up to do secretarial work and accountancy, for which she had a great aptitude. She had held very responsible posts, and was an exceptionally intelligent and efficient woman with a tremendous driving power. In fact she was so ultraefficient that she aroused anxiety and antagonism in other people; she could add up figures with lightning speed and accuracy and was merciless toward the inefficiency and essential dishonesty of those who did the same work as she and drew the same pay, but showed a lack of comprehension or enthusiasm. She had now a wide education, having compensated for the early deficiencies by attending evening classes in many subjects, including cookery, millinery, tailoring, and at least two foreign languages, apart from the specialized training in Company Law.

She gave up her career when she left home, and bought a shop in a country town, where she sold babies' woollies, knitting wools, embroidery materials, etc. It was in a moribund state when she took it on, but through her insistent driving, she not only revived it but by 1939 was running it as a real success. She took it in face of adverse advice from one friend who wanted to stop her from going and willfully accepting a piece of very unsound advice from another who wanted her out of the way. When clothes rationing came, she was not able to keep the shop going, but she kept up a connection and made and sold knitted garments.

PRELIMINARY PHASE AND PATTERN OF "WANDERING"

She installed two knitting machines in a workroom above her apartment. Each was bought during one of her flights from analysis.

At the time of my summer holiday, each time, she decided that she could not afford to go on with the treatment; it was too expensive to travel, and she could not bear to give up her apartment, so she must shut it up and take a job which would bring in enough to pay the rent. She would not consider letting it, although at that time apartments and houses in the country were at a premium, and she felt very sorry for those who couldn't get away from the bombing. She went far away from London each time: the first time she went as domestic help to a pregnant mother to look after an older child and stay till the new baby was born; the second, as secretary to a Cottage Hospital. Each time she was welcomed as the great helper, so kind, so capable, so willing; and each time she left after a few weeks, in a blaze of fury and recrimination, injured, insulted, underpaid, deceived, and ultimately retreated home, too ill to work again for many weeks.

But she did not go back there straight away; she went each time from these evil persecutors to her "good mother," Philippa, who would accept her help and help her in return. The second time Philippa herself was pregnant, and the same pattern was repeated there. I got letters from Theresa telling me how badly she was being treated: she was starved, not allowed enough rest, interfered with in every way; my letters to her were being withheld and even opened (I knew this to be *most* unlikely). Philippa was supposed to rest but wouldn't and then grumbled that she was tired; she was mean and improvident; everyone in the house except Theresa was allowed a priority milk ration, so there was plenty and it wasn't thought necessary to buy any for her, but as the others all drank the whole of theirs she got none. On top of this Philippa's husband, a doctor, would discuss his patients with his wife and her—the "domestic help"—laughing and joking about their "funny" ways.

Finally she left there, but fortunately this time the blaze was all on her side. She came to see me several times, and after a preliminary moan she began to tell me of the misdeeds of her neighbor downstairs.

This woman had been very friendly when Theresa had first gone to live there but was getting more and more troublesome. She always wanted to know everything and to comment on it, whether it had anything to do with her or not. She was everlastingly complaining of something, either the bathroom pipes in Theresa's rooms were leaking through her ceiling, or parcels for her were not being delivered, and she practically accused Theresa of taking them; she objected to the radio, to Theresa walking about her apartment in the evening, and to her hanging out washing in her own garden. But worse than all this was her interference with Theresa's visitors. Every time anyone came she opened her door to see who it was, she listened to their conversation, and if she got a chance she would ask them things about Theresa, or tell them something about her which might or might not be true. When Theresa had a friend to stay she complained to the friend that the dustbins were not being used properly; she insisted that there should be three dustbins, one for ashes, one for paper, and one for tins, and nothing else must go in them. One of the visitors put in a dead mouse and made great trouble, for she said "such things breed maggots."

I interpreted all this as relating, on an unconscious level, to Theresa's hostility to her mother, especially during her pregnancy with the next child, and over the cleanliness training, and I was able to get her to see how she had projected it on to Philippa.

It was here, when she could accept this, that I came to the conclusion that although she was very ill, this was not a true paranoia and analysis was possible. I told her that I was not willing to go on as we had done before, but that if she could not manage to come more often I would advise her to leave it, for the time being at least, as I felt it would be too disturbing for her otherwise. She decided to wait until the following autumn, and then to come four times a week.

ANALYSIS: FIRST PHASE
(BEGINNING IN OCTOBER 1944)

During that interval her mother died. Her account of the funeral sounds like a dream, but like a dream it contains fragments of childhood history. "There were crowds of people, and I was afraid of Daisy weeping and was concentrating all my will power on her to prevent it. I nearly fell into the grave, in fact I would have if Jim hadn't caught my arm. Then we went home, and it turned into a sort of party. I felt we were just like a puppet show. . . . I didn't want a great crowd and lots of big cars. They'd asked all sorts of people who hadn't seen mother for years and years, relations from all over the place. One of Mother's sisters asked Sally 'Who's that man over there? Is it my brother Alfred?' Sally said 'Yes, come and speak to him,' and to him she said 'Here's someone to talk to you.' He said 'Do I know you? I don't think I've met you before.' So absurd! But I just felt that Mother hadn't helped me, she hadn't wanted me, and it was too late afterward. I hadn't wanted those life insurance policies, and I didn't want to take them." Surely here is her visit to her mother and the new baby (the "puppet show"), just as she had felt it in childhood.

The others quarreled over what the mother had left, the house, what was to be done with her clothes, her furniture, etc. Her spectacles, for instance, were a source of difficulty (also, I suspect, her false teeth, for there was a dream in which four dentures were floating in a bowl of water). "Nobody wanted them, and they couldn't be sold. Why couldn't Tom just lose them or throw them away?" I asked "Why couldn't you?" and she laughed. Sally made a list of things "given to Sally," or "taken by Daisy." Theresa only wanted her father's pendulum clock, her eldest brother's gold watch, and a sandalwood box which had belonged to one of the sisters who had died.

Theresa was considered "not entitled" to anything because she had left home, although for years she had bought things for the house and had contributed to help support her mother. Sally wanted to keep the house for herself, though it was far too large, and insisted that the others should help her with the expense. She and Daisy quarreled for months as to whether they should live together or not, and the brothers advised first one and then the other.

During this phase of the analysis everything was seen "at one remove," so to speak, in terms of other people. Her neighbor downstairs appeared again as the tiresome, inquisitive, meddlesome child. She was once more talking to people about Theresa, wanting to know all her business, and waylaying and interfering with her visitors. She complained again about the leaking pipes, the noise, and the dustbins, etc.

Then Theresa invited her youngest brother, Jim, his wife, Susie, and their two-year-old adopted child, Michael, to stay, to get away from the rockets. She felt responsible for them, especially as Susie was now pregnant. They "used the flat as if it were their own," strewing things about, using up her stores of food, allowing the child to play with everything, to put coal into her armchairs, and generally smashing and messing. Her greatest treasures, a cut-glass rose bowl and a jam dish, were smashed almost deliberately, Susie's only comment being "I don't suppose it really matters." When Michael was about to smash something she warned him "You'll smash Auntie's jug, not that it matters." Theresa asked "Whose place is it, anyway? Anyone would think *I* was the lodger," and Susie retorted "So you are."

They would not tell Michael either that he was adopted or that there was another baby coming, and when he made it plain that he knew, by talking incessantly about babies and then reverting to being wet and dirty, Susie spoke of "Michael's baby, not Mummie's" and would not admit any responsibility for the coming child. "It's nothing to do with me" she said, "*I* didn't do it." Theresa's anxiety grew and grew, and it was with great relief that she saw them go after four months, for she had been afraid that Susie would insist on staying and having the baby there.

She felt that she must not cry while they were there; she could only allow it after they had gone, and only then could she go to the hairdresser and "spend three hours having my hair pulled about." She could not bring herself to use the room that they had had until it had been thoroughly cleaned out and all traces of them were gone.

She was aware throughout this time of her hostility to and fear of her father's genitals; she found difficulty in traveling except in "Ladies Only" compartments because she was aware of the men's genitals and of her wish to attack them, to stamp on them, and to destroy them. It became clear that she could accept Michael only because he was adopted and could not tolerate the new baby in the mother's womb because it was equated with the father's penis.

Just before they left Jim was taken ill with a duodenal ulcer and hemorrhage. Susie refused to believe it at first and could only think of her own fears and troubles, so Theresa's remark "He'll be all right if you feed him properly" (cf. her own early feeding) was not welcomed. He slowly recovered after their return home, and the baby arrived shortly after.

Then it became possible to bring some of the early situations more directly into relation with the transferences to Dr. X. and to me. Actual memories were still few and far between, and the representations of them meant that a good deal in the way of reconstruction was needed.

A month later (April) came my Easter holiday, which Theresa could only deal with by having a friend to stay "who badly needs a holiday."

SECOND PHASE: ILLNESS AND SEX

Now I come to the third interruption, and the situation in the transference which apparently precipitated it. One day at the end of May (1945) Theresa telephoned saying that she might not be able to keep her appointment next day. She had been to her doctor about her menorrhagia, and he wanted her to see a gynecologist, a woman. She wished her to go into hospital the following week for dilatation and curettage, and probably either radium treatment or hysterectomy. The menorrhagia was not news to me, but I had heard nothing about it for months; two years previously she had tried to get me to treat it. My reply then, "Why not see a general practitioner about it, and if necessary a gynecologist?" (for it certainly sounded severe) had been met with fury; she had been to several doctors already, one was drunk, another had been called up, there were two women who were "awful," and now I wouldn't take any notice. No further mention of it was made. Now suddenly, having hardly spoken of it since, she was "taking my advice."

She put off going into hospital for a fortnight on the grounds that a friend was coming to stay, and in that time we were able to make some progress in analyzing the whole situation. I remembered her saying once "I won't go and see a doctor about it because of the psychological side, and I won't talk to *you* about the physical side of it. When I've been to see a doctor I haven't always told everything, or else I've said things that weren't true." I thought it probable that she had painted an alarming picture of the symptom. Her general condition was obviously good, and I felt it unlikely that there was any serious organic trouble.

She was very anxious at the idea of an operation, and this was enhanced by fears of the anesthetic and of the preparation for it, particularly of being shaved and given castor oil or an enema. The unconscious significance of all this was that I was trying to get all she had out of her, and interpretation of it in relation to the transference relieved her worst anxiety.

The situation was that I had originally understood that she could afford to pay a full fee, and only later realized that she could not. From the previous October she was to come oftener than before, and as she was then just beginning slowly to rebuild her business I had suggested that she should pay me less, until she had had as many sessions at the lower fee as she had previously paid for at the higher rate. Then we would change again to a fee midway between the two, and by that means it would even out to the midway fee throughout the analysis. This should enable her to get a start with the business and make less of a strain while she was earning less. This second change was now due, and while she had felt guilty about accepting the reduction she was now regarding me as the persecutor who would tear out her inside. "When you reduced your fee I was determined not to accept it; I thought I'd pay the full amount, even if I had to sell my fur coat to do it."

Having interpreted this I asked her permission to write to the surgeon, and she finally consented after a further flare of anxiety at the thought of my telling the surgeon and the nurses that she was having psychological treatment and of their thinking her "mental." I interpreted this as relating to her early knowledge, hitherto denied, of her mother's genital (fur coat) menstruation, her parents' sexual intercourse, and her mother's pregnancies, together with the fear of discovery of her own infantile sexual activities of various kinds. I wrote to the surgeon explaining that she would benefit psychologically by not having hysterectomy or artificial induction of the menopause if it could be avoided. And so I became the person who *refused* her gifts, first money, and now her inside. And, even worse, I conspired with the surgeon to interfere with her sadomasochistic gratifications.

Dilatation and curettage were done and nothing abnormal found. She went to stay with a friend for convalescence and developed pleurodynia, which further delayed her return to analysis. From then until I went away in the following August the analysis was continually interrupted by excessive menstrual and intermenstrual loss which made further rest necessary. Bit by bit, however, I elicited the fact that the surgeon had advised her to "take things easy at those times," and what was her way of doing so. At the end of each day she was "whacked," or "dead beat." Compulsively she cleaned the flat and weeded the garden, tearing up armfuls of weeds; she made jam and bottled tomatoes. "I was very lazy over that; my kitchen has no chair in it, so I brought one in and sat down while I did it." She sat up in bed writing innumerable letters, but being tall and having a long back and scoliosis it was far more tiring than writing at her desk. She was surprised, hurt, and angry when I suggested that this was not the surgeon's idea of "taking things easy" and that she was in fact determined not to let the flooding stop.

Gradually the aggressive and hostile elements in this came home to her, with the self-punishment and the links with her suicidal tendencies. She had thought of not coming round from the anesthetic and afterward had felt an impulse to throw herself out the window in the hospital.

I have not yet mentioned her earlier illnesses. She had had appendicitis, and cystitis, both of which had necessitated operations. But besides these she had been knocked down by a car and sustained a badly fractured leg, which had given trouble ever since. This had happened on the day when she received a letter from her mother saying that as she had left home she need never return and never expect anything more from her. It was many months before she could admit to herself either that it was anything more than a coincidence that it should have happened on that day or that it represented castration and suicide.

Here is her account of one of the later times when she was nearly run over: "I nearly threw myself on the line today, and I nearly got run over at a pedestrian crossing yesterday. I see the traffic coming, and I know it's coming fast, but I can't look at it, so I don't know whether I'll get across or not, and I can't move any quicker." The element of provocation or invitation, which was clear in her approach to the gynecologist, is seen again here, and it is relevant that on each of these two days, on her way to me, she had seen her former therapist near the station. She then recognized that she had really invited Susie to smash the cut-glass dishes and that there were other acts with murderous or suicidal significance. Once she "managed to lose" a brooch which had belonged to her mother, a cameo, with a head on it similar to one of mine, and once during an analytic hour she almost sat on her glasses (without which she would have been practically helpless) and was furious when I intervened and rescued them. There was also a dream of smashing a gold watch, (perhaps her brother's).

The "lodger" theme continued to recur; she thought of taking in a man as permanent lodger when her brother and his family went home, but eventually decided against it. Then she thought of lodging with a friend in town during the winter and taking a secretarial post to avoid the difficulties and expense of traveling, but she could not bring herself to leave her home. She was as firmly fixed there as a winkle in its shell, but at the same time she was the eternal traveler, spending six hours on her journeys for analysis and "earning her living" in the time that was left.

After the summer holiday (an interruption of my making) she was very afraid of coming again. I had told her that I was changing most of the furniture in my consulting room, as what was there belonged to someone else. She was pleased at the disappearance of a large tallboy, which had a disconcerting way of juddering when any heavy traffic went by, and also of a large leather (man's) armchair in which she used to sit. But with the new arrangement she now sat facing the window, and this aroused great anxiety. She brought various reasons against going on with analysis, including traveling difficulties, expense, and the menorrhagia. Then she remembered that she had once more thought of taking a job which would have made it impossible, this time as secretary to a clinic. I asked whether she had bought a knitting machine again too, and she replied "No, I decided against it and went straight out and bought my season ticket," so this time she bought a machine which brought her to me.

"I'm afraid of coming, I don't like the room this way round so that I have to face the light. Today, when the train came out of the tunnel I found I was shaking" (like the tallboy). Earlier she had told me that she could never understand how a man could face a woman in the morning, "after doing *that* to her," and also of her fear of facing the window because of the impulse to throw herself out. A vague picture came to her of being in her cot, facing the window, and of her mother being in the bed beside her, with a new baby; her father was standing at the end of the bed. Sometimes she had seen him with his genitals exposed; sometimes she had seen her mother at the dressing table by the window. In dreams she had seen her mother pregnant, or with a penis, and in one dream her mother stood by the window and there were three babies in the cot (the three younger children), and she, Theresa, was going to Siberia. She had also had nightmares in which men or dogs broke in through the window.

The theme of hostile curiosity and breaking in was developed further. She told me of an "outbreak" of burglary in the town where she lived; police messages were being thrown on the screen in the cinema ("Did you lock your door when you came out?") and there were placards in the streets, "THE POLICE WANT YOU to help them" etc. She had been growing a vegetable marrow, and the only fruit on the plant was on a branch which grew through the fence into her neighbor's garden. Accidentally the neighbor cut the branch, and to make up for it she promised a marrow from *her* plant, but mysteriously that marrow withered and died. She went with two friends to see the play "Dangerous Corner," and when a few minutes before the end the stage was darkened one friend quickly went out, (as they both usually did when the curtain fell, so as to avoid the rush) then a shot was fired, and Theresa "found herself" outside. Only the third member of the party stayed till the end.

In the next day's session she was concerned with clothes and their significance for her: tailored suits, well-cut clothes, "dressy" ones with a lot of fullness or unstitched pleats, and then a dress which she had once made for her mother. She had altered it repeatedly but always left the sleeves the same, and finally had converted it into a robe. Long sleeves had already been seen to represent the male genital, and she herself rarely wore short sleeved frocks or blouses. One night she left the back door open, and when she found it she was anxious lest her stock of wool had been stolen. Her neighbor had been fussing about the dustbins again—"She wished I'd tell my visitors they mustn't put fish heads in, they breed maggots." I reminded her of the significance of "visitors" as a euphemism for menstruation and of her other fear about her wool (pubic hair) that the moths would eat it, and pointed out her invitation to the burglars, adding that "don't lose your wool" or "keep your hair on" means "don't lose your temper," and that I had said she should not be in a hurry when she had again spoken of selling her fur coat (her virginity; St. Theresa was a virgin) a few days previously.

An unexplained burst of fury and anxiety followed this. "You make me feel an awful person when you interpret everything sexually like that, only fit for Dartmoor. Oversexed, as if I thought of nothing else." My comment that the people who went to Dartmoor were mostly burglars or murderers, not sexual offenders, didn't help, but after she had gone I found that a pane of glass in the window of my room was cracked. Next day she was acutely agitated and unable to talk: she wandered around the room, growling, crying, and hiding her eyes. She finally drifted round behind me toward the window, at which point I was able to interpret that she had seen the cracked pane and thought of it as "pain", and she settled down again, to my relief, as I remembered her suicidal thoughts in the hospital.

MONEY AND LOVE

The following week she talked, almost for the first time, about her father. He had always refused to pay bills, especially doctors' bills and the rent. After years of difficulty over this the sons and daughters clubbed together and bought the house without telling him, when the existing lease ran out. They then rented it to him anonymously through a solicitor and insisted on the rent being paid monthly. They were always afraid he would find out; he was puzzled at the landlord's willingness to do repairs etc. One sister felt guilty about deceiving him, and the others had to make her keep quiet. This was all told as a joke, and the affect came only a week later. "You made me remember all the miseries of father's money dealings; I've tried hard not to let you know about it, but to tell you what I had to without any feelings. And then you seemed so pleased at *making* me get it out." (Like Dr. X., and probably her mother using laxatives, or taking things out of her mouth). "Having to hear father's anger when he was drunk, and not letting him know when bills came. I used to dread the postman coming and told mother to hide the bills from him. Father used to drink both consistently and in bouts." (She was surprised and suspicious at my knowing this, having forgotten that she had told me of his drinking.) His first remark every morning was "It's ten to eight," whatever the time really was, and this was the first thing that the youngest child learned to say. He ate his breakfast standing up or walking about the house, and he always had either whiskey or brandy in his tea. He came home at ten to seven in the evenings, usually drunk, and on Saturdays and Sundays and all holidays he was drunk the whole time and very quarrelsome. He was often unfit to go to work after a holiday, and one of the sons had to go to his firm and make excuses for him. One day an anonymous postcard came for him, "Whiskey interferes with business. Give up business."

Theresa never let me give her an account; she would add up the number of sessions at the end of the month, and ask whether I agreed. For a year after the operation she paid me nothing, asking if I would lend her the money. A few months later she reckoned up what was owing. At the end of the next month she found herself anxious about money again and thinking of selling the fur coat, but not to pay me—she needed to get her eyes and teeth attended to. She then realized the unconscious wish not to work and not to pay for things but to get them "for love"; this played a part in her not making much money by her work, as well as providing a grudge against her creditor.

The fur coat was an important thing. During the second summer that she was with me she told me one day that she was going to fetch it from the furrier's where it was being remodeled and that he had offered her £100 for it. She had paid £25 or £30 for it years ago. Later, about the time when she told me of the difficulty with her father over doctors' bills, she told me that she had been to see a doctor while she had been staying with Philippa, and on getting his account which she thought heavy, she asked Philippa what her husband charged his patients. Philippa said "What did you expect if you went wearing *that* coat?" and she was enraged. Philippa had two fur coats, so how could she envy Theresa hers? I reminded her that Philippa had not only two fur coats, but two babies, and yet was having a third. It was she who was envying Philippa the babies as she had envied her mother hers, and her "fur coat," i.e. her pubic hair. The coming of a new baby meant a revaluation, in which she felt her own value and that of her gifts to have gone down, while her mother's had increased. She was projecting onto Philippa the hostility that this aroused, as she had formerly projected it onto her mother.

About this time she took to locking her bedroom door, and then when I reminded her of her fears for her wool and its significance, she remembered that her father was not the only one who had made money a difficulty. Her mother had used the threat that her father's income might come to an end at any time, because of his drinking, as a means of keeping the children who were earning with her. When the eldest son was sent by his firm to Germany, she tried to stop him from going by that threat. When he insisted on going, saying that if he refused to go he would lose all chance of promotion, she said that she could not afford to spend anything on any training for Theresa. He said he would provide for it, whereupon Theresa vowed that she would not accept it from him—just as later she did not want to accept anything from me.

Throughout the year following the dilatation and curettage the menorrhagia continued as severely as ever. She had injections of various kinds, rested up at times, and finally was readmitted to hospital for radium treatment.

But before this happened she made one of the most important steps forward. She rediscovered her "good" mother in a woman standing behind her in a queue for fish, who supplied her with a piece of newspaper when, if she had had none, she would not have been served. The working over of this released a great deal of affect and brought great relief, so that when the operation came it had already lost much of the terror she had felt a year before.

Three months' rest once more followed this operation, and she resumed her analysis again in the autumn. Meanwhile I had told her that I was unwilling for her to increase the amount of her debt to me—not that the analysis was costing her nothing, but that the railway company was benefitting, and not I. I advised her that if she couldn't afford to pay as she went along to leave analysis for a while, until she was earning more. In the end we compromised by agreeing to three sessions a week and leaving the existing debt as it stood. Nevertheless, she paid me some of it straight away.

THIRD PHASE: FIRE AND LOVE

In the next six months there were continual interruptions first from inside, by minor illnesses such as tonsillitis, and then from outside, by the severe weather which made traveling impossible. But in spite of all this the analysis went on, and some most important material came, first in relation to her fear of fire and second in talking more freely than before about her grandfather and her eldest brother, both of whom appeared as substitutes for the loved father in the oedipal situation.

She told me how a serious fire had once broken out at her firm's premises through the carelessness of an employee who threw a lighted match on the stairs and then told a lie in court about the time at which he had left work. Arson was suspected, and she knew that a senior member of the firm had previously worked for another business where there had been a fire and arson had been proved. Her evidence, which she managed to give without implicating anyone, saved both her employer's good name and his money, and he was very grateful. But she felt that this had been forgotten, and she expressed her anger at the ingratitude of people who would accept services given and then allow the giver to go away, without caring.

After this she remembered that she had seen a spent match lying on my staircase that day, and then went on to tell me how she had once jumped off her mother's lap, when she was about eighteen months old, straight into the fire (possibly an early attempt at suicide, but also getting mother's attention). Both her hands had been badly burnt and had to be covered with flour and tied up in paper bags. She "could not think of those paper bags without feeling almost a physical pain." She related all of this to the radium treatment, and to the hot flushes and sweats which followed the artificial menopause. She was waking up soaked in sweat night after night and had to move her chair back from the fire in my consulting room. Interpretation of this in terms of fantasies about her urine and her fear of loss of control resulted in a marked easing of bodily tension: she no longer needed to sit with her legs tightly crossed throughout the analytic sessions and could lie more comfortably in bed. Shortly after this she began to use the couch regularly, of her own accord.

More important still, she began to analyze her relationship to her mother. For a couple of weeks there was a strong resistance, for no apparent reason, shortly after my return from my Easter holiday. Remembering that a similar resistance had on a previous occasion proved to relate to an anniversary, I drew her attention to the fact that at the same time the previous year and the year before that she had had her operations and that her mother's death had come at this time of the year. A few weeks later she brought me some lilies-of-the-valley, and after an hour of tears and angry silence told me that it was her mother's birthday and that these were the flowers she had always given her on that day.

So at last she could begin to think of love and particularly to analyze her sexual feelings and ideas. Love had been something so dangerous that it must never be mentioned. "I remember when grandfather died I shut myself in the toolshed and cried and cried, and I thought 'Whoever I love dies,' but I knew I didn't love him. I hardly knew him. And I cried when I heard the news of mother's death, and I thought 'You didn't really love her, so why cry?' Now I feel she died before I'd had time to learn to love her, and I wish she hadn't. She refused my love and she treated me differently from all the others." But any evidence of anyone else's love for her had to be denied too, and any expressions of approval or praise repudiated. The response to my suggestion of writing to the surgeon was a passionate outburst about her mother never having done anything for her, never having given her a proper education or training. It was only when I pointed out that what I was proposing to do *was* something for her, and that I had no intention of doing it unless she herself wished it, that she could begin to see how *she* had refused love. My own understanding of this was that love, to her, meant the kiss of Judas, the "familiar friend" who by it singled out from among the rest the one whom he had conspired to betray to torture and death, and her father's "It's ten to eight" was the crowing of the cock.

But love was there in spite of her. It was implicit in the work she had chosen, for she found real enjoyment in it for its own sake, apart from the satisfaction in supplying other people's needs. Her mother disapproved of her taking the shop for this reason as well as that it was a "trade" and not a "profession." Pleasure in any form was not allowed: reading or embroidery were condemned as "useless" and to sit doing either was "laziness." This "utility" view found its echo in Theresa. She remembered in childhood the intense satisfaction of sitting beside her little brother when he was ill and moistening his lips with grapes, but she condemned ferociously the people who came to her when war broke out to buy white wool for hospital stockings. "They said they liked the color better than khaki, when I said why not make scarves or cuffs?—things that would keep people warm for people who would live and fight."

Closely linked with this, I think, was another factor in her not being able to make much money by her work and presumably not wanting to allow me to either. She spoke once of her knitting as "having such a healing effect," and her guilt would not allow her to get either pleasure or gain from other people's needs or misfortunes, which is what doctors and other professional people did (and I think the idea of prostitution links with this, although she had not explicitly said so). Doctors in her view were all alike—they laughed at other people's miseries, like her brother. I am sure there was a repressed memory of sex play of a sadomasochistic kind with this brother, probably followed by a loss of excretory control, the "getting it out" which fused with the hostile wishes toward her mother and the fantasy of the baby in the womb possessing and controling her.

So I had to become "a devil, who keeps you at it" and the person who knew things about her "in an uncanny way." Sex (all knowledge of which had been shut out until, at the age of twenty-eight, she was examined by a doctor and suddenly realized she understood) could have nothing to do with love. "How could a man face the world after doing that to a woman?" She was the eternal wanderer, driven from within by the evil, all-powerful penis-child, which she had torn from inside her mother and taken into herself, yet always returning, like a homing pigeon, to prove to herself that the mother was still there, and the child (herself) still safe within the womb.

Every analytic hour she watched the clock; she dreamed of a stable (sic) clock that had stopped at ten to twelve. This Cinderella dreaded the stroke of twelve, when the glass coach would become a pumpkin again, the fairy prince would vanish, and she would find herself alone, through her own fault, like the orphan child her sister Daisy was always singing about, "out in the bitter cold and sleet," that is her wet bed.

MODIFICATIONS

So these themes were worked over and over as this stormy childhood was restaged and relived in the analysis. But as it went on modifications could be seen more and more plainly.

Subjectively Miss Cutter herself spoke of feeling better and less depressed. She slept better, and though she was more aware of the compulsive tendencies, she was less subject to them than she had been and more able to find enjoyment in the things she was doing. Her relationships with other people were easier, as she became more tolerant and less "bossy." "I don't feel the same responsibility for other people; I only *think* about helping them now instead of having to do so, and I used to try and *make* them do things, but now I can let them alone."

Objectively from the point of view of a nonanalytical psychiatric observer, she improved both physically and mentally. She gained weight and became less angular, her appearance improved, and her expression became both pleasanter and less anxious. One could not say that she was more feminine, but she was markedly less aggressive, and her reactions generally not so sudden or so violent. Her color schemes, which used to reflect the internal conflict, were easier on the eye.

Analytically, although she still had far to go, there were signs of ego development, of which perhaps the most important was the increased reality sense which allowed of the undoing of the projections. She began to let herself see me as a real person, for she knitted a wool suit as a gift for me which at first she made much too small, judging some measurements by her own and others by her mother's, only afterward asking for mine and being surprised to find them so different from what she had expected. There was a marked degree of libidinization, especially in later months. No doubt for a time she "bought" a freedom from anxiety by owing me money, but that she was willing to do this in itself showed an easing up of the omnipotent and sadistic superego, even though I came to play the part of that superego to a large extent. Her omnipotence was now of a more benevolent kind.

It was too early yet to expect to see much real alteration in her sexuality or to find sublimations free from ambivalence, but the sublimations were there and were well founded, both in her creative and artistic work and in the use of her great practical ability. Wandering was still her main form of acting out and line of defense, but where it was repeated in relation to a recurring anxiety situation (for example in her reactions to my holidays), it was less marked, and there were variations in the details. The tendency was more and more toward recovering childhood memories and bringing things into the analysis instead of repeating or dramatizing them.

CONCLUSION

It was too early yet to draw conclusions about this patient, but there are many questions and speculations which are worth considering.

The psychopathology was not clear to me, and I should be glad to understand why she was suffering from this type of illness rather than, for instance, either obsessional neurosis or schizophrenia. I am sure that constitutional factors played a large part in determining her personality; she was of markedly "schizothymic" and also masculine physique, and there was evidence of considerable abnormality in other members of the family, including the epileptic sister, but no definite history of manic-depressive illness. The parents acted *both* as genetic and environmental factors, which would probably tend to bring about a mixed type of illness in any case.

The predominating traumatic situation was surely her mother's guilt and excessive devotion to her in her babyhood and later rejection, culminating in pregnancy and the birth of the younger brother, when she was two years old, which coincided with the cleanliness training. At that time she introjected the imago of her "abnormal" mother, abnormal *to her,* that is, by reason of the increased size of her body. She also introjected the father, whose alcoholism threatened to destroy the home. Her mother's pregnancy was a normal happening, (in the sense that it was something that might happen in any family) and of itself would not be sufficient to produce such an illness in the older child. But her reactions to it and her difficulties were increased by the very real psychic abnormalities of the parents.

Where this is the case, reality testing cannot have the same corrective value as it has in other circumstances, and a further stage of reality testing must be necessary when the child comes into contact with a wider circle than that of her own family, to provide a kind of "cross-checking." In analysis may not this be the meaning of Ferenczi's "comforting preliminary treatment" (1930) and A. Freud's "preparation for analysis" (1947)?

I would be inclined to believe that such a "cross-checking" of reality is far commoner in the early phases of analysis than we are accustomed to recognize in adults and that it is closely related to the question of "acceptance" by the analyst, of which patients also need to be assured, as was pointed out by Ferenczi (1929). In this case the testing of that "acceptance" seems to be in the things she asked me to do for her, my refusal not necessarily being understood as nonacceptance for, although I did not always do them, neither did I get angry nor reject her for making the demands. I do not mean that this need for "acceptance" was the only reason for her making them. She wished, too, to keep me by showing her need of me, as she had wished to keep her mother by being helpless and so to prevent the birth of another child. This I saw clearly when in the midst of tears one day about Susie's pregnancy she said "Get me my handkerchief from my bag, will you?" And alongside the wish for these gratifications was great fear of getting them, the same fear that made her resolve never to ask me anything again when I replied "Yes, if you can't get in anywhere else" when she asked me to take her in for the night.

From the point of view of prognosis I think one of the most illuminating and important things was her allowing me to interfere in the matter of the operation. Had she not allowed it, in all probability either hysterectomy or induction of the menopause would have been done immediately. It would be the obvious thing, from the gynecological point of view, in the case of a woman of fifty with severe menorrhagia, even in the absence of definite findings by dilatation and curettage. It would have relieved her anxiety at the time, and she might well have broken off the analysis altogether. She would then have been liable to break down completely some years hence, by which time all link with the operation might have been lost. In these circumstances I take it that the paranoid tendencies, rather than the suicidal ones, would be most likely to predominate. (I am speaking, of course, of the possible results of an operation for which *in reality* there was no urgent necessity, and it is the delay, giving time for further analysis, that I regard as so valuable.)

The "wanderer" fantasy which Theresa acted out repeatedly is familiar to us all in many versions. Cain, the Wandering Jew, Dick Whittington, Peer Gynt, the "Cat Who Walked by Himself" are only a few of them. In some versions of the story the wandering begins either when a stranger comes to visit or someone dies. In her its focus seems to be in the mother's pregnancy with a younger child, with all that this meant in terms of loss, and the whole tangle of emotions involved.

Theresa, thinking of herself as the one "chosen" by her mother to be loved best, felt betrayed, devalued, and driven out. She sought to keep her mother's body for herself, to prevent intercourse between the parents and the resulting pregnancy, to "interfere" with her mother's "visitors" and to drive them out by violence. But she also wished to have "visitors" herself and yet feared to, because of her hostile impulses, and so by identification with both her mother and the baby and her father's penis, she possessed her mother's body, and was in it, and was pregnant, and so liable herself to be attacked both by her mother and her father. Through guilt and by a complicated series of projections and introjections, it was herself that she "got out" (born), returning only when the guilt and anxiety were either relieved or increased by the wandering, and the impulse to return became sufficiently strong. She was dramatizing a childhood happening, perhaps an actual "wandering"—an actual "getting out," of her own feces or urine, the memory of which was repressed, repeating it in later day's terms rather than undo the repression and reexperience the emotions in remembering it.

We are accustomed to think of truanting in children as meaning a search for the lost "good" mother, but I would say that the loss in these cases is often the loss by the devaluation through the mother's pregnancy. I had another patient who remembered wandering through the streets all day when her mother left home after a quarrel with her father; she too had a younger sister born when she was two and a half and in her case also this was the predominating trauma.

The wandering is at one and the same time a defense against both the hostile and the libidinal impulses and an expression of them. One purpose of it is to protect both the mother and the father's genitals (equated to the unborn child) from her own aggression. I would illustrate this by a story of a little girl talking to her mother who was pregnant. She was telling her of the naughtiness of her doll, which she had left upstairs. The mother said "I wonder you don't punish her. Why don't you smack her?" The child looked up at the ceiling and said "But I can't reach." For safety, the mother's "naughtiness" had been transferred to the doll and left upstairs, so that the child should not want to smack the mother whom she could reach and who could reach and smack her, in retaliation.

Theresa also wandered "to seek her fortune," which in the fairy tale is always marrying and living happily ever after, that is, reunion with mother by identification with father's penis and having father's penis by identification with it. In a magical way she brought father and mother together in herself. By her wandering she deprived her mother of the penis-child and by returning restored it, and herself, to mother.

The fantasy includes a denial of all knowledge of sexuality (that is a denial of genitality) and an assertion that children are fecal and that she can make them alone. For three weeks when I was ill and not able to see her, she occupied herself in making, to sell for Christmas, tea cosies and lavender bags by the dozen, little ladies with china heads and muslin skirts; she was "so happy" doing it. In this way she denied the reality of her parents' intercourse, that her mother could make babies as she could not, and her own depression.

Here we see the fantasy in an individual, but I think we can see it also and get some understanding of it, in a much wider range, though it is beyond the scope of this paper to do more than glance at this.

I am interested in the "clannishness" of this family. I have come across patients belonging to such families who showed either strong reaction formations or paranoid tendencies, and I believe that one can see these as a family neurosis or even psychosis.

I am reminded of the Scottish clans and their blood ties and blood feuds. One of the incidents in Scottish history about which the emotion remains unaltered to this day is the massacre at Glencoe of the MacDonalds by their "visitors" the Campbells, in writing of which Seton Gordon speaks of the "appalling violation of the recognised laws of hospitality." At Dunvegan the visiting Mac-Donalds were murdered at a feast by their hosts, the MacLeods. Such mass murders are the very things against which the "laws of hospitality" were the reaction formation, and we see the thing in action both ways, for in the first instance it is the hosts who are killed, and in the second the visitors. The aggressors in either case are henceforth bound to one another not only by the blood-tie of birth, but by the blood they have conspired to shed, and all other men's hands are against them.

Here we see it in terms of a family whose members are tightly related. But rightly or wrongly, like the members of a clan or tribe, those of a race or nation are often thought of as being related by blood, however distantly; and so in pogroms, Nazism, and fanatical forms of Zionism we see the same two aspects of this fantasy that were evident in the history of the MacLeods and the Campbells.

The "crime against humanity," genocide, for which men have been condemned, was the attempted extermination of all who were not "of Aryan blood," especially Jews and gypsies. It is, in world terms, the equivalent of this little girl's wish to plot with her brothers and sisters to kill the stranger, the "crime against the family," that is, against the parents and the baby they were making.

The denial of genitality, the assertion that children are fecal, is only too clear to us in Belsen and the millions of "displaced persons" in the world today, but it is in relation to a revaluation that these large-scale actings out of this fantasy are happening. Mechanization, air travel, television, and finally atomic energy and space travel (the outcome of man's curiosity linked with *both* creative and destructive impulses) have brought about, or accompanied, a revaluation of men's work and a new cosmology, just as for Theresa her mother's pregnancy and the cleanliness training did, and we see the corresponding regression as a reaction to the blow to narcissism which this revaluation brings.

But the individual who will play a "lone hand," as Theresa did, seems to have accepted separation and the recognition of whole objects to some extent at least. The person who will only act as a member of a gang, or as one of a family or clan, is denying this and asserting that there is no separation and so carrying the regression a stage further, insisting that he himself can be only a part-object, i.e. part of the mother. Melanie Klein (1935) puts forward the view that on this recognition of whole objects depends the difference between depression and paranoia, and here I think is a clue to the understanding of Theresa's paranoid condition, which yet is depression, and not true paranoia, and hence its accessibility to analysis, however intermittent.

POSTSCRIPT

From October 1944 to December 1946 Theresa came for four sessions per week; in 1946 they were reduced to three per week, and again from January to March 1948 to one per week. From then until the end of 1954 she came about once a month.

In the spring of 1948 she had moved her home, and traveling was both more difficult and more expensive. Her savings were exhausted, and she could no longer afford even the fares, still less to pay me a fee. Her health had deteriorated; she was living in real poverty, in premises which were virtually uninhabitable, and she could now hardly earn anything at all.

Nevertheless, she kept the contact, not only by coming occasionally to see me but by frequent letters. She wrote literally hundreds, telling me of dreams, happenings in her life, her health, and her feelings, especially those of depression and discouragement and the old, unhappy feeling of being singled out and unwanted, and despair with thoughts of suicide. Many of her troubles and difficulties were objective, and not always provoked or invited by her, though some were.

I answered many of her letters, making comments and from time to time suggesting possible ways of meeting the difficulties, whether external or internal. I even occasionally gave some kind of interpretation or a reminder of something from our previous work that could link with what she was now telling me.

At the beginning of 1955 she became entitled to a small retirement pension from the State, which made it possible for her to afford the fare to come to me once a week, which she did until the end of October 1956, when we agreed to terminate.

I had looked on the monthly sessions as something of "maintenance doses." The later, weekly, sessions clearly became more. The changes which I described earlier went on slowly; no ground was lost, but she was still obviously ill, in need of help, asking for it, and paying to come, even though the payment was not to me.

These hours brought little in the way of fresh material at first, but the old themes were worked over again. Her old grumbles and complaints went on, only in fresh surroundings with new neighbors and contacts. But in those last two years very great changes came about when she came to see that her fear of her loving feelings was far greater than that of her hate ("Whoever I love dies") and that the real "persecutors" were within—being essentially her feelings and her memories.

One day she had been complaining, as usual, of being unloved—nobody cared about her, and all anyone wanted was to get things from her. They had taken just about everything she had ever had.

I said "You know very well that that simply isn't true. Why do you suppose that I go on seeing you every week and listening to your complaints and accusations without charging you anything? Can't you see that it is just because *I do* care? The trouble is that if somebody does care about you, it calls for you to care about them, in return, and that's what you are afraid of."

This brought the most agonized reaction. "No. No. NO!" she howled and turned away from me, hiding her face in the pillow and weeping furiously. Finally she acknowledged that she had known it, of course, but had simply not dared to admit it to herself—still less to me.

Then she could see that it was her love of me, and her need of my love and of the recognition of it that had brought her still, in spite of both the increasing difficulties and of her ambivalence, which she could at last acknowledge and accept. She could see, too, that insofar as she was herself responsible for incurring and putting up with those difficulties, they represented both the hate and the killing love which she had turned against herself.

This freed her to tackle the difficulties actively: she found she could move the authorities responsible for rehousing her and could get appropriate treatment for some of her physical ailments (cho-lecystitis, hypertension, hypothyroidism, and the old trouble in her back) by taking a different approach.

Soon after this she took a short-term job, working as part-time secretary-housekeeper companion to a very high-powered woman, rather masculine like herself, who was engaged in both local govern-ment and various important charitable activities (incidentally, a Highland Scot with strong clan affiliations). This relationship de-veloped into friendship—the first real one of any depth that I had ever known her to have, and it lasted until her friend's death, and after, in mourning. They had many ups and downs in the course of the years but Theresa was able to express appreciation of her friend's fair-mindedness, kindness, generosity, and pleasure in her company. Other new relationships followed, her previously fixed, jaundiced view of all other people gradually mellowed, and she found herself living in a hitherto unknown world that was in general friendly.

Her attitude to me altered out of all recognition. She openly expressed gratitude to me for help and support and wished that "other people could feel the same comfortable regard" for her that she felt for me.

Two years after our termination she wrote rejoicing that she was able at last to have a real home and to find happiness in it. She no longer needed to wander; she had found herself. In spite of continued poor health she undertook and enjoyed doing a lot of voluntary work. She enrolled as a member of the Women's Voluntary Services (for which she made her own uniform), helped in clubs for old people, organized outings for children, and became an assistant librarian in the local library. She also earned a little again, by dressmaking and knitting.

Her relations with her family did not alter much, though she found she could be reasonably friendly with two of her sisters-in-law and grateful to them for helping her when she was ill. With her brother Jim's adopted son, Michael, she had a good relationship, for she understood his feeling of being "outside" and unwanted.

The clannishness continued, and she found it intolerable that all her brothers and sisters would go on living close together, moving like a flock from place to place, near her, but without her. But even about this she could become almost philosophical. "I am annoyed with *myself* for allowing myself to be upset, but felt rather grim when

I discovered that the whole family had gathered for a party at Christmas without my knowledge or inclusion. I could wish my health were better, but I have much to be thankful for in the warmth and comfort of my home. All my friends like it, and it is very easy to run." Her Furies had become Kindly Ones, Eumenides, and had found a home at last.

She still came very occasionally until the end of 1958, and I saw her once in 1961 and once in 1962. She went on writing often up to 1965, chatty, friendly letters, now even with a certain wry humor about the "dears" and "bastards," "brave folk," and "moaners" among her clients and neighbors; "life begins at sixty" she said once. She wrote at Christmas each year until 1972, when, owing to illness and other difficulties, sadly I could not reply and so lost the contact.

I do not know whether she is still alive or not, but I hope she lives in what I have written. For me she is a living memory, very much a person, to whom I owe a lot, for she taught and gave me a very great deal.

2

COUNTERTRANSFERENCE AND THE PATIENT'S RESPONSE

I

I will begin with a story:

A patient whose mother had recently died was to give a radio talk on a subject in which he knew his analyst was interested. He gave him the script to read beforehand, and the analyst had the opportunity of hearing the broadcast. The patient felt very unwilling to give it just then, in view of his mother's death, but could not alter the arrangement. The day after the broadcast he arrived for his analysis in a state of anxiety and confusion.

The analyst (who was a very experienced man) interpreted the patient's distress as being due to a fear lest he, the analyst, should be jealous of what had clearly been a success and be wanting to deprive him of it and of its results. The interpretation was accepted, the distress cleared up quite quickly, and the analysis went on.

Two years later (the analysis having ended in the meanwhile) the patient was at a party which he found he could not enjoy, and he realized that it was a week after the anniversary of his mother's death. Suddenly it came to him that what had troubled him at the time of his broadcast had been a very simple and obvious thing, sadness that his mother was not there to enjoy his success (or even to know about it) and guilt that he had enjoyed it while she was dead. Instead of being able to mourn for her (by canceling the broadcast) he had had to behave as if he denied her death, almost in a manic way. He recognized that the interpretation given, which could be substantially correct, had in fact been the correct one at the time for the analyst, who had actually been jealous of him, and that it was the analyst's unconscious guilt that had led to the giving of an inappropriate interpretation. Its acceptance had come about through the patient's unconscious recognition of its correctness for his analyst and his identification with, or nondifferentiation from, him. Now he could accept it as true for himself in a totally different way, on another level—i.e. that of his jealousy of his father's success with his mother and guilt about himself having a success which represented success with his mother, of which his father would be jealous and want to deprive him. (His father had in fact been jealous of him in his baby relation to his mother. He discovered later still that if left to himself he would probably have broadcast anyway, but for a different reason, and it would have felt quite different.) But the analyst's behavior in giving such an interpretation must be attributed to countertransference.

II

Surprisingly little has been written on countertransference apart from books and papers on technique chiefly meant for students in training. The writers of these all emphasize the same two points—the importance and potential danger of countertransference and the need for thorough analysis of analysts. Much more has been written about transference, and a lot of that would apply equally well to countertransference. I found myself wondering why, and also why different people use the term *countertransference* to mean different things. The term is used to mean any or all of the following:

a. The analyst's unconscious attitude to the patient.
b. Repressed elements, hitherto unanalyzed, in the analyst himself which attach to the patient in the same way as the patient "transfers" to the analyst affects, etc. belonging to his parents or

to the objects of his childhood: i.e. the analyst regards the patient (temporarily and varyingly) as he regarded his own parents.

c. Some specific attitude or mechanism with which the analyst meets the patient's transference.

d. The whole of the analyst's attitudes and behavior toward his patient. This includes all the others, and any conscious attitudes as well.

The question is why it is so undefined or undefinable. Is it that true isolation of countertransference is impossible while the comprehensive idea of it is clumsy and unmanageable? I found four reasons.

1. I would say that unconscious countertransference is something which cannot be observed directly as such, but only in its effects: we might compare the difficulty with that of the physicists who try to define or observe a force which is manifested as light waves, gravity, etc. but which cannot be detected or observed directly.

2. I think part of the difficulty arises from the fact that (considering it metapsychologically) the analyst's total attitude involves his whole psyche, id, and any superego remnants as well as ego (he is also concerned with all these in the patient), and there are no clear boundaries differentiating them.

3. Any analysis (even self-analysis) postulates both an analysand and an analyst: in a sense they are inseparable. And similarly, transference and countertransference are inseparable, something suggested in the fact that what is written about the one can so largely be applied to the other.

4. More important than any of these, I think there is an attitude toward countertransference, i.e. toward one's own feelings and ideas, that is really paranoid or phobic, especially where the feelings are or may be subjective.

In one of his papers on technique Freud pointed out that the progress of psychoanalysis had been held up for more than ten years through fear of interpreting the transference, and the attitude of psychotherapists of other schools to this day is to regard it as highly dangerous and to avoid it. The attitude of most analysts toward countertransference is precisely the same, that it is a known and recognized phenomenon but that it is unnecessary and even dangerous ever to interpret it. In any case, what is unconscious one cannot easily be aware of (if at all), and to try to observe and interpret something unconscious in oneself is rather like trying to see the back of one's own head—it is a lot easier to see the back of someone else's. The fact of the patient's transference lends itself readily to avoidance by projection and rationalization, both mechanisms being characteristic for paranoia, and the myth of the impersonal, almost inhuman analyst who shows no feelings is consistent with this attitude. I wonder whether failure to make use of countertransference may not be having a precisely similar effect as far as the progress of psychoanalysis is concerned to that of ignoring or neglecting the transference. If we can make the right use of countertransference, may we not find that we have yet another extremely valuable, if not an indispensable, tool?

In writing this chapter, I found it very difficult to know which of the meanings of the term *countertransference* I was using, and I found that I tended to slip from one to another, although at the start I meant to limit it to the repressed, infantile, subjective, irrational feelings, some pleasurable, some painful, which belong to the second of my attempted definitions. This is usually the countertransference which is regarded as the source of difficulties and dangers.

But unconscious elements can be both normal and pathological, and not all repression is pathological any more than all conscious elements are "normal." The whole patient-analyst relationship includes both "normal" and pathological, conscious and unconscious, transference and countertransference, in varying proportions. It will always include something specific to both the individual patient, and the individual analyst. That is, every countertransference is different from every other, as every transference is different, and it varies within itself from day to day, according to variations in both patient and analyst and the outside world.

Repressed countertransference is a product of the unconscious part of the analyst's ego, that part nearest and most closely belonging to the id and least in contact with reality. It follows from this that the repetition compulsion is readily brought to bear on it, but other ego activities besides repression play a part in its development, of which the synthetic or integrative activity is most important. As I see it, countertransference is one of those compromise formations in the making of which the ego shows such surprising skill; it is in this respect essentially of the same order as a neurotic symptom, a perversion, or a sublimation. In it libidinal gratification is partly forbidden and partly accepted; an element of aggression is woven in with both the gratification and the prohibition, and the distribution of the aggression determines the relative proportions of each. Since countertransference, like transference, is concerned with another person, the mechanisms of projection and introjection are of special importance.

By the time we have paranoia linked with countertransference, we have a mammoth subject to discuss, and to talk about the patient's response may be just nonsense unless we can find some simple way of approach. Many of our difficulties, unfortunately, seem to me to come from trying to oversimplify and from an almost compulsive attempt to separate out conscious from unconscious and repressed unconscious from what is unconscious but not repressed, often with an ignoring of the dynamic aspects of the thing. So once again I would like to say here that although I am talking mainly about the repressed elements in countertransference, I am not limiting myself strictly to this, but am letting it flow over into the other elements in the total relationship. At the risk of being disjointed my "simple approach" is chiefly a matter of talking about a few things and then trying to relate them to the main theme.

Speaking of the dynamic aspects brings us to the question: What is the driving force in any analysis? What is it that urges the patient on to get well? The answer surely is that it is the combined id urges of both patient and analyst, urges which in the case of the analyst have been modified and integrated as a result of his own analysis so that they have become more directed and effective. Successful combination of these urges seems to me to depend on a special kind of identification of the analyst with the patient.

III

Consciously, and surely to a great extent unconsciously too, we all want our patients to get well, and we can identify readily with them in their desire to get well, that is with their ego. But unconsciously we tend to identify also with the patient's superego and id, and thereby with him, in any prohibition on getting well and in his wish to stay ill and dependent, and by so doing we may slow down his recovery. Unconsciously we may exploit a patient's illness for our own purposes, both libidinal and aggressive, and he will quickly respond to this.

A patient who has been in analysis for some considerable time has usually become his analyst's love object. He is the person to whom the analyst wishes to make reparation, and the reparative impulses, even when conscious, may through a partial repression come under the sway of the repetition compulsion: it becomes necessary to make that same patient well over and over again, which in effect means making him ill over and over again in order to have him to make well.

Rightly used, this repetitive process may be progressive, and the "making ill" then takes the necessary and effective form of opening up anxieties which can be interpreted and worked through. But this implies a degree of unconscious willingness on the part of the analyst to allow his patient to get well, to become independent and to leave him. In general we can agree that these are all acceptable to any analyst, but failures of timing of interpretation such as that which I have described, failure in understanding, or any interference with working through, will play into the patient's own fear of getting well, with all that it involves in the way of losing his analyst, and these fears cannot be put right until the patient himself is ready to let the opportunity occur. The repetition compulsion in the patient is here the ally of the analyst, if the analyst is ready not to repeat his former mistake and so once more strengthen the patient's resistances.

This unconscious unwillingness on the analyst's part to let his patient leave him can sometimes take very subtle forms, in which the analysis itself can be used as a rationalization. The demand that a patient should not "act out" in situations outside the analysis may hinder the formation of those very extraanalytic relationships which belong with his recovery and are evidence of his growth and ego development. Transferences to people outside the analysis need not be an actual hindrance to the analytic work if the analyst is willing to use them, but unconsciously he may behave exactly like the parents who, "for the child's own good," interfere with his development by not allowing him to love someone else. The patient of course needs them just as a child needs to form identifications with people outside his home and parents.

These things are so insidious that our perception of them comes slowly, and in our resistance to them we are allying with the patient's superego through our own superego. At the same time, we are showing our own inability to tolerate a splitting either of something in the patient or of the therapeutic process itself; we are demanding to be the only cause of the patient's getting well.

A patient whose analysis is "interminable" then may perhaps be the victim of his analyst's (primary) narcissism as much as of his own, and an apparent negative therapeutic reaction may be the outcome of a counterresistance of the kind I have indicated in my story.

We all know that only a few of several possible interpretations are the important and dynamic ones at any given point in the analysis, but as in my story, the interpretation which is the appropriate one for the patient may be the very one which, for reasons of countertransference and counterresistance, is least available to the analyst at that moment. If the interpretation given is the one that is appropriate for the analyst himself, the patient may, through fear, submissiveness, etc., accept it in precisely the same way as he would accept the "correct" one, with immediate good effect. Only later does it come out that the effect obtained was not the one required, and that the patient's resistance has been thereby strengthened and the analysis
. prolonged.

IV

It has been said that it is fatal for an analyst to become identified with his patient and that empathy (as distinct from sympathy) and detachment are essential to success in analysis. But the basis of empathy, as of sympathy, is identification, and it is the detachment which makes the difference between them. This detachment comes about partly at least by the use of the ego function of reality testing with the introduction of the factors of time and distance. The analyst necessarily identifies with the patient, but there is for him an interval of time between himself and the experience which for the patient has the quality of immediacy—he knows it for past experience, while to the patient it is a present one. That makes it at that moment the patient's experience, not his, and if the analyst is experiencing it as a present thing, he is interfering with the patient's growth and development. When an experience is the patient's own and not the analyst's, an interval of distance is introduced automatically as well, and it is on the preservation of these intervals of time and distance that successful use of the countertransference may depend. The analyst's identification with the patient needs of course to be an introjective, not a projective, one.

When such an interval of time is introduced, the patient can feel his experience in its immediacy, free from interference, and let it become past for him too, so that a fresh identification can be made with his analyst. When the interval of distance is introduced, the experience becomes the patient's alone, and he can separate himself off psychically from the analyst. Growth depends on an alternating rhythm of identification and separation brought about in this way by having experiences and knowing them for one's own, in a suitable setting.

To come back to the story with which I began, what happened was that the analyst felt the patient's unconscious, repressed jealousy as his own immediate experience, instead of as a past, remembered, one. The patient was immediately concerned with his mother's death, feeling the necessity to broadcast just then as an interference with his process of mourning, and the pleasure proper to it was transformed into a manic one, as if he denied his mother's death. Only later, after the interpretation, when his mourning had been transferred to the analyst and so become past, could he experience the jealousy situation as an immediate one, and then recognize (as something past and remembered) his analyst's countertransference reaction. His immediate reaction to the analyst's jealousy was a phobic one—displacement by (introjective) identification, and rerepression.

Failures in timing such as this, or failures to recognize transference references, are failures of the ego function of recognizing time and distance. Unconscious mind is timeless and irrational, "What's yours is mine, what's mine is my own." "What's yours is half mine and half the other half's mine, so it's all mine." These are infantile ways of thinking which are used in relation to feelings and experiences as much as to things, and countertransference becomes a hindrance to the patient's growth when the analyst uses them. The analyst becomes the blind man leading the blind, for neither has the use of the necessary two dimensions to know where he is at any given moment. But when the analyst can keep these intervals in his identification with his patient, it becomes possible for the patient to take the step forward of eliminating them again and of going on to the next experience when the process of establishing the interval has to be repeated.

This is one of the major difficulties of the student in training or the analyst who is undergoing further analysis—he is having to deal with things in his patients' analysis which have still the quality of presentness, or immediacy, for him himself, instead of that pastness which is so important. In these circumstances it may be impossible for him always to keep this time interval, and he has then to defer as full an analysis as the patient might otherwise achieve until he has carried his own analysis further, and wait until a repetition of the material comes.

V

The discussions of Dr. Rosen's work—"Direct Analysis"—brought the subject of countertransference to the surface with a fresh challenge to us to know and understand much more clearly what we are doing. We heard how in the space of a few days or weeks patients who for years had been completely inaccessible had shown remarkable changes which, from some points of view at least, must be regarded as improvement. But what was not originally meant to be in the bargain, they seem to have remained permanently dependent on and attached to the therapist concerned. The description of the way in which the patients were treated and of the results stirred and disturbed most of us profoundly and apparently aroused a good deal of guilt among us, for several members in their contributions to the discussion beat their breasts and cried mea culpa.

I have tried to understand where so much guilt came from, and it seemed to me that a possible explanation of it might lie in the unconscious unwillingness to let patients go. Many seriously ill patients, especially psychotic cases, are not able, either for internal (psychological) reasons or for external (e.g. financial) ones, to go through with a full analysis and bring it to what we regard as a satisfactory conclusion, that is, with sufficient ego development for them to be able to live successfully in real independence of the analyst. In such cases a superficial relationship of dependence is continued (and rightly continued) indefinitely, by means of occasional "maintenance" sessions, the contact being preserved deliberately by the analyst. Such patients we can keep in this way without guilt, and the high proportion of successes in the treatment of these patients, it seems to me, may well depend on that very freedom from guilt.

But over and above this there is perhaps a tendency to identify particularly with the patient's id in psychotic cases generally; in fact it would sometimes be difficult to find the ego to identify with. This will be a narcissistic identification on the level of the primary love-hate, which nevertheless lends itself readily to a transformation into object-love. The powerful stimulus of the extensively disintegrated personality touches on the most deeply repressed and carefully defended danger spots in the analyst, and correspondingly the most primitive (and incidentally least effective) of his defense mechanisms are called into play. But at the same time a small fragment of the patient's shattered ego may identify with the ego of the therapist (where the therapist's understanding of the patient's fears filters through to him, and he can introject the therapist's ego as a good object). He is then enabled to make a contact with reality through the therapist's contact with it. Such contact is tenuous and easily broken at first, but is capable of being strengthened and extended by a process of increasing introjection of the external world and reprojection of it, with a gradually increasing investment of it with libido derived originally from the therapist.

This contact may never become sufficient for the patient to be able to maintain it entirely alone, and in such a case continued contact with the therapist is essential and will need to vary in frequency according to the patient's changing condition and situation. I would compare the patient's position to that of a drowning man who has been brought to a boat, and while still in the water his hand is placed on the gunwale and held there by his rescuer until he can establish his own hold.

It follows from this perhaps, a truth already recognized, that the more disintegrated the patient the greater is the need for the analyst to be well integrated.

It may be that in those psychotic patients who do not respond to the usual analytic situation in the ordinary way, by developing a transference which can be interpreted and resolved, the countertransference has to do the whole of the work, and in order to find something in the patient with which to make contact, the therapist has to allow his ideas and the libidinal gratifications derived from his work to regress to a quite extraordinary degree. (We may wonder, for instance, about the pleasure an analyst derives from his patients sleeping during their analytic sessions with him.) It has been said that greater therapeutic results are found when a patient is so disturbed that the therapist experiences intense feelings and profound disturbance, and the underlying mechanism for this may be identification with the patient's id.

But these outstanding results are found in the work of two classes of analyst. One consists of beginners who are not afraid to allow their unconscious impulses a considerable degree of freedom because, through lack of experience, like children, they do not know or understand the dangers and do not recognize them. It works out well in quite a high proportion of cases because the positive feelings preponderate. Where it does not the results are mostly not seen or not disclosed—they may even be repressed. We all have our private graveyards, and not every grave has a headstone.

The other class consists of those experienced analysts who have gone through a stage of overcautiousness and have reached the point at which they can trust not only directly to their unconscious impulses as such (because of the modifications resulting from their own analyses) but also to being able at any given moment to bring the countertransference as it stands then into consciousness enough to see at least whether they are advancing or retarding the patient's recovery—in other words to overcome countertransference resistance.

At times the patient himself will help this, for transference and countertransference are not only syntheses by the patient and analyst acting separately but, like the analytic work as a whole, are the result of a joint effort. We often hear of the mirror which the analyst holds up to the patient, but the patient holds one up to the analyst too, and there is a whole series of reflections in each, repetitive in kind and subject to continual modification. The mirror in each case should become progressively clearer as the analysis goes on, for patient and analyst respond to each other in a reverberative kind of way, and increasing clearness in one mirror will bring the need for a corresponding clearing in the other.

The patient's ambivalence leads him both to try to break down the analyst's counterresistances (which can be a frightening thing to do) and also to identify with him in them and so to use them as his own. The question of giving him a "correct" interpretation is then of considerable importance from this point of view.

VI

When such a thing happens as I have quoted in this story, to neutralize the obstructive effect of a mistimed or wrongly emphasized interpretation by giving the "correct" interpretation when the occasion arises may not be enough. Not only should the mistake be admitted (and the patient is entitled not only to express his own anger but also to some expression of regret from the analyst for its occurrence, quite as much as for the occurrence of a mistake in the amount of his account or the time of his appointment), but its origin in unconscious countertransference may be explained, unless there is some definite contraindication for so doing, in which case it should be postponed until a suitable time comes, as it surely will. Such explanation may be essential for the further progress of the analysis, and it will have only beneficial results, increasing the patient's confidence in the honesty and goodwill of the analyst, showing him to be human enough to make mistakes and making clear the universality of the phenomenon of transference and the way in which it can arise in any relationship. Only harm can come from the withholding of such an interpretation.

Let me make it clear that I do not mean that I think countertransference interpretations should be unloaded injudiciously or without consideration on the heads of hapless patients, any more than transference interpretations are given without thought today. I mean that they should neither be positively avoided nor perhaps restricted to feelings which are justified or objective, such as those to which Dr. Winnicott refers in his paper "Hate in the Countertransference" (1949). (And of course they *cannot* be given unless something of the countertransference has become conscious.) The subjectivity of the feelings needs to be shown to the patient, though their actual origin need not be gone into (there should not be "confessions"). It should be enough to point out one's own need to analyze them, but above all the important thing is that they should be recognized by both analyst and patient.

In my view a time comes in the course of every analysis when it is essential for the patient to recognize the existence not only of the analyst's subjective feelings: that is, that the analyst must and does develop an unconscious countertransference which he is nevertheless able to deal with in such a way that it does not interfere to any serious extent with the patient's interests, especially the progress of cure. The point at which such recognition comes will of course vary in individual analyses, but it belongs rather to the later stages of analysis than to the earlier ones. Occasionally mistakes in technique or mistakes such as errors in accounts, etc., make it necessary to refer to unconscious mental processes in the analyst (i.e. to countertransference) at an earlier time than one would choose, but the reference can be a slight one, sufficient only for the purpose of relieving the immediate anxiety. Too much stress on it at an early time would increase anxiety to what might be a really dangerous degree.

So much emphasis is laid on the unconscious fantasies of patients about their analysts that it is often ignored that they really come to know a great deal of truth about them—both actual and psychic. Such knowledge could not be prevented in any case, even if desirable, but patients do not know they have it, and part of the analyst's task is to bring it into consciousness, which may be the very thing to which he has himself the greatest resistance. Analysts often behave unconsciously exactly like the parents who put up a smoke screen and tantalize their children, tempting them to see the very things they forbid their seeing. Not to refer to countertransference is tantamount to denying its existence or forbidding the patient to know or speak about it.

The ever-quoted remedy for countertransference difficulties— deeper and more thorough analysis of the analyst—can at best only be an incomplete one, for some tendency to develop unconscious infantile countertransference is bound to remain. Analysis cannot reach the whole of the unconscious id, and we have only to remember that even the most thoroughly analyzed person still dreams to be reminded of this. Freud's saying "Where id was ego shall be" is an ideal, and like most other ideals is not fully realizable. All that we can really aim at is reaching the point at which the analyst's attitude to his own id impulses is no longer a paranoid one and so is safe from his patients' point of view and remembering besides that this will still vary in him from day to day, according to the stresses and strains to which he is exposed.

To my mind it is this question of a paranoid or phobic attitude toward the analyst's own feelings which constitutes the greatest danger and difficulty in countertransference. The very real fear of being flooded with feeling of any kind, rage, anxiety, love, etc., in relation to one's patient and of being passive to it and at its mercy leads to an unconscious avoidance or denial. Honest recognition of such feeling is essential to the analytic process, and the analysand is naturally sensitive to any insincerity in his analyst and will inevitably respond to it with hostility. He will identify with the analyst in it (by introjection) as a means of denying his own feelings and will exploit it generally in every way possible, to the detriment of his analysis.

I have shown above that unconscious (and uninterpreted) countertransference may be responsible for the prolonging of analysis. It can equally well be responsible for the premature ending, and I feel that it is again in the final stages that most care is needed to avoid these things. Analysts writing about the final stages of analysis and its termination speak over and over again of the way in which patients reach a certain point and then either slip away and break off the analysis just at the moment when to continue is vital for its ultimate success or else slip again into another of their interminable repetitions, instead of analysing the anxiety situations. Countertransference may perhaps be the deciding factor at this point, and the analyst's willingness to deal with it may be the all-important thing.

I should perhaps add that I am sure that valuable unconscious countertransferences may also very often be responsible for the carrying through to a successful conclusion of analyses which have appeared earlier to be moving toward inevitable failure and also for quite a lot of the postanalytic work carried on by patients when analyses have been terminated prematurely for any reason.

In the later stages of analysis then, when the patient's capacity for objectivity is already increased, the analyst needs especially to be on the lookout for countertransference manifestations and for opportunities to interpret it, whether directly or indirectly, as and when the patient reveals it to him. Without it patients may fail to recognize objectively much of the irrational parental behavior which has been so powerful a factor in the development of the neurosis, for wherever the analyst does behave like the parents and conceals the fact, there is the point at which continued repression of what might otherwise be recognized is inevitable. It brings great relief to a patient to find that irrational behavior on the part of his parents was not intended for him personally, but was already transferred to him from their parents. To find his analyst doing the same kind of thing in minor ways can give conviction to his understanding and make the whole process more tolerable to him than anything else can do.

There will of course be fantasies in every analysis about the analyst's feelings toward his patient—we know that from the start—and they have to be interpreted like any other fantasies, but beyond these a patient may quite well become aware of real feelings in his analyst even before the analyst himself is fully aware of them. There may be a great struggle against accepting the idea that the analyst can have unconscious countertransference feelings, but when once the patient's ego has accepted it certain ideas and memories which have been inaccessible till then may be brought into consciousness, things which would otherwise have stayed repressed.

I have spoken of the patient revealing the countertransference to the analyst, and I mean this quite literally, though it may sound like the dangerous blood sport of "analyzing the analyst." The "analytic rule" as it is usually worded nowadays is more helpful to us than in its original form. We no longer "require" our patients to tell us everything that is in their minds. On the contrary, we give them permission to do so, and what comes may on occasion be a piece of real countertransference interpretation for the analyst. Should he not be willing to accept it, rerepression with strengthened resistance follows, and consequently interruption or prolonging of the analysis. Together with the different formulation of the analytic rule goes a different way of giving interpretations or comments. In the old days analysts, like parents, said what they liked when they liked, as by right, and patients had to take it. Now, in return for the permission to speak or withhold freely, we ask our patients to allow us to say some things, and allow them too to refuse to accept them. This makes for a greater freedom all round to choose the time for giving interpretations and the form in which they are given, by a lessening of the didactic or authoritarian attitude.

Incidentally, a good many of the transference interpretations which are ordinarily given are capable of extension to demonstrate the possibility of countertransference; for instance, "You feel that I am angry, as your mother was when . . . " can include "I'm not angry as far as I know, but I'll have to find out about it, and if I am, to know why, for there's no real reason for me to be." Such things of course are often said, but they are not always thought of as countertransference interpretations. In my view that is what they are, and their use might well be developed consciously as a means of freeing countertransferences and making them more directly available for use (Searles 1965).

In her paper read at the Zurich Congress Dr. Heimann (1950) has referred to the appearance of some countertransference feelings as a kind of signal comparable to the development of anxiety as a warning of the approach of a traumatic situation. If I have understood her correctly, the disturbance which she describes is surely in fact anxiety, but a secondary anxiety which is justified and objective and brings a greater alertness and awareness of what is happening. She specifically states that in her opinion countertransference interpretations are best avoided.

But anxiety serves first of all another purpose—it is primarily a method of dealing with an actual trauma, however ineffective it may be in this capacity. It can happen that this secondary anxiety with its awareness and watchfulness can mask very effectively anxiety of a more primitive kind. Below the level of consciousness analyst and patient can be sensitive to each other's paranoid fears and persecutory feelings and become so to speak synchronized (or "in phase") in them, so that the analysis itself can be used by both as defense. The analyst may swing over from an introjective identification with the patient to a projective one, with a loss of those intervals of time and distance of which I spoke earlier, while the patient may defend himself by an introjective identification with the analyst, instead of being able to project onto him the persecuting objects.

Resolution of this situation can come about through conscious recognition of the countertransference either by the analyst or by the patient. Failure to recognize it may lead to either premature interruption of the analysis or to prolonging it. In each case there will be rerepression of what might otherwise have become conscious and strengthening of the resistances. Premature interruption is not necessarily fatal to the ultimate success of the analysis, any more than its prolongation is, for the presence of sufficient understanding and some valuable countertransference may make further progress possible, even after termination, by virtue of other introjections already made.

The ideal analyst of course exists only in imagination (whether the patient's or the analyst's), and can only be made actual and living in rare moments. But if the analyst can trust to his own modified id impulses, his own repressions of a valuable kind, and to something positive in his patient as well (presumably something which helped to decide him to undertake the analysis in the first place), then he can provide enough of that thing which was missing from the patient's early environment and so badly needed—a person who can allow the patient to grow without either interference or overstimulation. Then a benign circle forms in the analytic situation which the patient can use to develop his own basic rhythmic patterns, and on those patterns to build up the more complex rhythms needed to deal with the world of external reality and his own continuously growing inner world.

VII

I have tried to show how patients respond to the unconscious countertransferences of their analysts, and in particular the importance of any paranoid attitude in the analyst to the countertransference itself. Countertransference is a defense mechanism of a synthetic kind, brought about by the analyst's unconscious ego, and is easily brought under the control of the repetition compulsion. But transference and countertransference are still further syntheses in that they are products of the combined unconscious work of patient and analyst. They depend on conditions which are partly internal and partly external to the analytic relationship and vary from week to week, day to day, and even moment to moment with the rapid intrapsychic and extrapsychic changes. Both are essential to psychoanalysis, and countertransference is no more to be feared or avoided than is transference; in fact it *cannot* be avoided, it can only be looked out for, controlled to some extent, and used.

But only insofar as analysis is a true sublimation for the analyst and not a perversion or addiction (as I think it sometimes may be) can we avoid countertransference neurosis. Patches of transitory countertransference neurosis may appear from time to time even in the most skilled, experienced and well-analyzed analysts, and they can be used positively to help patients toward recovery by means of their own transferences. According to the analyst's attitude to countertransference (which is ultimately his attitude to his own id impulses and his own feelings) paranoid anxiety, denial, condemnation, or acceptance, and the degree of his own willingness to allow it to become conscious to his patient as well as to himself, the patient will be encouraged to respond either by exploiting it repetitively or by using it progressively to good purpose.

Interpretation of countertransference along the lines which I have tried to indicate would make much heavier demands on analysts than before, but so did interpretation of transference at the time when it began to be used. Nowadays that is something which is taken for granted, and it has been found to have its compensations in that the analyst's libidinal impulses and creative and reparative wishes find effective gratification in the greater power and success of his work. I believe that similar results might follow a greater use of countertransference if we can find ways of using it, though I must stress the tentativeness with which I am putting forward any of these ideas.

3

"R"—THE ANALYST'S TOTAL RESPONSE TO HIS PATIENT'S NEEDS

This chapter contains a number of themes each of which requires a paper to itself. In considering them together in their relatedness, I am having to condense, and am risking being misunderstood, owing to the inevitable distortion and loss of clarity. At the same time, I am making the one chapter long and weighty. I hope to do more justice to my themes later when I can develop them further separately.

The ideas that I am putting forward follow on from those expressed in chapter 2. They have come to me both through analyses of my patients and through my own analysis. I will illustrate them with some material from the analysis of one patient in particular.

Most patients I have analyzed come into the category known as "psychopaths" and "character disorders," some of them being quite seriously ill and disturbed people with a great deal of psychotic anxiety. Although much of what I have to say seems to apply mostly to patients of this kind, I do not think it is in any way limited to them, but can also apply to both neurotic and psychotic patients.

THE SYMBOL "R"

In chapter 2 I tried to find an agreed definition of *countertransference,* and found that "the term is used to mean any or all of the following":

   a The analyst's unconscious attitude to the patient.

   b. Repressed elements, hitherto unanalyzed, in the analyst himself which attach to the patient in the same way as the patient "transfers" to the analyst affects, etc., belonging to his parents or to the objects of his childhood; i.e. the analyst regards the patient (temporarily and varyingly) as he regarded his own parents.

   c. Some specific attitude or mechanism with which the analyst meets the patient's transference.

   d. The whole of the analyst's attitudes and behavior toward his patient. This includes all the others, and any conscious attitudes as well.

Humpty Dumpty said, "When I use a word it means just what I choose it to mean—neither more nor less," and when Alice questioned whether you *can* make words mean so many different things, he replied: "The question is, which is to be Master—that's all." Our difficulty here is to get one word *not* to mean as many different things as there are people using it.

Besides the confusion between these various meanings the term *countertransference* has also come to be invested with an emotional charge, which makes discussion difficult. It is obviously impossible to avoid either the confusion or the emotional charge altogether, but to reduce both to a minimum, I am introducing a symbol, *R,* to denote what I am talking about, defining it as "the analyst's total response to his patient's needs, whatever the needs, and whatever the response."

DEFINITIONS

Total Response

In using the expression *total response* I have deliberately chosen an omnibus word, and I want to make my position clear about it. I am using it to cover everything that an analyst says, does, thinks, imagines, dreams, or feels, throughout the analysis, in relation to his patient.

Every patient who comes for analysis has certain needs, and to these his analyst responds in a variety of ways. The response is inevitable, and valuable; it is an indispensable part of the analysis, providing a large share of its driving force. It is the resultant of the balance, interplay, and fusion between the analyst's love for his patient and his hate of him.

What an analyst says and does in the analysis of patients is often separated out into "interpretation" and "behavior," with the belief that only "interpretation" is of any real use to the patient. Such a separation in itself is false, for the giving of an interpretation is in fact a piece of behavior, as are its form, timing, etc. These are no less matters of behavior than are the analyst's shaking hands with the patient, or not shaking hands, the conditions he provides (both for the patient and for himself), his silence, listening, reacting, or not reacting.

All these things are the outcome of his feelings, whether conscious or unconscious. However much he is aware of, there is always far more that is unconscious, which exerts more dynamic pressure than that exerted by what is conscious.

Limitations can be imposed to make the amount of interpretation maximal and of other kinds of behavior minimal, but too great limitation leads to rigidity and stereotypy. Limitations cannot be absolute or standardized. It would not be desirable even if they could, as it would only too soon involve the negation of a basic principle—that of the value of the individual (both to himself and to society) whether that individual be the analyst or the patient.

Needs

Needs in this context is another omnibus word, also deliberately chosen. The ultimate need in every case, of course, is the gaining of insight with growing appreciation and apprehension of reality. But on the way to this many severely ill patients have other needs which have to be met; if they are not met, analysis becomes impossible. The most obvious is hospitalization, but short of this there are many times when an analyst has to intervene. Arrangements for care by the family doctor, control of drugs, contacts with relatives or friends, control of acting out (often necessary for the patient's safety)—all these may be needed, apart from the ordinary routine fixing of the conditions for the analysis such as money arrangements, times of appointment, and, of course, the initial choice of patient.

Without these things, in many cases no amount of understanding or of careful and accurate interpretation will make it possible for the analysis to be carried through. With them it may be possible, even though they may be felt by both patient and analyst as interfering and delaying; only the outcome of the analysis will show whether they really were so or not.

RESPONSIBILITY

Responsibility in analysis is not a simple thing; the analyst has not only a responsibility to his patient. He has also a responsibility to himself, to psychoanalysis, and to the community. There are many responsibilities which his patient or society would like to put on him, but there are also limits to his responsibility.

For the whole of his response to his patient's needs, the analyst's responsibility is 100 percent. I have considered this statement carefully to see whether it should be qualified or modified in any way and cannot find that it should. The analyst's words, ideas, feelings, actions, reactions, his decisions, his dreams, his associations, are all his own, and he must take responsibility for them even though they arise from unconscious processes. No responsibility for them can be shared with anyone else, nor can they be delegated. This seems to me to be true, unvaryingly, for every analysis.

What does vary comes within that 100 percent responsibility, i.e. the extent to which the responsibility can be delegated or shared, and to or with whom. The decisions when to delegate it, and how, are still the analyst's responsibility.

There are roughly three classes of patient, the outlines of the classes being ill-defined and variable; any one patient at different stages of the analysis may pass from one to another.

1. Frankly psychotic patients, for whom responsibility has to be delegated to other people—doctors, nursing staff, relatives, etc.—for purely practical reasons. Suicide risk, danger to others, general irresponsibility and violent acting out are the commonest reasons. In these cases the strain is largely carried by the patient's environment and so can be lifted temporarily from the analyst.

2. Plainly neurotic patients, where responsibility can be delegated to the patient himself. This depends on the presence of an intact ego and a good reality sense, for the taking of responsibility is one of the highest functions of the ego, and is closely related to stability. These cases are least strain for an analyst, as the patient bears his own strain to a large extent. But it is important that both analyst and patient recognize that there is this sharing or delegation of responsibility, and that the ultimate responsibility throughout the analysis is on the analyst. A time comes in every analysis when the patient needs to bear his own strains, and to take over responsibility for himself, but he needs to understand what is happening and why. In any case, owing to the conditions in which we work, some such sharing or delegation is unavoidable.

3. Between these two groups there lies the large group of "character disorders," "psychopaths," and "borderline psychotics," for all of whom any kind of delegation is extremely difficult and often impossible. It can be done temporarily as in either of the other groups, but usually only to a limited extent.

In this class of patient the therapist's responsibility can be seen most clearly, and the "management" of the case is of great importance. This is the type of case which puts perhaps the greatest and most continuous strain on the analyst himself, for the very reason that delegation is so difficult. Patients in each of the other groups involve it in certain phases of treatment, especially transition phases—e.g. when a psychotic leaves the mental hospital or a neurotic is in a temporary regressed state.

There are limits to the responsibility of the analyst: no human being can carry more than a certain amount of it. It is worthwhile remembering that no one is under obligation to do analytic work unless he chooses, and no analyst is compelled to take on very disturbed patients. He has the right to refuse to undertake an analysis in conditions which he considers unsuitable or unsafe, and to refuse to continue if the conditions are changed for any reason after the analysis has begun.

Two other self-evident things are often forgotten, even by analysts. No analyst has to attempt the impossible, and he does not have to have 100 percent ability to understand or interpret; even in a long analysis there will be many things left at the end, not understood by either patient or analyst.

Every patient needs at some point in the analysis to become aware of the responsibility which the analyst is taking (whether that includes the responsibility for his life, or his acting out, or not). It is surprising how few patients have any idea that the analyst takes any real responsibility whatever in regard to them. Various writers, from Freud and Ferenczi onwards, have described the way in which the patient uses the analyst as an ego; Phyllis Greenacre puts it: "The analyst acts like an extra function, or set of functions which is lent to the analyzand for the latter's temporary use and benefit." I think this is as true of the responsibility function of the analyst as of anything. Stability in the analysis depends upon it, and the patient's ultimate capacity for taking his own responsibilities depends on his having a reliably responsible person with whom to identify.

COMMITMENT

The taking of responsibility involves first of all the making of an accurate assessment of the patient, as regards both superficial levels and deeper ones. This does not, of course, mean immediate recognition of all that the deeper levels contain, but that they are there, and to what extent they are contributing to the success or failure of his life and relationships, i.e. to what extent and in what kind of way he is disturbed. This knowledge has to be gradually increased, widened, and deepened until the patient is as fully known as possible. It means, in effect, recognition of the patient as an individual, a person; the realities of his childhood and his present life need to be understood, as well as his fantasies. The analyst both enters and becomes part of the patient's inner world and remains outside it and separate from it.

To do this involves a willingness to commit oneself—100 percent at times. It is only possible to the extent to which the analyst is able to be a person himself, i.e. to have an outline, or limits, and to be able to bear loss of outline or fusion, that is, his capacity for making identifications and remaining uninvolved.

The analyst's commitment of himself is quite obvious in some respects: he undertakes to give the patient at and over certain agreed times his attention, his interest, his energy; all within the ordinary limits of human capacity. He stands committed to his words and decisions, his mistakes and failures as well as his successes.

There are occasionally other kinds of commitment which are

unavoidable. I have had to give evidence, on oath, in a court of law, in the patient's hearing. This does not happen often, fortunately, but commitment of this kind occurs in cases where acting out brings the patient into conflict with the outer world, which then takes action against him. It serves to demonstrate clearly the 100 percent degree of the commitment.

It is difficult to express what I mean by this 100 percent commitment, beyond these more obvious things, in such a way as to make it understandable. Most analysts feel that these things are not the limits of their commitment, but I have not found a complete definition or description of it.

Freud spoke of "evenly hovering attention," and it may be that I am really only speaking of the kind and degree of attention involved when I say that the analyst puts both what is conscious and what is unconscious in himself at his patient's service.

These have to be made available to the patient in forms that have meaning for him and that he can use. These forms may be verbal or nonverbal. The patient's capacity for symbolization and for deductive thinking largely determine the form, and these depend on what has happened to him in his early development. Different patients may need different forms, and for any one patient a form that is usable and meaningful at one time may be useless at another.

Ultimately, of course, the form has to be verbal and interpretative, but an object (apple, biscuit, blanket, etc.), as Mme. Séchehaye has shown, can have an effect *like* that of an interpretation and can be linked with verbal interpretations later, when the capacity to use symbols has been developed far enough.

The full implication of this is that the analyst goes with the patient as far into the patient's illness as it is possible for him to go. There may have to be times—moments or split seconds even—when, psychically, for the analyst nothing exists but the patient, and nothing exists of himself apart from the patient. He allows the patient to enter his own inner world and become part of it. His whole psyche becomes liable to be subjected to sudden unheralded inroads, often of vast extent and long duration. He is taken possession of, his emotions are exploited. He has to be able to make all kinds of identifications with his patient, accepting a fusion with him which often involves the taking into himself of something really mad; at the same time he has to be able to remain whole and separate.

Unless the analyst is willing to commit himself and makes that commitment clear, it is often quite impossible for a patient to commit himself to his analysis. To commit oneself means to give something and to waive one's rights. Very deprived people cannot give anything until they have first been given something; neither do they believe that they have any rights. It has to be made clear to them that something *is* given, that it is given willingly, and that it is part of the analysis for it to be given, and therefore they have a right to have it.

What is given is not given out of the analyst's need to give, but out of the situation where person-with-something-to-spare meets person-with-need. It is essential that the analyst fully admits that what is "to spare" and is given is limited; it is of the nature of a "token" or a "stand-in" and does not in fact really fit the patient's need (though the more nearly it can fit the better), as the deepest needs cannot really be met except by enlargement of insight and grasp of reality.

FEELING

This commitment, whatever its range, involves feeling. The analyst has to be willing to feel, about his patient, with his patient, and sometimes even for his patient, in the sense of supplying feelings which the patient is unable to find in himself, and in the absence of which no real change can happen. This is so where change is feared and the situation is controlled by the patient keeping his feelings unfelt—i.e. unconscious.

The analyst's real feeling for the patient and his desire to help (there has to be some feeling, whether we call it sympathy, compassion, or interest, to prompt the starting and continuing of the analysis), these need to be expressed clearly and explicitly at times when they are appropriate and are actually felt, and can therefore come spontaneously and sincerely.

Very disturbed patients, and at times even less disturbed ones, cannot make accurate deductions, so leaving these things to be deduced, or even talking about them, is meaningless; there needs to be some actual, direct expression as and when (but not whenever) they occur. In *The House of the Dead* Dostoevsky says, "The impression made by the reality is always stronger than that made by description," and I have found this to be particularly true in this connection. Pretended feeling would be worse than useless, but absolute restraint of intense feeling is of no real use either—it is inhuman, and it gives a false idea of the aim of analysis to enable the patient to have and express freely his own feelings. It gives the impression that expression of feeling is something allowed only to children or patients but forbidden in a "normal" or grown-up world.

From the point of view of the analyst absolute restraint of feeling is unreal, and it can make too great a demand on him. Self-imposed limitation there must be, but this is not the same thing as absolute restraint; there is no difficulty with less intense feelings which can find their expression comparatively easily in indirect ways.

I have been talking rather of the conscious expression of feeling, whether deliberately predetermined, or on conscious impulse. "Reacting" is something different. There are times when a reaction of quite a primitive type is not only not bad, but positively helpful. When an angry patient shakes his fist in my face, and I flinch, the reaction is in itself a reminder of reality. It quickly recalls him both to the fact that he could actually damage me and that I am only on one level the person he wants to hurt. Other reactions, not only bodily ones, can on occasion have similar effect and are not altogether to be despised; they can sometimes reach the ego in ways that are closed to interpretation, quite apart from the time factor of their speed.

It has been objected that expression of feelings by the analyst either gives too great gratification or is a burden to the patient. In my experience, neither of these things need be so, though of course they can. Provided the necessary oneness with, and separateness from, the patient are working right, such expressions of feeling tend to happen at the right times. If they are not, then any other way of treating the situation is also liable to make for difficulty.

Reactions, or expressions of the analyst's feelings, however, are not substitutes for interpretations although they may in certain circumstances act like them. They open the way for interpretation by making the patient accessible, i.e. by establishing contact in a fresh area which has hitherto not been reached. Interpretations have to be given as well later when they can be used, otherwise the only change achieved is that of opening the way. If interpretation does not follow, it closes again, and resistance is increased.

Having one's feelings available to this extent is at times a very great strain. To feel real hate of a patient for weeks on end or to be suddenly flooded with rage is extremely painful, as it is accompanied by guilt. It makes little difference whether the feelings are due to the patient's projections or whether they are objective and called forth by the patient's actual behavior. Real damage can be done if they remain unconscious, but there is little danger if they become conscious. Recognition of them alone brings some relief and the possibility of either direct or indirect expression. Dreams are often helpful in finding the unconscious, disallowed love or hate of one's patient.

Guilt or self-consciousness about these feelings for a patient can lead to both stereotypy and a false separating off of "the analyst" from the rest of the person (splitting, in other words, where it is not appropriate), with results that can be dangerous for very ill patients.

The range of feelings that can be aroused, of course, is enormous. I have spoken of rage and hate, but these follow such things as bewilderment or confusion, incomprehension, fear (of being attacked, that the patient will kill himself, of failure, etc.), guilt. Love, excitement, and pleasure can be as difficult: when a patient at last accepts an interpretation or makes real progress, even when from hating violently his mood and feeling change to something more friendly, a sign of relief may help him to become aware of a change which otherwise he might deny and not recognize. It may also help him to know something of what he is arousing in someone else— again something which he would otherwise be unable to believe.

Like responsibility and commitment, feelings for a patient have their limits. The claims of other patients and of one's own life assert themselves, the material changes, and the feelings change. Unless an analyst is "in love" with his patient, there is no real risk of his feelings getting fixed or of his having to go on and on expressing them, which is what people fear if any feeling is expressed at all.

The benefit to the patient, too, is limited in its extent. Sooner or later he has to realize that no one else can do his loving and hating for him; he has to feel on his own account and to take over the responsibility for it. But meanwhile he has had a feeling person there and the opportunity to identify with him, both by projecting his own unfeelingness and finding the projection, and by introjecting the feeling analyst.

LIMITS; "GOING ALL OUT"

I have shown that responsibility, commitment, and feeling all have their limits. These will of course vary with the different types of patient treated and the individual analyst. They are of great importance as they provide points of separation.

When a limit is reached and the patient becomes aware of it and aware of the impossibility of going beyond it even though his needs and demands go further, he becomes aware too of his separateness. If his ability to bear separation is very small, then every limit will be reached too soon. The demand on his ego will be too great, and a reaction of some kind (e.g. a piece of violent acting out or the development of a physical illness) may follow unless the situation is very carefully handled. Limits which are within the ego's capacity, whose logic and reality are within his grasp, provide growing points and places where the ego can be strengthened.

In contrast with the limits are the 100 percent of the responsibility, commitment, and acceptance of feeling and reaction. They correspond to the "no limits" of ideas and words allowed to the patient and help to make them a reality.

Some patients are so ill that their treatment cannot succeed without the expenditure of enormous effort, both extensive and intensive. In such cases the difficulty is to get the patient to make his own effort an "all out" one, and it is only if he realizes that his analyst is "going all out" on his behalf that he can find it worthwhile to do so himself.

MANIFESTATION OF THE ANALYST AS A PERSON

Each of these things, responsibility, commitment, feeling, etc., carries with it a manifestation or affirmation of the analyst's self as a person, a living human being with whom it is possible to have contact and relationship.

The idea of the impersonal screen or mirror has served, and still serves, a very valuable purpose in isolating the transference in neurotic patients. But it can be used defensively, even in an almost concrete, nonsymbolic way at times, by either patient or analyst.

For patients dealing with psychotic anxieties, and especially those suffering from actual psychotic illness, some more direct contact with the analyst is necessary. Symbolism and deductive thinking are needed where direct contact is minimized, and both of these are defective or lacking in such patients. Their development is impaired where the realities of the patient's childhood have coincided with the fantasies which he needed to work through. When this happens, projection becomes not only useless but quite impossible.

Every patient tests his analyst constantly to find out his weak spots and limitations. He has to find out whether the same thing is true of the analyst as of himself—i.e. that the relation of ego strength to instinct-tension is inadequate. If he can prove that his analyst cannot stand anxiety, madness, helplessness either in his patient or himself, then he knows for certain that what he feels must be true—the world will fall to pieces and be shattered by his discharge of tension, whatever the form it takes. Again, since he and his analyst are the same, then they must be one and indivisible.

It is therefore of vital importance to discover that the analyst not only can bear both tension and its discharge, but also can bear the fact that there are some things he cannot stand. The difference between anxiety and panic, and the difference between his own anxiety and fear of his patient's anxiety, can be seen when the analyst can fall, pick himself up, and go on again. This is where recognition of countertransference in the literal sense of the word (second definition) is of greatest importance. It may be necessary for it to be recognized by both patient and analyst, and denial of it by the analyst where it is present and the patient has seen it can have serious results. (Simple admission of it is enough; details are the analyst's own affair, but that there is countertransference affecting the analysis is the patient's affair, and he has the right to the acknowledgment.)

Every analyst, of course, has his own particular areas of difficulty about letting things happen, especially in himself. This relates to the whole problem of control, but it may be essential for some patients to see their analyst react or act on impulse. Remembering the biological origin of both reaction to stimulus and instinctual impulse and that not all ego activity is immediately conscious, I think it is a mistake to regard either as intrinsically undesirable or dangerous even in an analyst's work. In any case, when an analysis is moving swiftly and ideas follow each other in rapid succession, or mechanisms are changing, it is impossible to be always a step ahead of the patient or always to think before speaking or acting. One finds one has said something. If the unconscious contact with the patient is good, what is said in this way usually turns out to have been right. Unconscious countertransference is the thing that is most likely to prompt a wrong response, and the only safeguard against that is the analyst's continuous self-analysis.

The effect on the ego of conscious recognition of one or other of these things in an actual known person (as distinct from either a machine or a "type") is to make it accessible to transference interpretations and to other recognitions of reality. I have often found such a recognition to be a turning point in an analysis. By means of it a human being is discovered, taken in, imaginatively eaten, digested, and absorbed, and built up into the ego (not magically introjected)— a person who can take responsibility, commit himself, feel and express feeling spontaneously, who can bear tension, limitation, failure, or satisfaction and success.

The patient is enabled to commit himself to his analysis, his paranoid anxiety is relieved in a direct way, and transference interpretations can come to mean something to him. He begins to be able to meet reality and to deal with real people instead of with his phantasms. The development of relationship becomes a possibility, with its need for bearing both fusion and separateness and the risk of feelings being aroused in another person, or by another person.

CLINICAL MATERIAL

The material which I am using to illustrate my points consists of some episodes from an analysis. This involves compressing into the space of ten minutes things which belong to ten years. It can give only a very distorted picture, and I am aware that it is only understandable to a very limited extent.

The condensation of ten years into ten minutes is in fact quite appropriate, for my patient, Frieda, has been disorientated in time throughout the analysis, and she has used time in ways that are personal to her and that cannot be readily understood. This disorientation has been her main regressive feature; she has had no regressive illness and very little obvious regression in the sessions.

She was referred to me for difficulties with her husband and children; she also had a skin rash, affecting chiefly her face, vulva, and the inner surfaces of the thighs.

Frieda's childhood in Germany had been a very traumatic one. Her parents were Jewish. Her father was a very brilliant man, but vain, selfish, and megalomanic. His magical belief that no ill could befall him led to his remaining behind when all his family emigrated and eventually to his death in a concentration camp. Her mother is still alive—possessive to the last degree, mean, prudish, and insincere. She quarreled with her own relatives for years, and then with her husband, breaking up the marriage. She reviles him to her children, and now speaks of the marriage as always an unhappy one. She enjoys quarreling for the sake of sentimental reconciliations.

Both parents exploited their children. Frieda was made to be responsible for the younger ones. She was expected to wait on her father, forced to do things which she might have done of her own accord, if left alone, for she was very fond of him. In return for the mother's compelling her in this way, her father would punish any revolt or shortcoming by beating her severely, especially when she obstinately refused to say she was "sorry" for disobeying her mother. Her mother punished her by hitting her, dragging her upstairs by her hair, and locking her in a dark cupboard. When she was about four years old she was "cured" of masturbation by being put into a cold bath.

Her mother never forgot her crimes, even when they had been punished, atoned for, and ostensibly forgiven—they are kept in "cold storage" and brought out twenty years later, in all their original intensity. She still tries to exploit Frieda emotionally.

This picture of the parents came out slowly. At first they were described as loving, ordinary people, and it was with great surprise that Frieda found she had this other picture hidden away.

Frieda was the eldest child—she was a disappointment to her parents, who wanted a son. She was breast-fed for a few days only, as the milk "dried up" when her father joked to his wife about the child resembling someone else, not him.

At school she was unhappy, being often withdrawn, confused, and in a dream state. At one school she was made the subject of a lecture from the headmaster to all the staff and pupils for taking sweets and eating them under the desk. After leaving school she had one serious sexual relationship and finally married someone else and came to England.

Her friends found her capable, gifted, cultured, generous, and warm hearted. She is all of these, but behind a facade there was a deeply unhappy, wildly impetuous and impatient child, who could bear neither tension nor separation. Her children were extensions of her own body, as she had been of her mother's, and were unconsciously exploited as she had been.

After she had been coming to me for a year, she told me that a piece of furniture in my room reminded her of a cupboard in her childhood home. The jam was kept there, and she sometimes stole some. Then she told me that stealing was one of her real difficulties. It gradually appeared as part of a much larger pattern of impulsive behavior which brought her into various kinds of real danger. The impulsive actions happened when there was stress of any kind.

The first seven years of her analysis were characterized by failure on my part to make the transference real to her in any way or to "help her to discover it," as she put it later. The analysis was carried out along ordinary lines, within the limits of accepted analytic technique. Many transference interpretations were given, but they were all entirely meaningless to her. The only thing was that often she would give advice or comment to her friends and acquaintances based on things I had said, and even attributing them to me. But still they had no personal meaning for her, and the changes brought about were very slight. Her condition was certainly improved: there were fewer thefts, and her relationships were in general a lot easier. We were preparing to stop although both of us knew that the main difficulties still remained. I could sometimes get her to see where she was transferring something to her husband or one of the children, but never to me. Her emotional attachment to her mother was unchanged, and her mourning for her father never reached.

She had told me a story of a child who went into a room which was forbidden, and guarded, not by Bluebeard, but by the Virgin Mary. The child's fingers were covered with gold which she found there, and she was punished by being cast out. My interpretations about her curiosity, whether about her own body or about me, telling her of her idea about me as the forbidding, punishing Virgin with the hidden gold, meant nothing to her. It seemed that the key to her own locked door was lost beyond our finding.

Suddenly and dramatically the picture changed. She came one day beside herself with grief, dressed all in black, her face swollen with weeping, in real agony. Ilse had died suddenly in Germany.

I had heard of Ilse, among many other friends; there had been nothing to distinguish her from the others. Now I found that the

main part of the transference had been to her and had been kept
secret, apparently because of the guilt about the homosexual feeling
toward her. She had been a friend and contemporary of Frieda's
parents and had transferred her friendship to Frieda when Frieda
was six years old.

For five weeks this state of acute distress continued unchanged. I
spoke of her guilt about Ilse's death, her anger with her, and fear of
her. I said that she felt that Ilse had been stolen from her by me, that
she was reproaching the world, her family, and me, that she wanted
me to understand her grief as Ilse had understood her childhood
unhappiness, and to sympathize with her.

None of this reached her—she was completely out of contact. Her
family bore the brunt of it: she neither ate nor slept, and she talked
only of Ilse, who was idealized and whose photos were everywhere in
the home. She saw Ilse in buses, in the street, in shops, ran after her,
only to find that it was someone else. My interpretations that she
wanted me magically to bring Ilse to life again and that she wanted to
punish herself and her environment for her unhappiness fell on deaf
ears—nothing reached her. She could not lie down: she sat for a few
minutes at a time and ranged round the room, weeping and wringing
her hands.

After five weeks her life was in evident danger, either from the risk
of suicide or from exhaustion—somehow I had to break through. At
last I told her how painful her distress was, not only to herself and to
her family, but to me. I said that no one could be near her in that state
without being deeply affected. I felt sorrow with her, and for her, in
her loss.

The effect was instantaneous and very great. Within the hour she
became calmer, lay down on the couch, and cried ordinarily sadly.
She began to look after her family again and a few months later had
found the larger flat they had been needing for years, which up till
then she had declared was impossible. In fitting it up and moving into
it she found a happiness that she had never experienced before, and
that has lasted and grown. Her reparative impulses came into action
in a wholly new way.

I had often spoken about feelings in connection with myself, but
this had absolutely no meaning for her—only those feelings that were
actually shown and expressed meant anything at all. She remembered only too clearly having told her mother that she loved her, that

she was sorry for things she had done, etc., with her tongue in her cheek, to say nothing of her mother's exaggerated expressions of a love for her father, which was subsequently denied.

But I had also on two earlier occasions expressed my own feelings. The first was when I had sat listening for the hundredth time to an unending account of a quarrel with her mother about money and also for the hundredth time had struggled to keep awake. It was boring, and as usual no interpretation would reach her, whether it was concerned with the content of her talk, the mechanisms, transference, her unconscious wishes, etc. This time I told her that I was sure that the content of her talk was not the important thing, that it was defensive, and added that I was having difficulty in staying awake as these repetitions were boring. There was a shocked and horrified silence, an outburst of aggrieved anger, and then she said she was glad I had told her. Her accounts of the quarrels were shorter, and she apologized for them after that, but their meaning remained obscure. I now know that I was being to her the (dead) father whom she should have been able to tell how "awful" her mother was, and who should have helped her to deal in childhood with her mother's mental illness. I was also Ilse who should have been with her in all her difficulties. But if I had given this interpretation, I am sure that it would only have met with the same response as all the other transference interpretations.

The second time I had been having some redecorating done. She prided herself on knowing just how this should have been done and had often given me advice in a very patronizing way, which I had interpreted as her wanting to control me and own my house, to tell me things instead of having me tell her. This time I had had advice all day long from one patient after another, it was the end of the day and I was tired and, instead of giving an interpretation, without thinking I said crossly "I really don't care what you think about it." Once again the shocked silence was followed first by fury, and then a really sincere apology. Soon after this came the recognition that most of the good advice she gave to friends and people she met casually in the street or in shops might quite well have been resented and that in her anxiety to control the world she was, in fact, overbearing and a busybody.

After my telling her of my feelings at the time of Ilse's death, and linking it up with those earlier times, she told me that for the first time since starting her analysis I had become a real person and that I was quite different from her mother. She had felt whenever I commented on anything she did that I was her mother and was saying, as she had always done, "and you are an awful person." This I had known and had told her was a transference manifestation, but all meaning of this interpretation was denied—it, too, only meant "and you are awful." She called me "Lesson 56" in the textbook. Now she could link the textbook with the women's magazines which her mother had read and in which she found many of her fads and fancies. My feelings, being unmistakably real, were different from the counterfeit ones of her parents. They allowed her and her concerns a value which she had never had, except with Ilse. In other words, for her I had become Ilse in the moment of expressing my feelings.

From this time transference interpretations began to have meaning for her. Not only did she now often accept them when I gave them, but she frequently said "You've told me that before, but I didn't know what it meant," and even "I remember you saying many times . . . *now* I understand it," making the application herself of something which she had previously rejected.

Soon after this, for the first time, a pattern began to show in relation to the stealing and other impulsive actions. I was now able to see that they happened only when her mother was visiting her. But they were also increasingly dangerous. One day on her way home from analysis she was run over by a car and badly hurt. I don't know how she was not killed outright. Another time a neighbor of mine asked me, "Is that woman who runs out your gate across the road without looking one of your patients? She's very dangerous." Again, another day when she was expecting a visit from her mother, I went into a main road near my home, at a busy spot, and there was Frieda, twenty yards from a pedestrian crossing, leaping about among the cars, putting everyone in danger, including herself. I showed her the relation of these happenings to her mother's visits, and their suicidal and murderous character. She rejected this idea, as she rejected any idea of herself as ill, and as she had previously rejected all transference interpretations.

A few weeks later, while her mother was staying with her, she was caught traveling without paying her fare, being in a hurry and having no change. The consequence was being charged in the magistrate's court. I gave her a certificate stating that she was in treatment for her impulsive behavior and that essentially she was an honest and reliable person (which was completely true). This, like my expressions of feeling, made a deep impression, for I had said *openly* the very opposite of what her parents had said when they labeled her "liar" and "thief," and an "awful person." She began to recognize her dangerous acting out, and to be afraid of it, but it still continued.

The next time her mother came she stole again, and now I said I wondered if I should not refuse to go on taking responsibility for her analysis if she had her mother there again. I had already told her several times that I considered that she was taking risks in doing so. At her mother's next visit she stole once more, and I repeated what I had said.

I showed her that she had neither believed in the danger, in the reality of her illness, nor that I could have meant what I said. I assured her that I did, and that if she had her mother there again I could not take the responsibility for her—I would interrupt her analysis.

About this time she spent several sessions telling me of the bad behavior of a child who was visiting her. She had also told me of her little girl's' disobedience, and I had asked why she could not be firm and not allow them to go on doing the same things over and over again. This was an old story; she was never able to get obedience from her children without flying into a violent rage and frightening them into it. She let them do just what they chose, rationalizing it as being "modern," or "advanced," and they would stay up late at night, miss school, etc., and neither she nor her husband could do anything about it—in fact, unconsciously they encouraged it.

I asked her what would happen if I refused to let her go on telling me these stories. I was as tired of them as she was of the children's behavior. She "didn't know," and went on into another story. I said, "I meant that. I'm not listening to any more of them." She was silent, then giggled and said, "It's *awful.* And it's *glorious,* to have you say something like that. Nobody has ever spoken to me like that before. I didn't know it could be like that. You've often told me about telling the children that I won't have them do things, but I simply didn't know how to do it." And from then she began to be able both to accept "no" for herself and to say it.

Now I reminded her that I told her that I would stop her analysis if she allowed her mother to come again, and of her finding it "glorious." For the next three days she was in a panic and confusion. When it subsided she spent some time planning how to refuse to have her mother to stay. She put her off for some weeks and then the question came up again. Would I tell her what to say? Could she let her mother come, and she would go out and sleep at a friend's house? I showed her that this was no solution and that she had to find her own way of dealing with the situation. After more panic and fury she told her mother for the first time about her analysis and that I had forbidden the visit. This was tantamount to saying "You are an awful person" to her mother.

Next day she had an impulse to steal apples from a neighbor's garden. Just as she went to slip through the fence with her basket she stopped herself. She later sent one of the children to ask for some and was delighted and surprised to be given them.

I showed her that in seeing her mother at all she had in fact defied me, in a token way, as well as obeying me, and that her altered behavior over the apples depended on her having been able to accept "no" from me and to say "no" to her mother. She had found me reliable in that I meant what I said about this and that even if I did stop the analysis I would not be angry. She had begun to believe in the realities she had been denying. From here her feelings about her analysis changed a lot—she began really to suffer, as she never had before, especially at the weekends. One hour was not long enough— she was wanting me all the time and was living in her analysis all day long, even though she was doing her work more effectively and living her life differently. The transference became a reality for her at last.

She had difficulty in folding up the blanket, in deciding whether to bring up my milk when she found the bottles on the step. These were old difficulties, and she found she wanted to do quite the opposite things about them. Here I could show her how much of her feelings toward me had been put on to these things. She described herself as split (it was her own expression, I had not used it) and she showed me how far apart the pieces were, holding her hands about a foot apart. I reminded her that at one time part of her had been here and the other in Germany, in Ilse. She found that she wanted to look at me with "stolen glances," and discovered that she had had two beliefs, one that I was her mother, the other that I was Ilse—both had been held with delusional strength and with an hallucinatory quality which she could now begin to disperse by consciously checking up with the reality. The stealing came directly into the transference, and she found herself traveling without paying her fare on her journeys to me.

About this time she came into closer contact with my hate of her than she had been before, in a way that meant something real to her. One day we had met by chance at a concert, and she found me afterwards in the musicians' room, to her great surprise. "I didn't know *you* knew X," she said, angrily, and next day discovered that she had meant "What right have *you* to be here?" From there it became possible to show her (as I had often tried to do) how she had been trying magically to control me and to have me with her everywhere. Much of her concert going had been to go with me, and finding me there in reality had disturbed her fantasy. I showed her, too, what it would have meant *for me* to have met her often, to have come up against her possessiveness in that setting. For in her idea of herself, expressed in her behavior and previous talk, she owned not only me but all the concert halls—artists and composers as well.

Recognition of her omnipotent fantasy led to the realization that she had been expecting something unattainable and magical from her analysis. She had believed that it would make her husband, children, mother, brothers, and sister well, back in her childhood, and bring both her father and Ilse to life again. Her "stolen glances" enabled her really to see me as a person for the first time. "I've discovered something. It's very painful, and yet I'm so glad. I found that I know nothing about you, nothing at all. What a fool I've been. I've put all that tremendous effort into trying to make you be something you aren't. Whatever I thought I knew, however I struggled to make myself understand, reading Freud and Melanie Klein, all that effort was so futile. I feel so stupid. I was trying to force you. I'm so sorry." I said she need not be sorry. She glared at me and burst out furiously, "I *will* be sorry if I want to," and then she told me of her secret game of "associations" in which she thought of a scent, a building, a book, etc., to "associate" with me. Now her "secret glances" showed her how unreal it had all been.

Next day I had a cold, and she felt it impossible to talk as anything she said would be attacking me. She recognized that she was wanting something magical, two opposite things at once, to be there and to go away, to protect me and to destroy me. Now she had seen that no amount of analysis could make it possible. I spoke of the inner world of her imagining and the world of outer reality—only in an inner one could it be like that, and while her inner world and mine might meet in places, they could never be the same. She was silent and, I thought, nearly asleep. She hid under the blanket. When she came out she said she had been trying it out. She had thought, "If I keep quiet I can be here and not be here, and you go to sleep, dear, if you want to." She felt relieved and whole, for it had worked. I told her that she had brought together the inner and outer worlds, allowing herself to have her own and me to have mine. She had been a whole person, separate from me.

The following day she found that she had been able to do something in an unplanned and unarranged way, and it had been good. This had never before seemed possible. And she had discovered a new sort of feeling that she did not understand—she felt gratitude toward someone she did not love and had been able to help someone in a new way. It made her feel different, both toward other people and toward herself. She had been "arrogant'" before, now she could be friendly and could like herself. I said she had found that she could like and dislike the same person and so need no longer split me into two and put part of me elsewhere, magically.

Then she recalled an incident when she was four years old. She was out with her father, and she was holding a little stick in her hand, about the size of his penis. He took it and threw it into a stream, and showed her it floating away under the bridge. He said it was her "naughty temper." She could not feel that it had anything to do with her, as she had not been in a temper at the time. She now saw that she had really believed it to be his penis. She had seen it as that and had been disappointed and angry at his taking it from her. She knew now that it was true, as I had said, that she had never been able to mourn for him, as his death "had nothing to do with her." She had "not caused it by being angry" and yet believed that she had.

Here we could see more clearly than before how many things in the earlier part of her analysis had been difficult because of her failure to symbolize. For example, she had often fought with herself as to whether she should bring up the milk bottles she had found on my doorstep or not. It had been utterly impossible for her to decide and useless for me to interpret anything about it or to tell her that it didn't matter which she did. Only now could she see that to her the milk bottles not only represented me (as I had said) but *were* me, and that she had wanted to kick them off the step, as she had been kicked by her parents and by the car that had knocked her down. But in her delusion it meant actually kicking me. The blanket too, had had the same significance. At last she was free of them, someone else could fold the blanket and bring up my milk. It was no longer her responsibility.

Her ambivalence became clearer. "I hate you because I love you so much," she said; and again, "Damn you and blast you, and bless you, for loving you so much."

Separateness was so far accepted; fusion, or merging, loss of identity has been more difficult. Along with the difficulty in accepting it goes the difficulty of allowing herself only to hate or only to love me, wholeheartedly, now that I am the person toward whom both are felt instead of being the loved person while her mother is hated, or the hated one while Ilse is loved.

She described how she felt she was "inside a capsule and trying to get out, but altogether lost outside it." The capsule is transparent, even invisible. She recalled, as a child of six, having drawn a circle in the sand and sat inside it, believing herself to be invisible and feeling utterly bewildered when someone spoke of how she looked sitting there. A similar thing happened years later when she ate sweets in school not knowing that she could be seen.

Here at last, in her own description, is the basic delusion by which she has lived and which has been her main defense throughout the analysis.

I linked it with an observation which I had made several times before, that I thought she had at some time witnessed the primal scene in a mirror, being screened from seeing directly. I spoke of the difficulty in understanding about a mirror unless someone is there to show the child her reflection or unless there is some familiar and identifiable object that she can see both in the mirror and without it. She said "You've told me before about seeing my parents in the mirror, and I've never believed it. I don't remember it—but I know which side my cot is on—it's on the right side, and I *know* it. I can see a room, but all the furniture's strange—I don't know any of it." Then she recalled hearing that in the second year of her life for a short time the family stayed in an hotel. That was the only time she had slept in the parents' room as far as she knew, and the memory of it had been denied.

The "capsule" represents among other things her identification with her father, the magical father whom nothing could touch. It also represents the magical, invisible penis by means of which she could remain one with her mother and with Ilse. Ilse she kept invisible—until her death shattered the "capsule" and revealed her. My identification with Frieda in her loss and grief restored it, but with me inside it in Ilse's place.

It was this that made both mourning for her father and for Ilse possible, through the analysis of the transference which until then had been inaccessible.

For her to break the "capsule"—to discard her delusions—has meant annihilation, both by separateness and by fusion. Only if someone from outside could break through it forcibly and safely could she emerge as a living, feeling person and only a person with real feelings could do it by making her feelings available. Everything had to be held fixed, magically and invisibly, out of reach of the primitive, destructive love-hate impulses. Now she is sitting among the ruins of a world that she has shattered and is looking for ways of restoring it—not restoring it by trying to bring her father and Ilse back to life, or by trying to make her parents well and happy forty years ago and more, but doing so imaginatively by means of the new creative activities that are already at work in her, activities that we call sublimations.

She is happier now than she has ever been, but also unhappier. Her mourning is not yet accomplished, but she is well on the way to it. Her home is a more reliable place for her husband and children, for she can say a thing and keep to it, she can differ from her husband without having a furious row in front of the children as she used to do, and she can allow them to be individuals. The stealing has stopped altogether, even when her mother visits her. Other impulsive behavior is greatly modified. Her sex life has altered—she can now enjoy it and have genital and psychic orgasm. The skin rash rarely troubles her, and the world she lives in is becoming sane and ordinary (though there may be mad things in it), instead of it being hostile, anti-Semitic, and mad. She knows that it is through Ilse's death that she is getting well, she has accepted her pleasure in Ilse's death, and her hate, her destructive love, and her sadness. The analysis still goes on.

I have not gone into the very complicated psychopathology of this woman. For my present purpose it is enough to say that her capacity to develop a reality sense had been seriously impaired; symbolization and deductive thinking were largely replaced by concrete thinking. She was unable to distinguish between real visual and auditory impressions and hallucinations, or between reality and delusion. Splitting of the ego while it was still a body ego had resulted in persistent failure to make accurate perceptions, or accurate deductions from such perceptions as she made. The consequence of this was that all her transferences were delusional, and on them were based all her relationships.

She had to be reached, through layer on layer of splitting and denial, on the level of helpless dependence and no-separateness—the level of her paranoid delusion. This, like all other delusions, was not susceptible to transference interpretation: it had to be broken down in the most direct way possible, i.e. through the analyst as an actual person.

IMPLICATIONS FOR TECHNIQUE

The growing realization that there are many patients who cannot make use of transference interpretations until some change has taken place that makes the ego accessible leads to the question of what alterations in technique and in the theory of technique are necessary.

Difficulties in getting transference interpretations accepted, the arising of sudden, unpredictable tensions which often result in violent acting out have been regarded as due to some insufficiency in the analyst—insufficient analysis, failure to deal with his own anxieties, acting out on his part.

Verbalization, understanding, and interpretation have been regarded as all-important. But the need for "working through" has long been recognized as a necessary process in analysis. It is important to understand what is going on during that process and whether there is anything that can be done to help it on.

Looking at patients such as the one I have cited, we find that patients whose reality sense is seriously impaired, who cannot distinguish delusion or hallucination from reality, cannot use transference interpretations because the transference itself is of a delusional nature. Transference interpretation calls for the use of deductive thinking, symbolization, and the acceptance of substitutes. It is not possible to transfer something that is not there to be transferred, and in these patients their early experiences have not enabled them to build up either what needs to be transferred or a picture of a person on to whom transference is possible. They are still living in the primitive world of early infancy, and their needs have to be met on that level, the level of autoerotism and delusion.

Ways have to be found of presenting reality to these patients, many of whom cannot use it as it presents itself in their daily life.

The reality that is present, available, in every analysis is the analyst himself, his functions, his person, and his personality. It is up to him to find his own token ways of using these to meet the individual needs of his patients, to find out what is practicable, and to set his own limits in the handling of his patient's anxieties, as far as possible determining consciously what he will or will not do, but being willing to act on impulse, and on occasion to react. This is part of his acceptance of himself as he is.

In the early days of analysis no analyst had much personal analysis or much experience (either his own or other people's) to draw on, and in those days, "wild analysis" did in fact lead to danger situations which could not be dealt with. But conditions are different today, and the assertions that certain things are dangerous, or impede the analysis, can be tested out. Many such assertions seem to me to have the mythical or superstitious quality of superego judgments.

We have to recognize that the same paradox that we find in other areas of life is there too in analysis—that the same thing can be both bad and good, that what is most valuable can also be dangerous and useless. This is as true of transference interpretation as it is of answering questions, expression of feeling, acting on impulse, etc., by the analyst. The great need is for flexibility (which is not weakness), reliability, and strength (which is not rigidity), and a willingness to use whatever resources are available.

What I have tried to show is that the results that we all hope for and expect to get can be obtained if we are willing to approach the analyst's attitude to his patient from a new angle and to recognize some of the things that are in fact done in analysis, but often disregarded or not admitted.

My own awareness of them has been increasing. I have been evolving my way of working since 1937, before I began training as an analyst. Later, I tried to discard what I already had in favor of a more classical or less "unorthodox" technique and failed with a number of patients whom I still feel I would and should have been able to treat. In practice what I do varies widely from one patient to another. It is in itself an expression of the patients' individuality and a confirmation that I am not impressing something on them that belongs not to them but to me. This approach has both advantages and disadvantages. Quantitative measurement is never possible in analysis, but the usual tests and checks can be applied, as in all our work.

The original assessment of the patient's illness can be reevaluated, especially in the light of his response to transference interpretations. If such interpretations are consistently felt by him to be meaningless, even if in fact he shows that they do mean something somewhere, or if on the contrary they are accepted but no changes in behavior or ways of thinking follow, either of these I would regard as pathognomic of the presence of a deep split and a great deal of paranoid anxiety, the defenses against it being stronger in the second case than in the first.

This means that ways of making the ego accessible to transference interpretations have to be found. Whatever is found will have to be subjected to the usual scrutiny. My own questions run something like this:

Why do I do or say this?

How does it relate to things in myself—conscious or unconscious?

Why to X and not to Y?

Would I do or say it to this patient in other circumstances, another day, another time?

What effect does it have, and why?

Does the bringing of new material follow?

Is there any real ego development?

Could the same results be got otherwise? Quicker? Better?

If so, how, and why? and why have I not done something different?

One cannot always answer one's own questions right away. Sometimes the answers turn out to have been wrong; sometimes there is no answer to be found except that it felt right at the time or was the only thing one could find to say at a time when something had to be said. Subsequent events usually show whether it was right or not, and when one finds an analysis going on well where one has done something out of the ordinary, one's confidence in one's own unconscious processes increases. One's counter-resistances seem to break down more quickly, the work goes on often at a higher tension, and the analyst's greater spontaneity helps the patient to break down his own rigidity and stereotypy.

The main difficulty lies in a general state of unexpectedness. This does not mean everything being out of control, though it often feels like it to the patient. It is rather a state in which things can happen. The risk, of course, is that there may be a sudden "triggering off" in the patient or in the analyst when an unknown factor turns up. This again is something which can happen in any analysis and has to be dealt with when it does.

The account which I have given of one patient's analysis, condensed as it has had to be, could be a very misleading one. The variations in technique which I have shown do not always come off. When they do, the effect is very like that of any right interpretation: there may be rejection first and acceptance later or acceptance straight away. There may be no effect immediately to be seen, and it may appear later that there had been some. When they do not come off, again, as with ordinary interpretations, something may happen or not. And like ordinary interpretations, if the time is right and they are appropriate, their effect is good. If not, the effect is bad, and they are mistakes like any other mistakes. In Frieda's analysis the things I have quoted did succeed and were not mistakes. I think they were not just lucky flukes either, for I have experienced similar things in a number of other analyses with similar results.

The purpose of these things is quite clear, and limited. It is to make the patient's ego accessible to transference interpretation by breaking up a delusional transference.

Interpretation does not make any impression on delusion. The only thing that does so is the presentation of reality in a way that is comparable to waking up out of a dream—that is, finding that something that has been believed to be literally true is untrue, by confrontation with what is true. This does not make ordinary interpretation redundant, nor is it a substitute for it. It does not do away with all resistance. Ordinary interpretative work has to go on before such episodes as I have described, through them, and after them, and it still remains the main part of the analysis. Without it these other things would be useless but, in cases where the transference itself is of a delusional nature, they are the only kind of thing that makes transference interpretation meaningful and usable, for it is through them that a human being can be discovered behind the interpretations.

SUMMING UP

I have tried to show certain elements, some of which I consider essential, in the analyst's total response to his patient's needs, some ways in which they can be used directly, and the kind of effects that I have found from such direct use of them. They are things that in my opinion need to be made clear at some point in every analysis. They appear more obviously in the analysis of very disturbed patients and less so in that of neurotics. They are there, implicit or explicit, in every good and successful analysis that is carried out, and something of them is there in every analysis that is even partly successful.

The analyst's total love and hate of his patient, which provide the motive force of his total response, contain both some things that are basic and nonvariable and some that are variable. The analysis, as far as the analyst's share in it is concerned, depends mainly upon the quality of the basic, nonvariable part. This, in its turn, depends on the extent to which the analyst's world in which he lives is a sane and friendly one—i.e. on how far he has been able to deal with his own paranoid anxieties and his depression, anxieties that are inseparable from the work that he is doing. If he can rely on it, and consequently on himself, it will probably be safe for his patients to do so, and they will come to do so increasingly. If not, it will probably not only be unsafe but also impossible for them. Then there will be failure and perhaps tragedy.

It is this basic, nonvariable factor that provides the stability of the analysis (again, as far as the analyst is concerned). The variable things, the unconscious countertransferences, the day-to-day or hour-to-hour variations in the amount of strain he is bearing, his health, his outside concerns, all these tend to make for difficulty, especially if they have too wide a range of variation. These are also part of the analyst's responsibility—he has to see to it that the range of variation is not too great and that the variations do not get fixed or unfixed again too easily. But these things, like all the others that I have referred to, can be valuable as well as harmful. They are part of the analyst's life, and they make for life and movement in analytic work.

Analysis is a living thing, and like all living things it is changing all the while. Even in the few years that it has existed we can see many changes, especially in the field of technique. Patients are treated today who would have been thought unsuitable even a few years ago. Mrs. Klein reminded us that such things as analysis of children and interpretation of transference were once looked at askance. We cannot know what analysis will become in the future; we can know only that it will change, that we are contributing to its future, and that today's changes will look different to those who come after us.

"Countertransference," in the various meanings of the word, is a familiar phenomenon. At first, like transference, it was regarded as something dangerous and undesirable, but nevertheless unavoidable. Nowadays it is even respectable!

But I feel that it should be a great deal more than this. We do not know enough about our responses to our patients and have been (on the whole wisely) cautious in using them. But a very great deal of psychic energy goes into them, whether we wish it to be so or not, and if we are to get anything like the full benefit of this energy, either for our patients or for ourselves, we have got to be willing to experiment and even to take some risks. I am sure that experimenting by trained and experienced analysts is essential for the further growth and development of psychoanalysis, but it needs to be done against a background of responsibility, known and willingly taken.

4

ON DELUSIONAL TRANSFERENCE
(TRANSFERENCE PSYCHOSIS)

I

In practice one finds certain patients who cannot use transference interpretations—the difference between these and other patients is qualitative, not quantitative. They do not form a defined group, but include people suffering from character disorders, sexual perversions, some psychosomatic conditions, psychopaths, etc., i.e. sane people with a great deal of both persecutory and depressive anxiety.

When a transference interpretation is given to such a patient, either (1) it is experienced by the patient as meaningless, and no use can be made of it, or (2) it is accepted by the patient with apparent understanding, but the analyst realizes later that it has had no effect; no change happens, and no insight has been gained.

In the analysis of these patients several other characteristics are found.

a. Ordinary analysis of their dreams does not work. They bring dreams of two kinds. Of one, the manifest content leads to innumerable associations, but no meaningful latent content can be found. Nothing exists in the dream but the defensive mechanisms. In the other type of dream the manifest and the latent content are one, and the manifest content is the dream thought.

b. There are defects of thinking. The capacity to symbolize is deficient, there is "symbolic equation" ("primary process symbolization"), and concrete thinking, and the capacity to make accurate deductions or inferences is largely lacking.

c. Acting out is violent, or the violence appears negatively as passivity. These patients call a good deal of attention to themselves, involve other people in their affairs, and interfere in the affairs of others.

d. They tend to be very dependent and find someone else to carry out as many of their ego functions as possible. There is neither real separateness nor real fusion, no mutuality, only reciprocity—"tit-for-tat," "you scratch my back and I'll scratch yours." Their relationships turn out to be folies à deux in which each partner claims preference and precedence; both are violent, or one dominates and the other is passive, sometimes alternating.

The analytical relationship is understood only on this kind of basis, and attempts are made to establish a folie à deux with the analyst. Unequal relationship or give-and-take on someone else's terms seems to be something which has never happened before; the idea is met with blank incomprehension, going on to fury when the patient has to give way; if the analyst gives way it may not be perceived at all, but if it is perceived it produces great satisfaction, and guilt.

e. These patients seem to develop a sort of addiction to analysis. They have an insatiable need for love and attention by means of which they seek magically to control their limitless hate and destructiveness.

This "addiction to analysis" leads to a ruthless, repetitive searching for something, at any cost to either patient or analyst. But this very quality sometimes makes an unpromising-looking analysis successful in the long run, if only that "something" can be recognized and got, at least in token measure. The gap between the need and what is got has to be fully acknowledged by the analyst.

f. These conditions seem to have arisen out of a situation where the mother herself was infantile, and as incapable of bearing either separateness or fusion as her baby, a mother whose anxiety and inadequacy acted as real persecutions to the child. The depressive position could not be reached, as in these circumstances the ordinary mechanisms of projection and introjection are distorted. (This is an oversimplification, of course, but I cannot enlarge upon it here.)

II

In these patients the character of the transference is essentially delusional.

As in neurotics, the transference is ambivalent and is therefore twofold, though it often appears only in its positive aspect as what has been called "erotized transference," the purpose of which is to keep only the idealization and to deny that the opposite exists.

But a neurotic can recognize the analyst as a real person, who for the time being symbolizes, or "stands in" for his parents, either as they actually were, or as he experienced them in his childhood, and he is accessible to verbal interpretation of the transference.

Where the transference is delusional there is no such "stand-in" or "as-if" quality about it. To such a patient the analyst *is,* in an absolute way, with a quality of "authenticity," both the idealized parents and their opposites, or rather, the parents deified and diabolized, and also himself (the patient) deified and diabolized, for the analyst is assumed absolutely to be magical.

To resolve the transference, the patient has to be enabled to bring together his love and his hate onto one person, to find both good and bad aspects of his analyst, his parents, and himself as human beings, and to know the difference between imaginative and objective reality.

The main mechanisms used in the production and maintenance of a delusional transference are splitting, denial, isolation, projection, introjection and repetition.

But it seems to be chiefly a failure of integration between psyche and soma (with consequent failure of integration between weakly organized ego and id) rather than a "split" that makes the ego inaccessible to transference interpretations, so they cannot either result in altered behavior or bodily activity or lead over from inner to outer reality. Their false acceptance or rejection depends on the insistence on identity between analyst and parent-imago: "Of course, how could it be otherwise?" or "Fancy thinking that!"

This failure of integration depends upon very early body experience, when awareness is essentially body awareness, at a pream-bivalent, presymbiotic, preverbal, preobject relation stage. Tension is experienced as something intolerable, threatening life itself. Dis-charge is experienced according to the setting in which it happens and its effect on the environment. Response by the environment may be felt to be good or bad; absence of response of a positive or active kind may be felt to be either, according to the patient's need and his previous experience of response, and, where bad, as a persecution.

The transference delusion hides a state in the patient which he both needs and fears to reach. In it subject and object, all feeling, thought, and movement are experienced as the same thing. That is to say there is only a *state of being* or of experiencing and no sense of there being a person. There is only an anger, fear, love, movement, etc., but no person *feeling* anger, fear or love, or moving. And since all these things are one and the same, there is no separateness or distinction between them. It is a state of undifferentiatedness, both as regards psyche and soma, experienced as chaos.

To reach this state is a terrifying thing, as it means losing all sense of being a person and all sense of identity. The patient who reaches it becomes for the moment only a pain, rage, mess, scream, etc. and is wholly dependent on the analyst for there being anywhere a person who feels or acts. There is, in fact, identification with the analyst of primary kind, but the patient cannot be aware of it.

This state has to be reached so that the unreality of these identities can be recognized, but the reaching of it is felt as utter annihilation—hence the need to maintain the delusion in the transference. At the same time, the inner reality of these identities has to be preserved. In a neurotic where the relation between inner and outer reality is established, the inner reality of these identities is already axiomatic, and survival can be taken for granted, but in a deluded person any fresh recognition of reality is felt as a threatened destruction of everything, and both inner and outer reality seem shaken to their foundations when the delusion is disturbed.

The quality of the disturbance is cataclysmic and can be compared to orgasm. It might be described as an "orgasm of pain," with tension rising to a climax, discharged in an impulsive movement, and followed by relief. It is not an agonal state, as there is no person suffering it, no functioning ego. In effect it is a state of frenzy, and the discharge, an *acces de rage,* may take the form either of an attack upon the self, self-injury or suicidal attempt, or of a maniacal attack upon the analyst. It is a moment of very real danger. When the movement is outward, toward the analyst, contact is made with a person who is separate from the feelings and movements and uninvolved in them: he experiences them, but his experience is different from the patient's, and this brings a new situation. The delusion cannot be maintained and is no longer needed.

With the movement has come differentiation. The giving up of the delusion starts from the discovery of a body moving in response to an urge and finding contact. This is the beginning of recovery, for the primary identification breaks up, secondary identification becomes possible, and through that again can come the ability to take the consequences of a happening.

III

It follows that the analysis depends upon breaking up the delusional transference. To do this, reality must be presented undeniably and inescapably so that contact with it cannot be refused, and in such ways that the patient does not have to use either inference or deductive thinking. It might be compared to the waking from a dream of a tiny child, but someone must be there to help the waking.

Regression to a very early dependent level is unavoidable, and there are many patients who cannot manage without some regressive illness. In my experience this is usually so where an existing folie à deux has to be destroyed for the analysis to be carried out. Dependence is both demanded and rejected, and it is not always easy to get a patient to accept the care that is needed for safety.

Body memories of very early infantile experiences of primitive "orgiastic" quality, both good and bad, have to be found, i.e. both of real satisfaction and of real frenzy. These have to be linked with experiences in the analytic situation, also of a body kind, otherwise both the separation between psyche and soma and the limitless destructiveness and insatiable need for love persist unchanged. The early experiences have to be reconstructed as convincingly as possible and linked with the analytic experiences through whatever cover-memories can be found to serve this purpose; any element of conjecture must be admitted.

The analytic setup provides something toward these body experiences, though its importance in this respect is often overlooked; e.g. the couch, warmth, shaded light, quiet, etc. Where there is regressive illness or a lasting psychotic episode more may be needed; hospital or nursing care in intercurrent illness can give a good deal in this way. These things need to be firmly linked with the transference, appearing as and being used as extensions of the analyst himself, on the delusional level, he taking full responsibility for them in the realm of psychic reality, whatever may be the actual reality and however much the patient may be aware of it in another area of himself.

Verbalization has to go back not only to nursery and onomatopoeic words but to very primitive sounds and mouth movements, from where other movements and body happenings can be reached, so as to make the contact between inner and outer reality and to help the change over from concrete and magical thinking to the acceptance of substitutes and symbolization.

Since transference interpretation is found to be ineffective, other ways of bringing the patient into touch with reality have to be found and used—ways that are out of place in the analysis of neurotics. In order to reach both preverbal and body levels and to enable the patient to reach the state he dreads the analyst's ego function has to be maximal and his object function minimal. He has ultimately only himself to use, since the help from the outer world is small and has to be related to him—psychically it has to come *from* him.

The analyst's own instinctual impulses have to be used as fully and directly as possible. Very primitive emotions are suddenly aroused in him, often leaving him no time for conscious thought before he has to speak or act. Provided his own analysis has gone far enough for sublimations to be established, provided he is mature, knows his limitations, and is not depending on, or exploiting his patient, the dangers which are admittedly there are fair risks, especially considering the seriousness of the illness.

He may sometimes have to use body activity and movement, e.g. to hold a destructive patient in a frenzy. He may have to allow his feelings to be plainly seen, as the only meaningful way of conveying the truth about a situation to a patient to whom words cannot convey it and who cannot make deductions from the less personal, less direct "signs" to be found in the analytic room and ordinary analytic technique. There are times when nothing can reach a patient but a direct expression of what the analyst is feeling at that instant and times when such expression has immediate and profound effect—just because it is meaningful.

It is through these things—feeling and movement—that the patient finds himself as a separate person, with likenesses to and differences from other people, as his analyst is like others and yet different from them. But the recognition that it is true when the analyst says that feeling and its expression are right comes most clearly when the patient finds it happening, experiences his feelings and his analyst's separately, finds who is feeling what, and that the relationship is not destroyed as he had expected.

I have only touched on the question of technique in analyzing a delusional transference. Ordinary interpretative technique forms the main part of the analysis; it cannot be superseded or replaced, but it can be supplemented in the ways I have indicated, to make the ego accessible to interpretation. The technique needs to be flexible, with free use of imagination (and flexibility does not mean sloppiness, any more than rigidity means strength). The fundamentals of analysis must be observed, and the analyst's own analysis must be continued, actively, throughout.

POSTSCRIPT

A number of speakers at the Paris Congress[1] (in particular those taking part in the discussion on neurotic ego distortions) described patients for whom it was impossible to make analysis mean anything, patients whose ability to use it appeared to be blocked in some way, for whom some new method of approach seemed to be needed.

I have tried to put forward something of a new approach, and I want to link it with the work of other analysts besides these. There are, of course, many who have touched on these problems either directly or indirectly. I will mention only two people, Ernest Jones and Freud.

In the *International Journal of Psycho-Analysis,* in a short communication entitled "Pain," Ernest Jones (1957) describes how "when the white-heat peaks of intense pain are reached localization disappears, and the entire self is filled with nothing but pain," and he

1. International Psycho-Analytical Association, 20th Congress, July-August 1957.

goes on to describe the ego's reaction to it. This is the state of a person suffering pain, but at this point it borders on the state which I have described above, where unbearable stimuli break through the defensive barrier *(Reizschutz)* at a very early level of ego development, and the sense of being a person is lost. He speaks elsewhere of *aphanisis,* giving the term different meanings for the individual at different stages of his ego development. He does not refer to it in this communication.

But the state which I have described, in which there is loss of all sense of being a person, is a state in which the ego's defensive functioning is temporarily suspended deliberately, through the analytic process, and id drives are released.

In the *New Introductory Lectures* Freud described the id as "all that the ego is not . . . a chaos, a cauldron of seething excitement." "Instinctual cathexes seeking discharge," he said, "is all that the id contains."

But Freud has also described the breaking up of a delusion, and he has done so in much the same way as I have. I have not consciously followed him here. I read Delusions and Dreams during my training as an analyst. I have only reread it in the last few weeks and found that I had forgotten it almost entirely. Wilhelm Jensen's novel *Gradiva* tells the story of a young man's temporary delusion and its cure. His sufferings when the delusion is disturbed differ from those of a patient whose delusional transference begins to break up only by being less in degree. It is clear that he is in danger at this time: he perceives a threat (real or imagined) to the young girl whom he is both seeking and avoiding, and in averting the danger, by impulsively "swatting" the insect that might sting her, he touches her arm with his hand, and in doing so finds her reality. The final breakup of the delusion, and his recovery, come about as the result of this body movement and contact.

Freud traces in detail the processes involved, in the light of psychoanalysis. His account is penetrating, self-consistent, and convincing, but he does not suggest the possibility of resolving a *fixed* delusional state in this way. I was astonished to find that the analysis of my patients whose transference is delusional follows this exact pattern, but of course, since the delusion in these cases is neither temporary nor recently developed (nor are the patients characters in a novel), recovery does not come about through a single episode of this kind. It has to happen repeatedly, and with each repetition it becomes more meaningful and more effective.

This word *meaningful* was often used by speakers at the Congress, and I think that *its* meaning for us in this context is really "ego enlarging." It seems that in these delusional cases the ego enlargement can only come about to all intents and purposes traumatically, which partly accounts for the difficulties encountered.

I want to go on to something more about the state of undifferentiatedness which the delusion hides. It is a very complex subject and calls for a separate paper which I hope to be able to write. It is not a new or original theme; only my approach to it may be new.

The terms *primary identification* and *primary narcissism* to my mind do not fit it, nor does *paranoid-schizoid position*. I would rather describe it as a state of primordial undifferentiatedness, or of *basic unity*, in which a primitive identification might be said to be included. What I want to convey is that the undifferentiatedness is absolute, in both degree and extent. Nothing exists apart from anything else, and the process of differentiation has to start from scratch.

From this unity a body happening (such as movement, salivation, etc.) crystallizes out, and emotion follows it, according to the response of the environment. These happenings are largely painful ones. The discovery of pain helps to differentiate between self and not-self. Discovery of positive pleasure seems to help only secondarily by making the discovery of pain tolerable at all; primarily it tends to increase the cohesion between the undifferentiated particles, and so to make for stability. But the discovery of pain is already a differentiation in itself, and the process, once started, tends to continue, progressively and cumulatively, and can do so as long as there is sufficient stability inside and outside the analyst/patient entity.

The analyst's task, then, is to enable the patient to suspend the defensive functioning of his own ego, to let the analyst function for him, and let happen what happens, the analyst being in charge and looking after things, otherwise chaos develops. This process can come about through this same basic unity, for the patient feels "What you want is what I want, since you are me and I am you." We have here, too, I think, the explanation of the compliance which we so often find in our patients, and its negative, defiance.

The further task, after the delusional transference has begun to be resolved, is that of enabling the patient to take over his own ego function of suspending his defenses, recognizing for himself when he is deluded, and dealing with what lies behind the delusion in his own individual version of the way in which his analyst has done so for him, before.

Being able to do this involves perception of the analyst and his ways of doing things, going on to internalization of him on the primitive pattern of eating (which is a body experience, not magical introjection), digesting, absorbing, building up into the self, so that the analyst is no longer there recognizable in his original, unchanged form. All of this depends on separation from the analyst, i.e. differentiation out of the basic unity.

For this purpose the analyst must accept fully the basic unity, being at once indistinguishable, psychically, from the patient, and still preserving his identity. He must find what he feels right for himself (i.e. what he wants to do or say), and assume that it is equally right for the patient. It is a point at which he must be able to commit himself, even sometimes risking making a mistake, but remembering that the biggest mistake of all at this point may be *not* doing just this. He has to be very plain and definite in saying certain things, but leave the patient free to take or leave them. Refusal on the patient's part often only means delay until once more the basic state can be reached, when he feels "if you think that, then I do."

It is sometimes difficult to avoid the appearance of "cashing in" on the patient's compliance and dependence, but waiting usually brings acceptance (though this acceptance, of course, does not of itself guarantee the analyst's rightness).

This state of basic unity is the unconscious basis of the whole of the transference phenomena; it can account, too, for such things as suggestibility under hypnosis and the mysterious "confessions" we often hear about. Where pleasure, promoting love, has contributed enough to its strengthening, it is there, axiomatic, and taken for granted. It becomes the basis of marriage, mothering, and such sublimations as child care, and psychoanalysis itself.

Where it has been too early or too extensively disturbed by pain, whether bodily or psychic, in infancy, with the balance of ambivalence tipped in the direction of hate, and chaos develops, it can be seen for instance as the basis of the less attractive features of ideologies and of class and racial strifes. Where it has to be asserted (in order to deny its absence or insufficiency), we find bonhomie and brotherhoods.

In this paper I have talked about what and why rather than about how. The how is not easily described in ways that convey meaning. Once one begins to describe ways of doing things that are unfamiliar to one's hearers, anxiety is inevitably aroused, with consequent misunderstanding and distortions. We have to rely largely on empathy, which *is* relying on this basic state, but enlarged by experience. Each of us has to find his own how, by trial and error, letting happen what happens in himself and finding out for himself the realities of analysis.

5

DIRECT PRESENTATION OF REALITY IN AREAS OF DELUSION

I

In other papers I have described patients in whom areas of primary total undifferentiatedness ("basic unity") have persisted into adult life as a delusion—borderline psychotics; and how in analytic work with them they are unable, in those areas, to use the sophisticated processes of deductive thinking, drawing correct inference, symbolization, or metaphor.

This comes from the undifferentiatedness itself, as here, the symbol and the thing symbolized are absolutely one, as are the deduction, its source, and its consequences.

For this same reason these patients are not able to test reality in many areas; they have first to *find* it. They are engaged upon processes of differentiation and integration, and not upon such things as projection and introjection, identification and repression, all of which presuppose a separateness of subject and object. This is where the psychotic annihilation anxiety lies, as separateness and merging are *both* apprehended as identical, inevitable, and annihilating. The simultaneous conflicting aims are to maintain and to destroy both identity with, and total separateness from the therapist, identity and separateness between subject and object, thought, and feeling. It is a complicated and all-pervasive state indeed where such undifferentiatedness obtains.

Reality, then, has to be presented to these people without the need for deduction, inference, or symbol, i.e. via the actual and concrete; the mode of presentation will be specific both to the individual patient and to the immediate context. Once the reality has reached the patient's awareness, the nonpsychotic part of him, which has had to be suspended temporarily, can come into play, and whatever capacity for deduction etc. he has can then be used. But this has to be secondary to the finding of the reality.

Most of the realities that need to be presented belong to a very early level—the level where differentiation between psyche and soma is beginning and long before verbalization is possible. Linking with words becomes possible only later, but is then essential.

This is the level of the undifferentiated state, where body experience is of first importance; on this level experience which can have meaning for the patient has, in fact, exactly the same kind of effect as a correct and well-timed interpretation has in the analysis of a psychoneurotic, as I hope to show through clinical material.

II

Sometimes if a particular body experience is not found the analysis jams up completely, and further progress cannot happen.

Charles had great difficulty in keeping his analysis going at all. He missed every Monday's session, and in many weeks at least one other. When he did come he was often unable to say anything. After months of this the analysis was really threatened with breakdown.

One day he found that he wanted to throw something at a certain jug on my mantelshelf. Any attempt to understand why, or to imagine doing so was useless—he did not know why, or what was stopping him talking about it, but *something* was. At last I gave him a ball of crumpled newspaper, which he threw over and over again, missing wildly every time. He became quite desperate, something was stopping him from aiming properly. He went to throw again, and when his arm was raised he suddenly said angrily, "Don't *do* that." I asked, "What happened?" "You pulled my arm," he said. He threw the ball again, and hit the jug squarely.

Then he remembered his mother doing this, he had felt her pull; now he had hallucinated it. This linked with experiences of being stopped from putting things into his mouth, and of keeping it firmly shut to prevent something being pushed in or taken out, and from there to interruptions of breast feeding and memories of being forced to take medicine.

His mother seems to have organized confusion, artificially bringing conflict from outside; two texts hung on the wall: one read, "Don't worry, it will never happen," and the other, "Cheer up, the best is yet to come."

She confused him about his identity, "My *nice* little boy wouldn't do that. This can't be Charles," and "*You* don't want that, do you?" He had never been able to establish the identity of his own body, and many body memories had never been assimilated.

I put my hand where he had felt the pull, and he found that he could distinguish between the real contact and the hallucination, and between me and his mother. She might quite well have touched him and denied it, or suddenly distracted his attention and confused him about what had happened. He saw her doing this kind of thing now with her grandchildren. In fact, he had been seeing it for some time with them, but only now could he deduce that she must have done it with him.

The same kind of release can come when a reality of another kind is found.

Henry had been for a holiday with his brother a few years older, a special one that he had looked forward to for a long time, to a place where he knew I had not been. He had imagined going there with me in my car. It had involved missing a few sessions.

I had shown him beforehand that there was a risk of his having an accident, because of his anger with me for not taking him on my holidays, and his expectation of retaliation. He had had car accidents before, in this kind of context. We had then been working over memories of earlier outings with his brother, from which he had come home sopping wet, cut, and bruised. I spoke too of the unconscious hate between the brothers.

When he came back he was very offhand and noncommittal about the holiday. It had been "all right" (rather grudgingly), and then he lapsed into one of his long silences, looking deeply unhappy.

I waited, and then said, "You know, I'm very glad you enjoyed the holiday so much." He opened his eyes, stared at me, and said, "Good lord! That had exactly the same effect as an interpretation." His mother had grumbled at the wetness and the cuts; she had tried to stop him from going with his brother ("You don't want to, you won't enjoy it"), and he had had to hide his excitement and enjoyment. This had been one of the factors causing the accidents, but talking about it beforehand and relating it to the transference had only been an intellectualization, whereas my telling him directly what I felt at that moment had real meaning for him.

After this he remembered being taken out by his older sister (who until then had come into the analysis as no more than a name), and being upset out of his pram. This was recalled with acute fear, giddiness, and headache. I related it to the sensations experienced during and just after birth—the original massive "upset"—and also to later excretory "accidents," exciting, and enjoyable, but punished severely by spanking.

What I want to convey is the way in which a piece of reality presented so, inescapably and unmistakably, not only breaks up delusion but helps to bring about differentiation which has hitherto been prevented. As the experience becomes usable, misapprehensions and wrong deductions etc. can be sorted out by using words.

In his commentary on Jensen's *Gradiva* ("Delusions and Dreams") Freud points out that to attempt to convince someone of the falsity of his delusional ideas is useless; it only arouses hostility. It is necessary to accept their truth *for him,* to enter into the delusion, and then break it up from inside by a direct presentation of what is real.

This entry into the delusion by the analyst (without, of course, his being deluded too, or accepting the truth of the delusion as actual) is an important element in finding the form of presentation best suited to the particular patient at any given moment.

Alice had been for a fortnight in an unshifting resistance and unbroken silence, and unmoving. Today she lay twisting and writhing on the couch. Suddenly she said, "I feel trapped; I can't move, I'm caught by the leg." She went on wriggling and turning, in a frenzy, but holding one leg out stiffly towards me. I waited and then put my hand lightly on her ankle. She gave one flip with her foot, which I allowed to push my hand away. I said, "I was the trap."

She then began to talk freely; she told me how in childhood she had seen a rabbit with its leg caught in a trap and how her dog pounced on it and killed it—how very dead it had looked, motionless and silent. From there she went to primal scene material and memories of finding bloodstained clothes after her sister's birth when she was two years old. An older boy cousin caught and tormented her, and there had been some sex play with him which had been both exciting and frightening.

When I put my hand on her ankle I took over being the trap, (on the delusional level) so that she no longer had to be both trap and rabbit. That liberated the energy of the part of her that was being the trap, (the mouth) and so let the "rabbit" part be strong enough to break free and move and speak.

In the nonpsychotic part of her Alice was, of course, fully aware that her leg was *not* caught in a trap, that my hand did not really restrict her movement at all, and that I knew this too. But in her psychotic area there was absolute belief that I *was* a trap that was holding her, that I was the cousin who had held her forcibly, the mother who had often restrained her, and also the drive of the birth forces. But since I could move, and she and I were one, then she could move too, and *in moving* she became aware of being separate from me. There was a delusion of being caught in a trap that meant destruction and annihilation, and to move meant to be annihilated. There was delusion of being identical with me. Only when I accepted the reality for her of the delusional ideas and their *psychic* reality for us both, could she recognize their *factual* unreality.

To have said anything like, "You feel yourself caught and you think I am the trap, as you thought you were the rabbit" would have been quite useless to the psychotic part of her, which was not joined up with the nonpsychotic part. Only showing her on the level of body sensation that she could move safely could break up the delusion and bring about the necessary fusion of psyche and soma, and of her psychotic and nonpsychotic parts.

An alternating rhythm develops of merging psychically with the patient, imaginatively becoming one with him, and then separating out again, which enables him in his turn to find oneness with me, and separate himself out again from there.

I know that this sounds like projective and introjective identification, but the word *identification* already implies separateness between subject and object. I am trying to make clear a rhythmic process of differentiation out from a homogenous mass, followed by a reattachment or assimilation back to it, a process which is both repeated many times and can later be varied. It is the forerunner of projective and introjective identification.

The importance of such movements as I have been describing lies in the fact that memory is primarily body memory and that movement plays a great part in bringing about differentiation and the discovery of realities about both self and the environment. Movements which are met in the right way can be psychically elaborated; they are assimilated and join up with other experiences, becoming something to be repeated, something creative, and a starting place for new movements and new experiences. Most important of all, perhaps, they become assertions of the self and a starting point for developing relationships.

If an infant puts out a hand and meets the mother's hand, or breast or face, he ultimately discovers, through many repetitions of the experience, something about the existence, nature, and activity of a part of his environment and his relation to it. He comes to know that he has a hand, that it moves, and something happens. If he only meets hard cot bars, a slap, or the smothering of the mother's body in a restraining "absorption" (as described by Bonnard) the experience will mean something quite different, and unavoidable repetitions of it will not help him in his differentiation/integration processes, nor in his sorting out of reality from delusion, or inner from outer reality. What should be there only as fantasy becomes reality for him and cannot then be subjected to the ordinary processes of projection and introjection. Ego organization may be seriously impaired in this way.

Martin had infantile eczema, which persisted throughout his childhood, and his hands were always bandaged. His mother avoided all body contact as far as she could and brought him up according to the Truby King method. She told him that it hurt *her* when he cried, and he had not understood that he cried when something hurt *him*.

He would lie on the couch with his head almost in my lap and hold my hand, which he would explore with his own, and smell, saying "soap," or "onions" etc. according to what he found. In a frenzy he would move his hand so as to get his wrist held by me, and then make punching and lunging movements. I let go, being pushed away. His fear of hitting me was so great that he hit the wall on his other side. I

pointed out that he was hurting himself—that he didn't seem to know
the difference between me and the wall—if he thumped the couch he
would hurt neither of us, but would be hitting something of me—my
couch—which could be an imaginative extension of my body, as the
wall was. I took his hand and brought it first to touch my face, and
then to touch the couch, which he thumped and thumped, till he was
satisfied.

Next time, when he was angry he pushed my hand away, with a
minimal movement, which I showed him was effective, as he needed
it to be, otherwise he would never find that he could be effective. He
made an unrehearsed movement suddenly and hit my face about as
hard as a baby might, and I showed him the importance of this for
differentiation and reality appreciation. He found great relief from
this, and joined it up with his difficulty in passing a driving test, an
accident he had had in which a man died (where the police had had to
determine whether he had been responsible or not), and my having
spoken of a car as a lethal weapon. He hardly even knew that he had
hands, let alone what they were doing or might do. Then he could
find, too, that although I minded things hurting him that didn't mean
that his crying hurt me.

III

In analysis body movement is limited to some extent by using the
couch, and in psychoneurotics the tendency to verbalize is increased.
But borderline psychotics cannot always verbalize and often have to
move first. When any patient lies down, regression occurs automatically to whatever level contains the predominant anxiety at that
time; in borderline patients it is most often to their psychotic level.
The movements, although made with a fully grown body, are
essentially those of an infant: an infant whose movements have been
so inhibited or made so meaningless that they have remained ineffective. When an effective movement is found, it can be linked with
speech.

Lack of experiences which most people take for granted, and
indeed hardly believe could be missing from any childhood (such as
the free kicking of a naked baby, or crying oneself to sleep), and the
presence of other experiences (such as being left tightly rolled in a
shawl with the feeding bottle propped up on a pillow, all limb

movement being prevented), over too large an area, reinforce the lack of basic unity or its premature interruption, and so prevent differentiation and the assimilation of experience.

Finding these new experiences and reliving the memories of the old ones in the new setting of the analysis restores the unity, though the immediate effect of disturbing the delusion is that of shock. Relief, restoration and change come later.

Hilda arrived early for her session in an obviously excited state. She lay down while I was still drinking my mid-morning coffee.

"Will you give me some of your coffee?" she asked; I drank some more and then handed her the mug. She held it between her hands for a few moments, then gazed at me in amazement, drank the coffee quickly, and handed back the mug. "What did you think I would do with it?" she said, and I replied that I had not known, but had half expected that she might throw it in my face. She said she had thought she would pour it over her own head, "But when I felt the lovely shape of the mug in my hands, and the warmth, and smelt the coffee I found I just wanted to drink it." The excitement was discharged, and we went on to something else.

Hilda's infancy and childhood had been so traumatic that in order to survive she had had to hide her feelings both from other people and from herself. She had also had to imagine pleasurable happenings, but disaster followed whenever she tried to bring them about. Different standards prevailed in her childhood home between grown-ups and children. She had thought of my coffee as belonging in the world of the grown-ups and that what she would get from me would be a rebuff, or something from the "nursery" world. She would show her revolt in the kind of way she had always done, by pouring the coffee on her head. But she found my spontaneous response different, and this changed her feelings altogether, and her behavior. She could then join sensation and emotion together and link both with words, through movement, mine and her own, without disaster.

IV

I use my hands a good deal, both in gesture and in touch, in analyzing delusion, but it is not easy to convey just how, when, and why I move or touch a patient. Most often it is simply putting my hand somewhere, according to the context, as when I put my hand on Alice's ankle when she felt caught in the trap, or if there is severe headache I may put my hand on the patient's forehead.

I was once asked, "When do you touch a patient?," and I said then, "When I can't bear *not* to any longer." Since then I have been able better to judge whether it is fitting or not, but also to be less afraid of spontaneity.

It has been believed that any physical contact between analyst and patient must inevitably be understood as a sexual seduction. As students we were taught this, and that it is not so could only be found in this way, by actual experience.

Dick was unable to talk at all in one session; he had a "splitting" headache and was plainly suffering. I put my hand on his head, and after a while he moved, showing me that he no longer wanted it. Then he gave a little laugh, and I made an enquiring sort of sound. He said that when I put my hand there his first thought had been, "Good God! the woman's a nympho!" and then he had found that there was nothing sexual in it. He then told me a dream which related to his real "headache," the imminent split-up of his marriage, which he had not mentioned before. He had assumed that I knew about it, as he did, since we were one.

(An experienced colleague once told me of his surprise at finding when a patient took hold of his hand that it was "just like holding a small child's hand—not sexual at all.")

If an analyst feels guilt about touching a patient, then his action may have come though unconscious countertransference (using the term in its strict sense, as I have defined it elsewhere), or it may be that he has realized too late that it was inappropriate. If the patient feels guilt it must somewhere relate to the transference and may be to do with either an aggressive or a sexual impulse.

A hand can become a "stand-in" for a nipple, penis, etc., sometimes for the whole body; but I have come to realize that on the delusional level it often becomes no longer mine, but something of the patient's own, beginning to be differentiated out. It is also a token, but a token equated with what it stands for, like so many other things, the couch, blanket, or coffee. It is in something of this way that I understand both the phenomena described by Mme. Séchehaye as "symbolic realization," and those of "symbolic equation."

It is important, of course, to know when and when not to touch a patient, e.g. if a patient develops excitement out of touching or holding the analyst's hand he does not usually want an active response. But if he is already excited and cannot find release otherwise, then contact may enable him to find it; if it is being expressed there is no occasion for the analyst to touch him and to do so would be an interference. Contact may be needed *after* the discharge to show that both analyst and patient have survived it and to preserve the (psychic) unity between them.

When it is remembered that the body happenings I am describing belong to earliest infancy and that by the time that anal or genital levels for instance are reached words have already begun to be used, it may be easier to understand that the usefulness of body contact is limited, and why in psychoneurosis it is both unnecessary and unhelpful.

I have to be aware of any excitement that I may experience myself, to find out whether it belongs with my own infantile experiences and is material for analysis, or whether it is objective, belonging to the immediate situation in the analysis of the patient. Doing analysis is often very exciting, and the excitement may well be appropriate.

But just as the usefulness of and occasions for using movement and body contact are limited, so too are the uses and occasions for letting the analyst's emotion (including excitement) be seen. Feeling of one kind or another in the analyst does belong to many situations which arise, and in fact it is a large part of the driving force in any analysis.

Occasionally the full force of feeling turns up in direct impact, and to restrain its expression then could only put the brakes on the whole movement of the analysis. These moments are important for both partners, and they are often remembered as outstanding. The whole course of one patient's analysis was altered when I showed her my feeling about her intense grief for the loss of her mother. It was the point at which I entered into her delusion, though I did not recognize this at the time. And I once shouted at this patient, in a fury. She had often *heard* what I said as shouting, but this time she heard the difference, and it mattered. A turning point for another patient came when I moved my chair from behind the head of the couch so as to sit facing him, where he could see me. He had expected to be looking at me all the time (and that I would be looking at him) but found that after the first few minutes he only looked occasionally, when he needed to for some specific reason.

Apart from direct expression of the analyst's feelings, talking about them in a simple, straightforward way, what they are now, or what they were at a particular time often helps someone who, because words or actions are seen only in the light of a set of delusional ideas, cannot deduce what another person is thinking or feeling. The truth can only be found if it is presented "straight."

In speaking of letting my feelings show, or expressing them, I do not mean only positive feelings, love, friendliness, appreciation etc., I mean the whole range of feelings that turn up, from laughter to tears and from love to hate. What matters is that they are *real*. Nor do I mean that any and every feeling is disclosed as and when it is there, only that it has its place, and that in that place it is right and valuable. Far more often its use and expression are indirect, even when the feeling itself is fully conscious. Nor again do I mean that an analyst's feeling is stronger or better than another person's, only that it is important that whatever is there should be freely available for use, whether in direct or indirect expression.

This calls for a straightforwardness in the analyst that matches what we ask of our patients, and that is surely desirable in all our dealings, though in our ordinary lives and with less ill patients reticences and reserves are no obstacle and can be taken for granted. If, as sometimes happens, we cannot avoid being less than truthful—to safeguard someone else, or even for self-protection—it is essential to recognize both the fact and the reason for it, otherwise we make difficulties for ourselves as well as for others.

In working in this way I have found two safeguards, and it is rare for both to fail. The first is that the patient will stop me when he wants to, as Dick did by moving. The other is in myself, a limit that I find automatically. This second one may fail either through my unconscious hate of the patient or through failure to recognize the element of delusion, but the effects usually show soon, and when I do realize it there is something I can do about it.

But these two things relate to the basic unity—the point where the patient stops me is the point where he is separating himself from me. Where I stop it would feel bad to me *for myself* to go on, and I know that it would not be right for him; i.e. where I experience him as if he were myself or myself as if I were he, and that to stop is right for both. To me this is one of the clearest examples of empathy that I know.

It is surprising how little detail a patient will want. "How do you know these things about being ill?" I have been asked, and my answer, "By having been ill myself and got well" was enough. Only "Were you as ill as I am?" and the answer, "Yes" or "No" was all that was further needed.

Talking over his illness, its severity, and prognosis with the patient, what is meant by "breakdown" and perhaps especially the question of suicide calls for the same directness. He needs to know the truth as far as his analyst knows it, even though somewhere he already knows it himself.

If he were to kill himself, what would the analyst feel? His right to do so must be admitted, but only a clear statement that the analyst *would* care, that he would feel grief and loss, not guilt (though even that may have to be there about the times when he could actually wish for it, because of the hate the patient has aroused in him, most often objective hate) can convey the fact that he takes the question seriously and feels the responsibility, but he would neither die nor kill himself if it were to happen. And the ultimate responsibility must be shown to rest with the patient himself. If he does *really* want to kill himself the analyst cannot prevent it and it would be final. (To a small child dying means merely going away and coming back when wanted, so the finality must be stated.) All this is true and fitting, and it allows of both oneness and separateness between the two.

But it is also an assertion of the analyst as a real person, allowing the patient his reality too. Nothing can be lost through such an assertion, even if it is exploited by the patient many times and in many ways. In my experience it brings so much clear gain, in recognition of truth that stands.

In the end, of course, the patient has to find that my feelings, words, or movements are of no use to him as a substitute for his own, and it is this that finally breaks up the delusion of our being identical. He discovers that while he and I may feel the same way about some things we feel quite differently about others, and that although we share many happenings our experiencing of them is not the same. But these can only come about through my first accepting fully the truth *for him* of his delusion of identity with me and then showing its objective untruth, but also its truth *in inner psychic reality for us both*.

This principle of oneness of patient and analyst cannot be shown unless it is honestly accepted, though it is there to some extent in every analysis. The two are *in fact* part of one another's lives over a long stretch of time and deeply engaged in the analysis in which they have both common and mutual interest. This the patient can experience as something so close as to obliterate any boundary between them—a parallel to the body closeness of his face and the cushion when, lying on the couch, he cannot perceive where his face ends, and the cushion begins.

V

In the analysis of areas of delusion, then, reality is presented in a very direct way, on the same level as that of the delusion—a primitive, preverbal, preambivalent, preobject relation, body-experiencing level. The disturbance of the delusion is experienced as a painful shock because one of the patient's "catastrophe" points has been reached, but the outcome is relief when the cathexis shifts from the delusion to the reality. The delusion loses its here-and-now immediacy and may remain as a memory, or be forgotten. The altered modes of perception result in altered ways of thinking and behavior. Energy which has hitherto been used in unending struggles against destructiveness and despair comes free for creative purposes; the ego begins to function in a more coordinated way; it becomes accessible to verbal interpretation, so that ordinary analytic technique is appropriate and can be used.

Delusion can still turn up, on the old pattern, in times of stress, for it is not done away with in any area that remains psychotic—there it remains unchanged. The difference is that it has become possible for the patient to recognize for himself that a state of frenzy, for example, disproportionate feeling, or inappropriate behavior must relate to delusion if ordinary reflection cannot change it, and he can then seek it out and understand it as his analyst has done before. He comes to be able to find the movement that will bring him out of his frenzy, or the relevant memory, and to trust to the basic unity within himself.

I have said elsewhere that these delusional ideas not only come from the factual reality of the oneness of mother and fetus before birth, but also that they have a positive value. It seems to me that the idea of a fundamental oneness, or "basic unity" is in fact the basis of not only stability in the individual and society but also such things as family life, home, and any sense of belonging. All transference phenomena, symbolization, and empathy are rooted in it. The implications are enormous, once the idea is grasped, and it can throw light on many things hitherto not understood.

POSTSCRIPT

Such episodes as those I have described usually come after long and careful work. Trust in the analyst has had to be built up through experience of his reliability and general predictability. A good deal of repetition is often needed in the working through.

What I am chiefly talking about is dealing with a patient's "catastrophe areas" (Galatzer-Levy 1978) or "catastrophe points," where sudden changes come about through the analyst's constant pressure ceasing to have consistent effect and *reversing* the patient's reaction. Aggressive impulses can change to flight, expressions of hate to expressions of love, and vice versa.

The experience is not, in my view, "corrective." The original damage cannot be undone, but providing other experience to put alongside the earlier ones enables the patient to bring his more mature, nondelusional self into action.

But, of course, the patient is an individual in a setting, and consistent pressure in the outside world, where he is faced with a reality hitherto unacknowledged, can bring about sudden change in exactly the same way. This can be dangerous, precipitating a psychotic episode, which the analyst should be ready to meet if it comes.

The variables are almost infinite, and so are the potentialities for change; but both must be *real*, not matters of fantasy, and a very large degree of stability in the analytic situation is essential, as the "uncertainty principle" is also involved. One can neither measure nor accurately predict the changes, for even in observing them one alters both the changes themselves, and the events that follow, by one's own unconscious reactions.

This brings in the matter of the analyst's integrity. His responsibility for changes, whether good or bad, resulting from his work is that of the researcher to his material. It means that an analyst working in catastrophe areas or areas of delusion must be willing to know and use similar areas in himself; otherwise his countertransference will make difficulties for both his patient and himself, and there are enough there already.

I will end with two quotations from Rudyard Kipling's *Captains Courageous* (1908).

"When Disko [the skipper of a Cape Cod trawler] thought of cod he thought as a cod."

When I am analyzing a borderline psychotic patient I have to think not only *like* a borderline psychotic, but *as* a borderline psychotic, i.e. using my own psychotic areas.

"Dan did things automatically . . . as he made his dory a part of his own will and body, but he could not communicate his knowledge to Harvey."

One's technique becomes a part of oneself, but it is difficult to communicate it to others. Every analyst has to find things for himself and to develop his own individual ways of working.

6

ON BASIC UNITY (PRIMARY TOTAL UNDIFFERENTIATEDNESS)

I

In the analysis of patients whose transference manifestations are of a psychotic rather than a neurotic kind, I have found two characteristic phenomena which I want to examine. One is a particular position which they attempt to force me to accept; the other is the supreme importance for them of body happenings, as shown in their acting out—i.e. body memory.

These patients are people who cannot in any circumstances take survival for granted. There exist in their unconscious memories experiences of something which we must really regard as annihilation; in many cases there has been in early infancy some actual threat to life—illness of the infant or mother, hostility in the environment, etc.

They have been variously described: objectively, as suffering from, e.g., a "basic fault" (Balint 1955) or "psychological catastrophe, or disaster" (Bion 1958) and, subjectively, as by themselves—"I am cut off from my roots," or "I have a fracture-dislocation."

Their insistent, prolonged, and exhausting efforts to repair this condition have been described by a number of writers as attempts to establish a "symbiotic" relationship with the analyst, but I think this use of the word is a misleading one. In my experience it is not a state of symbiosis that the patient seeks to establish but rather one of total identity with the analyst and of undifferentiatedness from him.

Some clinical illustrations may help us at this point.

1. *Miss E.* told me that, when I first went to the hospital where she was, in place of the doctor who had been treating her, she had thought to herself "Here's a new doctor; she wants a patient."

At first sight this could be seen as a piece of realism, and secondly it can readily be understood as projective identification. It was in this way that I interpreted it to her, and she accepted my interpretation. Only after many years of analysis did I come to recognize that it had meant much more than that, and that although she accepted the interpretation she could not really use it. She had understood my need of a patient and her need of a doctor to mean absolute identity of person between us. Her acceptance of the interpretation also meant identity of person, as did my acceptance of her for treatment, whereby I tacitly confirmed her in her belief, asserted that I too believed it, and was therefore, once more, one with and inseparable from her.

Many years later, when moving towards termination, this patient found it almost impossible to leave me at the end of every session. She would experience agonizing pain in her buttocks and would scream, as she had screamed in childhood when severely beaten. When I recognized the hate aroused in me by her attempting to prolong the sessions in this way and making me feel guilty for not doing so, I could separate myself out from her. Then I could see, and interpret, that she felt *in her body* pain that she believed she was inflicting on mine (as, in her hate, she wished to do). The pain she experienced was remembered in a bodily way and was now psychic, not somatic. Temporarily there was no differentiation anywhere— only massive identity.

This patient's breakdown had followed a threat of separation from her sister with whom she believed herself, in a delusional way, to be identical. Their relationship was a folie à deux. Her recovery has been based on this delusion of total identity with me, which has had to be gradually broken down, as far as factual reality is concerned, while the psychic reality of it has had to be preserved with the greatest care. I will refer to the technical aspects again later.

2. *Mrs. M.* was referred for psychotherapy, as being "very ill mentally, with various psychosomatic symptoms; if not treated she may develop a serious physical illness and die."

She was unable to lie on the couch. She found great difficulty in keeping her appointments because she lived a long way off and had a little girl, aged seven. Although the sessions were arranged to fit in with the child's school life, Mrs. M. started bringing the child with her and then tried to get her husband to come too.

She painted three portraits of me, all of them with large dark eyes, like her own. She told me that her mother, whom she was said to resemble, had also had them. I drew her attention to the eyes in the pictures and asked if she thought mine were really like that. She looked intently into mine and said "But that's how your eyes *are*." (They aren't.) I would contrast this with a neurotic patient who got up off the couch, after spending an hour talking about my white hair, and laughted at his picture of me, finding that it was fair.

Mrs. M.'s mother had died when she was born, and her father had laid her beside her mother's dead body "so that she would have known her, at least for that time." She drew me a picture of this episode so that I would also have known her.

She gave me enormous bouquets of flowers, usually white ones, circumventing any attempts on my part to understand the unconscious significance of the gifts, and at Christmas she brought me a large card, with a picture of a cat, and the caption "From one cat to another."

After a few weeks of treatment she left her husband and child and took a flat where she expected me to live with her. When she found that I did not, she interrupted her treatment altogether and found a lover. He stayed only a few weeks, and shortly after he left her she went into a sanatorium suffering from tuberculosis.

I did not analyze Mrs. M., but I came to understand something about her through work with other patients.

In chapters 4 and 5 I have described as "delusional transference" this tenaciously held, absolute belief in the analyst's total identity with the patient himself, and with his parents, both deified and diabolized (i.e. having magical qualities, good and bad). It also extends to everyone with whom either the patient or the analyst has any relation. In effect, it extends to the whole world, both of people and things, of thought, sensation, emotion, and movement. The state of total undifferentiatedness I have called "basic unity." It is, actually, a delusion, but a valuable one, and as I shall show later, it is founded in certain factual realities of whose memory it is the psychic representation. It is also a state to which the patients concerned apparently need to regress in order to repair the "basic fault" or psychic "fracture-dislocation," i.e. to find their psychic roots.

This unconscious delusion, of course, only exists in certain areas of the patient's psyche, otherwise he would be totally insane; in other areas he is well aware of the reality of the analyst as a different and separate person from himself and from his parents, and nonmagical. This awareness of the reality is used as defense against the delusion. Such a use of one reality against another is, in fact, the most difficult of the defenses to penetrate, because giving it up exposes the patient to acutely painful states of increasing confusion and depersonalization, which are experienced as chaos or annihilation.

The fear of annihilation, however, is dynamic and all-pervading and therefore governs the patient's reactions and his behavior, both in relation to the analyst and to his environment. This fear, and the drive to establish identity with the analyst, lead him both to avoid these states of depersonalization and undifferentiatedness and at the same time to seek them, at any cost to himself or to the analyst. By reason of the life-and-death quality of the patient's experiences, his concrete thinking, and inability to make deductions, and the fact that events belonging to earliest infancy are being lived out in a grown-up body, these phases of the analysis contain a large element of actual danger (suicide, death, or attack upon someone, often the analyst), which calls for great care in the management of the case. In fact, the management becomes a vital part of the analysis itself, psychically if not actually, and the body events may become the interpretations. Verbalization then becomes the second stage in a two-stage process, both stages being necessary for real insight to be attained, but the second being effective only as a result of the first, i.e. of the body happening.

These states of depersonalization appear temporarily in the course of the analysis of a transference psychosis as states in which, psychically, nothing is differentiated from anything else. There is apparently awareness of one thing only, distress or pain of an overwhelming intensity, such that all else is annihilated, including any sense of being a person, even that of being a person suffering.

Discharge, and consequent differentiation, comes through some body event—a movement, a scream, salivation, etc.—by means of which some kind of bodily contact with the analyst occurs. Through repetitions of such events the patient comes gradually to recognize the difference between his body, his sensations, and his emotions, while those of the analyst are discovered as separate from his. The event has concerned two people, and the patient discovers himself as a person who has moved, screamed, etc., in relation to another person, whose separate existence, experience, movements, and responses can also be recognized. The delusion breaks up, recovery begins, and relationship becomes a possibility.

The importance of these body happenings lies in the fact that in those areas where the delusion is operative the patient is to all intents and purposes literally an infant, his ego a body ego. For him, in these areas, only concrete, actual, and bodily things have meaning and can carry conviction. These areas are separated off from those where deductive thinking, inference, and symbolization operate, but not through splitting mechanisms. The "basic fault" is a failure of differentiation and integration, splitting being an ego activity belonging to a later stage of development.

What appears to happen in these patients through their states of frenzy and depersonalization is a process of alternating differentiation and integration in which a kind of first awareness or discovery is experienced, which might be regarded as "personalization." The person can then go on to "reality testing" later, in connection with verbalization.

This "first awareness" is often a first awareness of the body, or of some part of it, for these patients behave as if the body were only some kind of appendage to which they happen to be linked, which is more a nuisance than anything and not an essential part of the self. The body is thrown around, in unawareness of sensation, function, or purpose, like that of an infant, and surprise is expressed when these things are found.

The quality of this first awareness has led me to understand the body happenings to which I refer as relating to body memories of prenatal and earliest postnatal life which have not been assimilated. It seems to me that in these patients there is a discontinuity between those earliest body memories and later experience, and that this discontinuity must be repaired before survival can be taken for granted. Only when this has been brought about can certain other processes follow, one of which is the development of the pleasure principle, for pleasure is not a reality and can have no meaning except in survival.

I would like to illustrate what I mean by talking about a lump of plasticine.

A lump of plasticine is homogeneous; it may have shape perceptible from outside, but not from within. Outside it may in fact be related to other objects, but it takes no account of them. Within itself it is nothing other than itself. A piece of it may become protruded, or nipped off, formed into another shape, and stuck on again—i.e. assimilated back to the lump, but differentiated from it, retaining its new shape or character. Here is the beginning of differentiation and integration, and of creation. The basic unity of the plasticine is first broken and then restored; there is coherence and stability, and a fresh place to go on from, but the essential nature of the plasticine (its *physis,* in the original meaning of the Greek word) remains unaltered.

In speaking of the undifferentiated state as it appears in the analysis of adults, I mean such a "lump of plasticine" state, one to which the patient has needed to regress in order to come forward again by means of new differentiation and the assimilation of new experience, finding and extending his basic unity. (This state of undifferentiatedness may of course be used defensively against the recovery of repressed memories and ideas, but this is not what I am attempting to discuss here.)

The analogy with the lump of plasticine can be strained too far, but I am using it to show the difference between a very early state, where psychically, the patient-infant is, so to speak, a lump of plasticine, and a much later one, where ideas of inside and outside, or "me and not-me," have begun to develop. He may then believe his whole inside to be full of homogeneous plasticinelike stuff, which he can imaginatively put outside himself, filling the whole world with it. In this earlier state nothing exists but himself: it is a monistic state of autoerotism, or more accurately perhaps "panautism," by which I mean a state in which nothing but the self exists.

Ideas such as projection, introjection, identification, subject, or object can have no meaning in relation to something totally undifferentiated, except from outside it. Differentiation comes about through movement, contact with the outside world (discovery), and assimilation back to the lump, or integration. At this point "autoerotism" may begin to change into narcissism, narcissism being by definition concerned with the self as both subject and object.

I am thinking here of a passage in Freud's paper "On Narcissism" (1914): "We are bound to suppose that a unity comparable to the ego cannot exist in the individual from the start; the ego has to be developed. The autoerotic instincts, however, are there from the very first, so there must be something added to autoerotism—a new psychical action—in order to bring about narcissism."

In my view this "new psychical action" is the beginning of the rhythmic processes of differentiation out from the primordial, undifferentiated state, and integration, or assimilation back, of the differentiates. The tendency toward it is inherent, but when these processes are disturbed, narcissism fails to develop, autoerotism (or "panautism") remains, and ego development may be seriously impaired, with grave risk to the psychic life of the individual.

As far as objective reality is concerned, I would repeat, this undifferentiated, "panautistic" state is a delusional one, and it remains unconscious in transference psychosis until it is uncovered in the analysis; no patient is in fact an infant, or wholly undifferentiated. The delusion, although accepted as true for the patient, is not shared by the analyst (unless, unfortunately, he has something of a countertransference psychosis).

It follows, then, that in the patient's delusion, patient and analyst are one and indivisible, identical and continuous, and without differentiation either within the entity or between the entity and anything in the outer world.

II

I want now to consider the primordial state of the fetus in intra-uterine life. There is at this time a unity with the mother which is broken up by the birth process. Up to the time of birth, although the fetal circulation is distinct from that of the mother, the mother's respiratory, digestive, and excretory systems are functioning for both, i.e. for the entity.

The fetus is in fact wholly dependent upon the mother, without whom it could not continue to exist. The mother, of course, is not dependent at all upon the fetus. The state of affairs, then, appears more parasitic than symbiotic, but to look upon it in this way is to do so from outside rather than from inside. From inside, as it were from the point of view of the fetus, it is a state of unity, or absolute identity, between fetus and mother.

This intrauterine state, with its continuity with the mother, provides the infant with the stability which is needed at the outset of life; the total birth experiences, and those which immediately follow, seem to set the pattern which tends to persist. At birth the first major contact with the environment is experienced, and it appears that only if something near enough to the intrauterine state is reestablished and maintained long enough without further disturbance can the experience be assimilated (i.e. linked with prenatal body experience) and become a useful one. Assimilated it can lead on to further differentiation and integration; it can be psychically elaborated and become creative, not disruptive. It becomes in any case a point of reference for every subsequent experience.

That is to say that every subsequent experience tends to become psychically *either* a restoration of the undifferentiated state, out of which differentiation and integration can safely occur, or dissolution, bodily dismemberment, and chaos.

"Return to the womb" has been thought of as something universally desired, a state of bliss and absence of demand; it sometimes happens that a patient who regresses in analysis is looked down on and thought of as lacking in something positive, that is of value for life. In my experience this view is mistaken. The matter of psychic return to the undifferentiated state (or rather of finding again still existing areas of undifferentiatedness), basic unity, is a matter of life and death; psychic, if not bodily, life or nonlife, and new integration between the psyche and the soma depends upon it. The regression is in fact extremely painful and frightening.

Certain realities of the analytic situation can be used in building up the psychic unity between analyst and analysand. For example, it is a fact that analyst and analysand are parts of one another's lives for the whole duration of the analysis (which concerns both) in an inseparable way. One room and one hour serve both together, as an entity; there are times when one of them thinks, feels, or acts for that entity, rather than for either as a separate being, or even for both as linked together.

The entity is, of course, an imagined one, whose reality for the analyst is limited and different from that of the analysand, who seeks to make it actual. If it be recognized and accepted imaginatively by the analyst, it means that he goes the whole way with the analysand psychically. If not, there is repeated failure to reach the basic unity, repetition of original failure, and repeated hopelessness, out of which nothing comes. The analysis drags on to eventual failure, either in abandonment, or in pseudosuccess, which is only a papering over of the cracks.

III

In this next part of the chapter I am concerned with questions of analytic technique. The underlying principle I have already stated: acceptance by the analyst of the truth *for the analysand* of his delusion of absolute identity between them, his entering into it, and demonstrating both its psychic truth and its objective untruth.

The presence of delusion makes necessary the use of certain extensions of ordinarily accepted technique, and I want here to gather some of them together.

1. Analysis of transference psychosis can only be carried out in regression, and regression to dependence for life (though this does not mean regressive illness in every case). Where ordinary conditions are not enough, some adaptations may be needed to make analysis possible, such as hospitalization, the analyst visiting the patient, altering his room or his timetable, interviewing relatives, etc.

2. Those who look after the patient (in factual reality) become psychically not only extensions of the analyst but identical with him. At times, at least momentarily in the sessions, he takes over (in the delusion) being various aspects of the patient, his ego, his fear, his love, etc., sometimes, even, his body, or part of it.

3. In the areas where the patient cannot use inference, analogy, symbolization, or deductive thinking, realities that are actual, concrete, and bodily are used in order to show the unreality in fact of the delusional ideas. These things are linked secondarily with words, which bring them into relation with those other areas where the delusion does not obtain.

I am speaking here of such things as answering questions, touching or being touched by the patient, or using objects as if they were the things they represent ("symbolic realization," as described by Mme. Séchehaye [1951]), or direct use of the analyst's own emotions. These have been regarded as dangerous, or in some way destructive of the analytic situation itself, but in my experience this is not true. It is true that a much more "fluid" situation is produced by using them and that this may provoke much more anxiety in the analyst, but that is a different matter.

4. Interpretations are not all verbal. I spoke earlier of a two-stage process of interpretation, in which the first stage is nonverbal, the body happenings or objects becoming the actual interpretations, whose result is discovery, and the second being verbalization, out of which come reality testing and insight. It is as if one were dealing first with a psychotic and then with a neurotic layer, though the transference phenomena remain at a psychotic level until both stages have been passed.

5. In adapting to the needs of the individual patient in this way, the analyst is limited only by the limits which he finds in himself, or in his patient. There can be no "absolute" or "canon" of analysis, or of any particular technique, only the application of the fundamental rule must be allowed to become flexible and extensible.

Limits are in fact found, and there is no occasion for the fear that if once a patient is allowed gratification in a regressed state there will be no end to it. In his regression the patient is psychically an infant, and infants do need gratification and *are* frequently satisfied. It is necessary to remember, and to acknowledge to the patient, that it is not possible to satisfy fully his infant needs in his grown-up body, and that even if it were, it would be at a cost to his mature self, which would be offended. But this very acknowledgment to some extent offsets the lack of satisfaction and is itself a gratification that he can use when combined with the partial bodily satisfaction.

The finding of these limits actually depends upon the unity which does exist between analyst and analysand. It is a difficult thing to describe, but once it has been experienced it becomes understandable.

If the analyst is sufficiently one with his patient psychically, he experiences him at times as himself, or himself at times as the patient. But because of his unity with himself he also experiences what he says or does to be himself. "What I do is me; what is not me I do not do," and "I do this, here, now, with this patient; I do not do it with him at another time, nor ever with that other patient." It is a part of owning himself, for the patient is his work, and his work and actions are himself.

Conversely there are points at which the patient experiences the analyst as himself, or himself as the analyst and, accepting the analyst's unity unconsciously as his own, will find a limit which the analyst then recognizes as appropriate to himself.

6. These extensions serve the limited and specific purpose of the analysis of delusion, and their use for this purpose is founded in, and inseparable from, classical technique, of which it is a logical development. Without such foundation it would be merely "wild analysis," or something mystical and truly dangerous.

For a longer or a shorter time the analyst (or some psychic extension or part of him) is all that stands between the patient and death, and at some moment he has to stand aside and allow the patient to take his life into his own hands, separating himself out from the entity, integrating with himself, and becoming either a living person or a corpse. The analyst can do nothing but be there, a whole and separate individual, with his own unity which he has made available to the patient.

From this moment the delusion breaks up from inside, as it were; the adaptations are gradually discarded, and verbalization increases. I would like to remind you again here of Freud's description of the breakup of a delusion in his commentary on Wilhelm Jensen's story *Gradiva,* entitled "Delusions and Dreams" (1906).

The outcome of the analysis of a transference psychosis is that the analysand finds and retains a psychic unity with the analyst, while establishing a true separateness from and independence of him. Once this comes about, he becomes capable of forming mature relationships, and of carrying out his analysis within himself.

IV

In my last section I want to say something about the implications and applications of this idea of basic unity, both in the analytic situation, and as we find it in ordinary life, as a normal and as a pathological thing.

It is of course more obvious as a pathological thing. As regards analysis, here is another piece of clinical material. I know that it can be taken in several different ways, but I am asking you to consider with me only the one aspect, that relating to the earliest level of development, the level that is preverbal, existing before object relations are developed, where body experience is all-important. Any kind of differentiation is only just beginning there, so it is also preambivalent and conflict-free.

"I find I haven't told you something, and that it's because I thought you already knew it," says *Rosemary*. "It's so much easier to talk to you when you aren't really there than when you are."

Rosemary has never sorted herself out from her sister Joyce, who is two years older. All childhood happenings, ideas, or feelings are told of the entity "we" ("We did this. We hated that"). She and Joyce are indivisible; she "never feels a person" but is often "two people," and sometimes "half a person." At the beginning of a session she frequently doesn't "know how to begin."

Three months after starting analysis, on her way to a session with me, she went into a big store to buy food, to entertain a favorite aunt who was visiting her. She collected some things, as much as she could hold, and then put into a string bag on her arm a bar of chocolate and a box of small cheeses. She paid for everything except these, which she forgot. On leaving the store, she was stopped by the store detective, who accused her of stealing them. Police were called; she was taken to the police station and locked in a cell for some hours, while her identity was checked. Next day she was charged in the Magistrate's Court, where she appeared without a lawyer, and was remanded for a week.

It never occurred to her to say that she was in treatment, nor, although she asked to be allowed to telephone to say that she had been prevented from keeping her appointment, did it occur to her to let me know what was happening. Several days elapsed before I knew.

Her movement, putting out her hand to take me (in the nonhuman form of cheese and chocolate) brought her up sharply against the environment, society, and the whole machinery of police, court, etc., and this interfered with the assimilation of the movement. The chain of events that followed effectively disrupted a process that was just beginning in her, and so repeated the happenings of her earliest infancy. They represented all that she most dreads and is constantly expecting.

Rosemary has not yet differentiated her mouth out from the rest of herself, or herself from her devouring surroundings. She suffers from anorexia nervosa, and she describes herself as "cut off from my roots."

At the time of her visit to the store Rosemary was functioning separately on at least two different levels, and I am understanding the separateness as being due to a failure of fusion, rather than to a splitting mechanism. There was a person who could choose and arrange a meal which she would provide for another person for whom she felt affection. This argues both a high degree of differentiation and organization and the existence of object relations. At the same time, on the earliest level she was not yet differentiated out from her environment or aware of its existence. She was an infant, in whom a movement happened which should have been creative, leading to differentiation and integration, becoming an assertion or statement of herself. But the movement was met by the environment in such a way as to bring about disruption instead.

Although to all outward appearance she was entirely composed and self-possessed, and gave her evidence in court simply and clearly, it was a matter of years before she could talk about this episode, and verbal interpretations given at the time brought no response. When she did finally talk about it it became clear that the only things that had had any reality for her were my presence in the court and what I actually said and did on her behalf. It was important that the magistrate in discharging her said "I believe your doctor when she tells me that you are ill," and not "I believe you when you tell me that you did not steal."

Some months later she told me of the only time she had stolen in childhood: Joyce was ill, and Rosemary (age eleven) did not even know whether she was alive or not; nobody told her, and she could not ask. The separation was absolute. Rosemary was sent to stay with this same aunt. In a shop she saw a little shell purse lined with red silk. She took it and kept it secretly for years, always feeling guilty, as if she had committed a murder.

Last year I was away from her for some time, and I was very doubtful whether she would kill herself or get ill and die. I lent her a book of poems by Walter de la Mare. Some time later she told me with great difficulty that two years before that she had found a poem in a magazine in my waiting room; some of the words "seemed to belong to her," and she had cut it out and kept it. When she showed it to me I could see why it had so much meaning for her, as the shell purse had had. I could also understand why she did not tell me at the time about the incident in the store. She believed that I knew it, as she and I were one.

Throughout her analysis she continued to be paralyzed with terror, and unable to find any starting point other than something happening in me. She would clutch my hand, and I would speak of it as showing me this terror and relate it to material of the previous day, or to other occasions when she had done the same. Only when I pointed out that the pressure was so great as to be painful to me, or that my fingers had "gone dead," could she begin to talk. Her silence and immobility would remain total for weeks on end, and only after I showed signs of life in some explicit way (for anything merely implicit was useless) could she begin to tell me what had been going on. It was a matter of amazement to discover that the person to whom she talked when I was not there did not reply, for it was herself, and not me; also that her own part in some of the childhood games was clearly distinguishable from that of Joyce. Her "we" began to break up.

At last I began to find something of how her analysis could perhaps be done. She began to talk comparatively freely and to feel a person, and the analysis became steadily a more ordinary one. I may add that in the outside world she did not give the impression of being a schizoid or withdrawn personality at all; she was much liked by her fellows and had a good sense of humor and fun.

In the light of this idea of absolute identity between patient and analyst I think we have to reconsider our ideas of such mental mechanisms as projection, introjection, condensation, displacement, and all that Freud included in the term *dream work*.

I spoke earlier of the analyst who experiences the patient as his work, and his work as himself. It is like the poet who speaks of 'my love,' meaning both his loved one and his own emotion, which is himself; we can see here how what we have considered to be condensation becomes instead a regression to the primordial, un-differentiated state. Similarly, in the first clinical example I quoted, what appeared to be projective identification turned out to be an assertion of absolute identity with me.

For this same reason, that to them everything is one, patients who show a transference psychosis bring dreams whose latent and manifest content are the same.

I have said more about the need to reach the basic unity than about the fear of it, though I have mentioned this. Fear of the idea arises from its very nature, for the point of unity is also the point of annihilation; it is the point of paradox, of chaos, or absolute ambivalency, where opposites are simultaneously the same thing and utterly different. It is not only the analysand who experiences this anxiety; the difficulty is shared by the analyst, whose task of being simultaneously absolutely one with, and separate from the analysand, deeply concerned—or *engaged,* to borrow Michael Fordham's expression (1960)—but not involved with him is so difficult already. This fear results in abhorrence of the word *delusion* and in rigid adherence to verbal technique alone.

I am postulating that a universal idea exists, as normal and essential as is the oedipus complex, (which cannot develop without it), an idea of absolute identity with the mother upon which survival depends. The presence of this idea is the foundation of mental health, development of a whole person, and the capacity for holistic thinking. It is to be found not only in the delusions of the mentally sick, where it takes the form of transference psychosis, but also in the sane and healthy.

The most obvious and immediate example is here, right now. You and I can only understand each other insofar as we possess an area of unity which is a psychic reality, to which temporarily we unconsciously regress. This is how empathy works. The finding of agreement, or consensus of opinion between individuals or in any group, depends upon it; in turn agreement strengthens unconscious belief in survival and so provides the necessary security for tolerating differences and disagreement elsewhere.

Professor I. Ramzy, in discussing a paper I presented in Topeka in 1958, drew attention to the absolute need to preserve our most primitive modes of functioning for the actual survival not only of the individual but also of the human race. What I have here called "basic unity" seems to me to be one of those essential primitive modes.

Contact or communication between the artist and his public depends upon the presence of, and regression to, this unconscious delusion in both. To the artist his creation is his work, is his feeling, is himself; to the the hearer or the viewer what is heard or seen is *his* feeling, is his response, is himself. So each psychically *is* the work of art, and *is* the other, in the area where they overlap.

Other manifestations that I would regard as normal can be found in such things as provision of school uniforms, existence of the flag as a national symbol and the behavior of gardeners who give each other plants, until their gardens contain the same things but still remain essentially different and individual.

Where the basic unity has not been established, either in infancy or through analysis, annihilation anxiety persists, and unity will be sought, and avoided, in such things as ideologies, organized religions, secret societies, folies á deux, etc.

I have not the space to go into this in detail here, but it seems to me that in *Group Psychology and the Analysis of the Ego* Freud (1921) has talked about this very thing, especially in his reference to organized groups with a leader.

The relationship between the members of the group is an attempt to deny separateness and difference, while the relationship between the members and the leader simultaneously asserts it. These groups are largely concerned with self-preservation, i.e. with survival, but the price of that survival is loss of individuality. Juvenile gangs of various kinds are largely composed of members who feel not only that their existence is precarious but that it is not real, and that the only certainty is annihilation.

Organized religion offers a defense of a kind against the death that is the certain fate of the isolated. Those who use such a defense but cannot submerge their individuality enough seek in such things as mysticism or pantheism to lose their identity in "mystical union" with the "Wholly Other," and to find survival in a life that is merged with that of the cosmos.

Freud quotes Robertson Smith (*Kinship and Marriage,* 1885): "Identifications which lie at the root of clan feeling rest upon the recognition of a common substance, and may even therefore be brought about by a meal eaten in common." Here again we have the substance, the concrete thing, and bodily experience. The Christian idea of Communion rests upon the concrete symbols of bread and wine, which are believed to provide a means of resurrection after death, i.e. survival of the body.

I know that this could be understood in terms of relationship of an oral kind, but I want to remind you of the two points from which I started: (1) the attempts made by patients to establish union or identity with the analyst and (2) the importance for them of body happenings.

To sum up:

Within an individual both survival and the ability to find objects with which relationships can be formed depend upon the existence of a unity which comes from the entity mother-infant (or analyst-analysand). From it a rhythm of differentiation and reassimilation or integration comes. It provides the "stillness at the center" which allows of movement and perception; it is the sine qua non for living continuously in one's body, for having an identity, and for being identical with, and able to make assertion or statement of, oneself.

PART II

THEORETICAL AND TECHNICAL EXPANSION

7

THE POSITIVE CONTRIBUTION OF COUNTERTRANSFERENCE

My views come very near to those of Dr. Winnicott (1960). In fact, I would agree with all that he has said. I too think it very important that the term *countertransference* be reserved for the specific part of the analyst's total response to his patient's needs that has remained unconscious and under repression. I would make a very clear distinction between what the analyst does in treating neurotic patients and in treating patients of other types, who cannot use the analyst's professional attitutde as neurotics can and do. I will use another word and talk about patients whose behavior and reactions are *unpredictable*. What I am going to say now is perhaps rather obvious, but I do not think it has been said very clearly by the other speakers. The affects and anxieties aroused in the analyst by patients of the two types are different, both in quantity and in quality.

I think we are probably all agreed that unconscious countertransference does not present any very great difficulty in the analysis of neurotic patients, except in the case of inexperienced analysts (students, or those who have not been qualified for very long). Any involvement that does occur is usually detectable fairly soon and can be analyzed without producing any very drastic effects.

But with patients whose reactions and behavior are unpredictable, it frustratbe very great; on occasion the outcome of the treatment may remain in doubt for a very long time, and the type of anxiety aroused in the analyst, apart from his objective anxiety, is often largely psychotic anxiety, both depressive and paranoid, in particular survival anxiety.

An analyst may be well able to work with neurotics as Dr. Winnicott (1960) describes: "with easy but conscious mental effort. Ideas and feelings come to mind, but these are well examined and sifted before an interpretation is made." What Dr. Winnicott is describing here is the action of his conscious ego, and it is surely how we would all like to be able to work, most of the time at least.

Patients of the unpredictable type do not always allow it to be so. There are two ways in which this desired way of working is frustrated. The first is that what to the analyst are "interpretations" are often merely meaningless remarks to the patient. He may sometimes accept them on a basis of "well, if you say so I must believe you," but this, of course, is not conviction, and next time he will behave exactly as if he had never heard the interpretation. The second is that he will frequently present the analyst with a situation that does not allow time enough for this examination and sifting to happen before some remark or action must be made to forestall him in some way if a dangerous piece of acting out is not to happen.

Whatever the analyst says or does in these circumstances must have some interpretive effect as far as the patient is concerned; that is, it must convey to him something of reality which he had been unable to perceive for himself. Fortunately for these patients many things of which we are ordinarily unaware have such an effect, and if we are willing to let them happen the results are often very enlightening to us as well as to our patients.

I should like to give an example here. It refers to the analysis of a very disturbed patient, who could not possibly be regarded as a psychoneurotic.

During one of her sessions there was a disturbance in the house. My rather excitable cleaning woman had an altercation with someone who came to the door. The patient stopped short in what she was saying and waited till it was over. She looked at me and then asked: "What were you thinking? I've seen that expression on your face before. What does it mean?"

I had plenty of time to consider, and I decided to answer her question. "I was just thinking that I would like to knock their two heads together," I said. She laughed and then said rather seriously: "I know now what you meant when you said that it isn't necessary to *do* what you feel you'd like to."

I had tried many times to get this across to her, but for her thinking of a thing and doing it were so much the same that not to do it had meant not even to have the fantasy of doing it. Now, when she was allowed to enjoy this fantasy and could see that it did not mean that these people's heads were actually knocked together, she could make use of it as an interpretive happening.

Some time later she arrived one day in a state of frenzy. She looked wildly round the room, and said, "I *must* smash something, what about your sham mink pot?" I realized she was talking about a flowerpot that I had recently put in the room, but I had no time to think out what to say. I did know not only that she could smash the pot in question, but that she might then damage herself. But none of this was conscious to me until later. I was aware only of sudden anger, which was expressed before I knew it. (I had had many of these episodes of frenzy with her without reacting. The emotion had been sustained, and I was pretty tired of them by then and so was she.) I said, "I'll just about kill you if you smash my pot." There was sudden silence, which lasted quite a time, and I then said, "I think you thought I really would kill you, or perhaps that I had done so." She said, "Yes, it felt like that, it was frightful, but it was also very good. I knew you really felt something, and I so often thought you didn't feel anything at all. But why did you get so angry about that pot? Is it something special?"

I showed it to her, and explained what it was, and that I did care about it. I then reminded her of my earlier remark, about knocking heads together. She said, "Yes, I thought about that, and then I knew you wouldn't really kill me."

The interpretive effect of this did not stop there. She came to see that something she had despised had a value not only for me but in the outside world as well (for she examined the pot closely and found it quite different from what she had imagined); that her judgment was not infallible; that I would defend something I cared about and that included her; that her feelings and mine about the same thing could be different; and that we could both survive the separateness that this involved.

What is the moral of all this? I am *not* advocating saying, consciously and deliberately, things like this to any patient. What I *am* trying to get across is something about the functioning of the unconscious part of the ego, something that I think is of very great importance for us, that we seem to ignore. This is, that the unconscious part of the ego *does* function as ego, albeit appearing in id fashion sometimes, that it exerts some control over id impulses (for I only *spoke* of killing her, and would not have done so), and that it can be relied on, not only in this controlling way but also through the carrying on of the analytic process within the analyst. Provided that the analyst has gone far enough with his own analysis to be able to deal with his paranoid anxiety, and that anxiety about survival is not a serious problem, his own analysis will go on automatically, not always in consciousness, as an activity of his unconscious ego (Kramer 1959).

The unpredictable reactions provoked by the behavior of such a patient as this are in fact met by the ego as well as by the id. The superego should have no part to play. Where it does, it does so as part of the id rather than as part of the ego, and this, again, manifests unconscious countertransference. Ella Sharpe, who was one of the first to speak about countertransference, stressed this aspect of it in her lectures to students.

This is where I would question Dr. Heimann's belief (1960) that to tell her patient the reason for her inattention would do harm. She seems surprised that it did not; she seems to have accepted without question the idea that it would, and not to have tested out the reality. This looks to me like a superego judgment. It might be that if she examined the episode further she might find that it had even done good. That is what I would expect in the case of a patient such as I have described, though in the case of a psychoneurotic I would not expect it to be necessary. I wonder what harm she expected to follow in her patient. Has she ever seen this happen, except with students in supervision?

The analytic process does not, in fact, suffer in any way, provided there is a follow-up, such as I have described, where, having discharged the emotion and having then had time to consider what to say next, I said to my patient that she had thought I would really kill her. Had I been overcome with guilt at my own outburst she might have been unable to go on, or not have recognized this for herself.

Dr. Winnicott (1960) referred to the need sometimes for the analyst to merge with the patient. I think that this was such an occasion, for my patient was regressed to the stage of doing something first and finding out about it after (that is, to an id or primary process level), and I had to regress there too, so as to know what was going on and to enable the id and the ego to come together. But my regression was of a different order from hers; it involved a much smaller part of me, and I could come out of it under my own steam, so to speak.

At this point it is relevant to look at one particular difference in approach between Dr. Heimann on the one hand, and Dr. Fordham and Dr. Winnicott on the other. Dr. Heimann asks "What is the patient doing, and why is he doing it?" Dr. Fordham and Dr. Winnicott, in dealing with patients whose behavior is unpredictable, ask "What am I doing, and why am I doing it?"

In the case of neurotic patients the former approach is enough. In other kinds of patients it is not, and the answer to it must include the latter approach. My own feeling is that both are right and necessary, and appropriate.

My last point concerns Dr. Fordham's question (1960) about how he can use his countertransference in the analysis of patients when it is in fact unconscious. I would say that he, and each one of us, is using it all the time. Countertransference is a fact of analysis, and as such it is essentially neutral, or rather, perhaps, has ambivalency. That is, it is potentially both good and bad, valuable and harmful. But far more than that: those very experiences of infancy and childhood, whose memories are so important to us, provide the possibility of our understanding our patients. These memories, and the memories deriving from the therapy that was the main part of our training, are the source of the very drive to do analysis, and without unconscious countertransference there would be neither empathy nor analysis itself. It is a tool, and skill and satisfaction lie in using it fully, trusting in the safeguards that the ego supplies.

Here is the importance of Dr. Fordham's understanding of analysis as an interaction between two people. Without such interaction, though the patient might grow, the analyst would not, and only work that promotes growth and ego development in both is worth what analysis costs both to do.

8

TRANSFERENCE IN BORDERLINE STATES

Not the thing itself, but the sense of other and contrary things makes reality. . . . East is West.
> —Freya Stark, *The Valleys of the Assassins* (1934)

Beatrice, a highly intelligent, highly trained teacher came to me for analysis in her late thirties. She was analytically sophisticated, having already been with an experienced psychoanalyst, a man who, as she made intolerably clear, was far superior to me. Sound external reasons appeared to account for the ending of her treatment with him, as also for the ending of her various sexual relationships.

She had suffered from severe infantile eczema beginning about the age of three months. The eczema had apparently aroused acute anxiety in her mother, who "lost her milk" and weaned the infant, thus bringing about a premature loss and separation. This was not told to me until she had been in analysis with me for three months, when I realized that she was scratching at the couch, her own hands, and even the wall, whilst crying in an irritable "grizzling" way, without tears and without relief.

This symptom became increasingly noticeable until it became apparent that everything that I said or did, every new and unfamiliar thing about my clothes, my room, my house, acted as an irritant and as something useless, painful, and to be got rid of. In fact to her I *was* her eczema, the source of all her troubles and the prime cause of the general ineffectiveness, loneliness, and despair which had brought her into treatment; I was the loneliness itself, and also, as appeared later, her mother's loneliness, anxiety, and despair.

She turned out to be a patient of the highly narcissistic kind, whose transference was psychotic in type, not neurotic; she destroyed whatever I said or did, making ordinary transference interpretations into nonsense, gibing and sneering sarcastically at everything, producing helpless rage and exasperation in me, whilst she avoided all feeling. She coolly blamed and reproached me for my anger and for her failure to improve, a failure which I gradually realized was quite unreal.

The symptom appeared soon after I had pointed out that although she had had analysis before she was rejecting my interpretations as if she had never heard of unconscious processes. This enraged her, but the rage was expressed only in the whimpering and grizzling, and then scratching. I came later to recognize this reaction as the only form of communication she could use.

The small piece of material which I have quoted shows certain characteristics of a delusional transference in a borderline patient.

To outward appearance this woman was fairly well integrated. She had done well academically, professionally, and socially, but under the surface was a limited range of absolutely fixed ideas belonging to a very early level of development.

In this area, to her, nothing was real except failure, inadequacy, and hopelessness; any change from this threatened her very existence; all emotion, and specifically all bodily experiences of emotion, were a threat of annihilation, against which she defended herself by means of organized hate and persecutory anxiety; primitive bodily movements were used to substitute for them and to ward them off.

Her acting out, which was limited to the destructive rejection of everything offered to her, provoked in others the feelings she avoided in herself. The bodily activity of scratching was a primitive form of memory. She could not recall the eczema; she had been told of it, and her own memory of it was solely body memory, reinforced by hearsay.

She showed no concern for others, and in fact very little for herself. Her narcissism had failed to develop, even her pain barrier being useless to her. Her sense of reality was undeveloped—she could not distinguish between her feelings and mine, using mine as a substitute for her own and, in fact, having an unconscious delusion of identity with me, which consciously she strenuously denied.

Her capacity for deductive thinking was impaired; this showed in her work and in contacts with other people. She could not carry over the idea of analyzing unconscious materal from one analyst to another, but discovered later that she had assumed that I already knew what she thought and felt and what had gone on in her previous analysis. This had concerned areas of psychoneurosis, and it had ended where the uncovering of areas of psychotic anxiety threatened. External reality was used to conceal this and provided the "reasons" for the interruption, even while she was aware of continued need and demanding to be passed on to someone else.

She had had a good deal of sexual experience, and genitality appeared to predominate. This again turned out to be defensive; forepleasure was absent and orgasm inhibited; she used, and abused, her sexual partners with whom no real relationships existed; and she broke up the affairs impulsively when she could not make her partners accept her ideas as theirs or share a folie á deux with her.

She showed very clearly the qualities of persistence and insistence so often found in these patients, and the ambivalence associated with them. One analysis having failed, she demanded another and set to work immediately to destroy that. She insisted that the analysis be done in her way (which was, of course, right for her) but that it also satisfy her in every way. She demanded absolute control, while refusing all responsibility, and experiencing guilt with no moderation.

My own powers of persistence and insistence had to match hers, and simultaneously I had to make identifications with her and allow her to make identifications with me which felt so foreign to me that I was many times on the point of refusing to go on. In fact, only the knowledge that I really did not *have* to do so and a determination to succeed, where I felt that success *should* be possible, saved the analysis! I was, of course, aware that there was a worthwhile person there, aware of continuous progress throughout, and also of the hidden, unconscious idealization of me.

I will come back to her again when I come to the question of technique, and specifically of countertransference.

Borderline state is an imprecise descriptive term used to label any mental illness which is neither clearly neurotic nor so obviously psychotic that the patient concerned has to be treated as insane.

The range of patients is a very wide one. And not only the range of patients but also the range within any one patient, who may in the course of weeks or months, or even in one analytic hour be neurotic, psychotic and "normal" by turns and simultaneously, being psychically on several levels at once, sometimes sliding almost imperceptibly from one level to another, sometimes going with a sudden jolt, according as an appropriate interpretation, or some happening either within himself or impinging from outside relieves existing anxiety, or breaks down a defense and uncovers a fresh layer of new material together with the anxiety belonging to it.

The essence of the borderline state is partial fixation in the undifferentiated phase. There is not enough differentiation between psyche and soma, and failure of fusion between ego and id, making adequate development to the depressive position and the early oedipal situation impossible. Failure in the early oedipal situation leads to interference with development of the later (classical) oedipal situation, and hence ordinary psychoneurosis is not developed.

At the same time the degree of differentiation and fusion are sufficient for the condition not to be psychosis.

The determining factors are both quantitative, i.e. the size of the areas affected, and qualitative, i.e. the localization; whether *all* excitement becomes a threat of annihilation, or only some; and, if the latter, whether oral, kinaesthetic, visual, etc.

Nevertheless, certain characteristics which distinguish neurosis from psychosis have to be considered in greater detail because of their bearing on the question of the suitability of any patient for analysis and the kind of transference phenomena one may expect to find.

A person who has been able to build up a body of experience that enables him to take survival for granted may yet suffer from castration anxiety and fear the loss of a part of his own body. In defense against this he may regress and show separation anxiety, fearing the loss of love objects which he recognizes as whole, real, and distinct from himself. Anxieties of this kind (neurotic anxieties) are different from those of a person who is *not* able to take survival for granted. Separation anxiety in such a person involves fear of loss of objects which are not recognized either as whole or as distinct from himself, but which are regarded as *identical* with himself, i.e. he fears annihilation. Anything which comes to be perceived as separate or different from himself is perceived as dangerous, threatening to annihilate him by virtue of its very separateness, and therefore as something to be destroyed by him. Yet his own destructiveness is feared as soon as it attaches to something other than himself, and hence loss, i.e. separateness, must be avoided at all costs. Such a person's anxieties are psychotic in type, and there will always be a tendency to regress toward anxiety about survival.

Where annihilation anxiety predominates, only one idea can have any meaning, and it is presumably this that brings about a state in which *everything* relates to survival or nonsurvival and where the patient's ideas are found to be fixed with an intensity which must be recognized as delusional. Only a series of experiences which have for the patient the *psychic* reality of annihilation, and yet in which he discovers the actual survival both of himself and whatever object he is related to (in analysis the analyst), can alter this state in any degree whatever. The alteration which comes about as a result is a reduction of the area in which delusion holds sway and an increase in the area of reality sense, not a total abolition of the delusion itself.

Where the predominant anxieties are those concerned with castration or object-loss, false ideas are held only with the lesser tenacity of illusion, not delusion, and the contact with factual reality needed to bring about an alteration is less both quantitatively (less repetition) and qualitatively (less violence and less intensity). The more primitive the form of anxiety the more primitive is the form of defense against it, and correspondingly, of course, the less effective in fact.

Magical thinking, "omnipotence," and simple denial are in effect the only possible defenses against annihilation anxiety, and they match the magical quality attributed to the annihilating force, which is of the order of Fate, God, Life, etc., representing probably in the first instance the birth process itself, and anything which later comes to join up with it, in bringing about total helplessness and passivity.

The more sophisticated anxieties, for example, fear of loss of an object, of the object's love, or of his own self-esteem, of castration etc. are met with the more sophisticated defenses of splitting, displacement, secondary identification, repression, etc.

The more primitive the prevalent form of anxiety the nearer the chief pattern of acting out will be to the single pattern of addiction, and the more fixed will be the object of addiction. An addict who can use only one object or "drug" may be nearer to psychosis than one who can accept any one of several things, though the latter often needs several all at once. He will eat, drink, smoke, play the radio, and telephone a friend all at the same time; in the analytic situation alcohol, cigarettes, sweets, girl friends, etc. will be used interchangeably (thereby asserting identity between them), to avoid awareness of the necessary addiction to the analyst. This phenomenon is already partway toward the development of object relations, and such a patient can the more readily find and use a transition object.

Similarly, the more primitive is the anxiety the more the acting out can ultimately be seen to be a primitive form of memory of the early environment, accurate and specific in all its details, whereas the acting out of a psychoneurotic, although it tends to be repetitive, is usually more varied both in form and content, relating not only to traumata belonging to the earliest time of life but to later ones as well.

The dreams of a person who is dealing with material belonging nearer the psychotic end of the spectrum than the psychoneurotic are often not analyzable in the ordinary classical way. They may present the problems and conflicts quite directly—i.e. the dream thoughts are manifest, not latent, and there is no secondary elaboration—or the dreams may be wholly defensive, consisting only of elaborations, and no amount of analysis of such a dream gets anywhere. The dream thoughts are split off in such a way as to be inaccessible until something else happens that brings them within reach.

In the so-called borderline states everything is found, from the total self-absorption of concern only with bodily happenings, through autoerotism and primary narcissism, to areas where secondary narcissism is well developed, and a capacity for altruism exists. At the one end of the scale concern for another person or thing hardly exists, even the existence of another person being to all intents and purposes denied, everything being subordinated to the avoidance of separateness (and, of course, also of its complement, fusion), while at the other end, where both separateness and fusion can be accepted, concern and the capacity to mourn are already present. (Something which closely resembles a borderline state is often seen in adolescence and also in convalescence after physical illness. These, of course, are temporary states, but the recognition of this similarity can often enable the difficulties to be resolved.)

The first appearance of any illness, or the first thing that may lead an analyst to regard a patient as being a borderline psychotic may be a faulty perception, an inaccurate inference or deduction, a failure to use symbols or analogy, the presence of symbolic equation or other evidence of concrete thinking, or a piece of totally irrational, often irresponsible, behavior in a person whose ways of perceiving, thinking, and behaving are otherwise quite ordinary, though he may have other symptoms of neurosis. Areas of primary and secondary process thinking can exist side by side and will be present or absent according to the predominance of survival, pleasure, or reality principles.

When survival is the main or only possible consideration, pleasure and pain are meaningless, sexuality of any kind is irrelevant, and the only kind of reality recognizable is psychic reality. External reality exists in these areas only in the form in which it existed in the patient's actual infancy. The adult form of memory—recall—will be found to be missing, or meaningless. Whereas a psychoneurotic, as Freud pointed out, is suffering from repressed memories, in a psychotic, and in the psychotic areas of borderline patients, the past is literally reproduced here and now, which accounts for both the patient's inappropriate behavior in the outer world and the special quality of the transference phenomena other than those also found in psychoneurotic patients.

The lives of these patients may have been eventful and colorful, showing a pattern of destructiveness and fragmentation, or they may have been limited, insipid and colorless where the destructiveness has been compulsively controlled and yet is expressed in the control itself. Both the destructiveness and the control tend to have a magical quality, and often a "looking-glass" quality, cause being effect and effect cause. The destructiveness is that of an infant, but is combined with all the bodily and mental resources of an adult.

Much of what is usually only found in the deeper layers of the personality may appear on the surface, and the illness then is unmistakable; or there may be no illness apparent. Polarities are kept absolutely separate—good and bad, male and female, love and hate, childhood and maturity. Everything is seen only in black and white; there are no shades of grey. The compromises which characterize psychoneurosis are absent wherever psychotic anxieties predominate.

All these things together add up to the matter of ego development and ego strength, or their absence, and what I am saying is that in what we call borderline states ego development is, in greater or less degree, patchy, uneven, and unreliable, so that a person who appears to have a fairly well-developed ego may turn out to be relatively unstable, and vice versa. Ego nuclei are present and functioning, but the ego does not function as a whole.

All the things that I have mentioned will be found in the analytic work to have their importance in the development of the transference, which will be at times neurotic and at other times psychotic, shifting from one to the other, resolving in some places and in others remaining fixed and irresolvable.

The work shifts and changes continually and calls for a high degree of sensitivity, stability, and flexibility in the analyst. His task in following these shifts and changes is not an easy one; the whole range of his own anxieties is at risk at any time, and he needs to be aware of whatever is going on within himself and to possess as wide an understanding of psychoanalytic ideas as he can encompass. Freedom of imagination, ability to allow a free flow of emotions in oneself, flexibility of ego boundaries, and willingness to consider the views and theories of colleagues whose approach may be different from one's own (which is perhaps the same thing) may all prove to be vitally important in the treatment of any patient.

I come now to the vexed question of technique in the analysis of transference psychosis. There are roughly three schools of thought in the matter of technique at the present time:

1. The strictly "classical," in which it is believed that verbal interpretation *alone* will achieve the desired result; that any departure from this confuses the patient, clouds the issue, and makes recovery more difficult if not impossible; and that patients whose analyses carried out in this way are unsuccessful are unanalyzable. Some analysts of this school of thought (not all) tend to stress the importance of unconscious fantasy and to disregard external reality, as if the actual happenings experienced either in infancy or in analysis were unimportant and the only things that mattered were the fantasies, imaginative elaborations, concerning them. It seems to

me that this view ignores the fact that fantasy is futile apart from its roots in factual reality, and vice versa. Alternatively it implies a belief in a greater capacity for reality testing and a greater overall reality sense than I have found in the many patients I have treated.

Some of these analysts have attributed failures in analysis ("un-analyzableness") to constitutional or innate factors in the patients concerned, without apparently questioning the possibility of either the analyst or the technique being at fault or inadequate.

2. Analysts who consider that some new experience must be supplied to the patient and that this will in some way supplant his previous experiences or undo the pathological effects of them, without the need for linking with words the new and the old, fantasy and reality, or the inner and outer worlds (Corrective Emotional Experience, Direct Analysis, etc.). This seems to me to be more a matter of treatment of symptoms than of the illness of which they are part. By not taking account of the need for working through and for linking the emotional experience with intellectual understanding, such therapy (valuable as it may be in certain circumstances) remains psychotherapy, not psychoanalysis.

3. A more scattered collection of analysts, with less homogeneous views, of whom I am one, who believe that these borderline patients by reason of ego defects, resulting from not-good-enough mothering in earliest infancy, cannot use verbal interpretations in the areas where psychotic anxieties and delusional ideas predominate, and that a new set of experiences of good-enough mothering needs to be supplied before the ego can become accessible to verbal interpreta-tion, which nevertheless is then a necessity, as a means of integrating the whole person. These analysts are willing to use such nonverbal adjuncts ("management," "parameters," etc.) as they find helpful, allowing the individual patient a greater freedom to direct the analysis to suit his personal needs. This can of course put a far greater strain on the analyst than the strictly "classical" technique, but in his most advanced areas, or even to know what is, or has been, view it does not confuse the patient or cloud the issues, and in fact makes possible certain analyses which would fail where a less flexible technique was used, not through something in the patient but through something in the analyst.

I will go on now to set out some of what I think and feel and do about technique in analyzing the transference in borderline patients, and I will illustrate it as far as I can by clinical material.

I find that I have to be willing to take things as they come, often without being able to foresee what may happen next except in the most advanced areas, or even to know what is, or has been, happening in the most primitive areas of these patients. The important thing is often only to have some idea in what kind of area or areas one is concerned at any given time, to know which of perhaps several-all-at-once may be the most important at that moment, and to be able to switch over almost instantaneously from one to another, without notice. This of course is in effect dealing mainly with the most primitive layers; it calls for modification of classical technique— "parameters"—using nonverbal things to carry interpretive effects and then linking them with words to make the interpretation complete and to join up the primitive with the advanced layers.

James is a doctor. He had repeatedly injured himself in the same way, every time attributing the injury to a piece of furniture which needed a simple repair. He knew intellectually that he had brought it about himself, and we had both thought we understood the unconscious motivation. At last he accepted it emotionally; in despair he turned away and hid his face under the blanket. After a few moments one hand moved across, over the other shoulder, and rested with the fingers just showing. I put my hand on his. He took a deep breath and burst into a storm of weeping, and great relief followed.

I showed him that unconsciously he had reached out toward me, though not being able to perceive until I touched him either that I was there or that he needed me.

A few minutes later he told me about one of his patients in childbirth. Now he was an adult, well integrated with his infant self, whom it would have been an affront to treat otherwise. I made some comment on that level and then waited a bit. Then I said that unconsciously he was showing me that he could treat patients as well as I could and was competing on the oedipal level with me, a specialist, i.e. a father with a bigger penis, but also as a boy, with the mother who could conceive and bear children.

This material would not have been reached but for the body happening of his hand movement, accepted both verbally and nonverbally by me. It was the body injury that showed me the need for body response, though I only realized this later. Since this he has been near to self-injury again, but he has avoided it because the memory of my hand has turned up, either recalled consciously or as a sensation in his own body. This material shows the rapid change from level to level and from non-verbal and bodily to verbal and psychic.

One of the essential needs of borderline patients is to find and experience in some degree the early mothering care, the "protective shield" which was missing or defective in their actual infancy. This may range from the very earliest 100-percent dependability needed for the first few hours or days following birth, the restoration as nearly as is humanly possible of the intrauterine state, to such things as a hurt child being held by the mother and comforted simply and unemotionally.

This was James' need. When he had hurt himself in childhood he had either been scolded and told that it was his fault, or he had been first overwhelmed by his mother's anxiety and then stood on his feet again as soon as she found he was not seriously injured. I remembered from my G.P. days a scalded child, so held, crying over and over "I want my Mummie. Where's my Mummie?" It was useless to say "Mummie's here, she's holding you." What he needed was not a person but a state of being, of unhurtness, which she could not then give him; she could only hold him, and say "There, there."

Hospitalization is one of the ways in which the missing or defective early mothering care can be supplied. A psychotic episode may make it necessary, or a psychosomatic illness or the psychic accompaniment of a somatic illness may provide an occasion for care; the latter are both frequent transference manifestations, becoming more recognizable as such as the analysis goes on.

Patients will insist either that the illness is entirely somatic, or entirely psychogenic, trying to keep psyche and soma apart. Or part of the body may be disowned and invested with its own autonomy—"My leg hurts me"—as if it existed separately. These somatic things must be properly cared for, and the analyst must join up with that care, becoming psychically continuous and identical with it. How far this joining up can be in symbolic or token form (flowers, letters, etc.) and how far it must be actual (visiting, contact with doctor or nursing home), depends upon the individual patient and his psychic state at the time.

Peter (formerly a "battered baby") decided after some years of analysis to have a minor operation, which he needed. I referred him to a surgeon whom I told of his mental illness, as I thought it possible that he might have a short psychotic episode if not given very careful attention after the operation. He might tear off the bandages or run away.

He was delusionally afraid, but determined to go through with the operation. During recovery from the anesthetic he felt an impulse to tear the bandages from the patient in the next bed, but was too drowsy to be able to do so. He wanted to discharge himself prematurely, but allowed himself to be dissuaded, partly through his delusional fears.

When he came back to analysis (ten days after admission) every detail of that time had to be recounted, and related to the multiple traumata of his childhood and adolescence.

After long and difficult working through he found that the experience, besides being terrifying, had been very good indeed. He had been able to regress to *total* dependence and to find himself *totally* held and cared for. Then he could recover memories of good caring which had hitherto been repressed together with much that was intolerably painful. Attention to his bodily needs made it possible to reach material which could not have become accessible in the consulting room in ordinary conditions.

There are patients who avoid illness; they may go through an influenza epidemic, for instance, nursing everyone else without becoming ill themselves. These present a special difficulty, for until they can become ill the mothering care is fought off and when they do there is often a real risk to life.

But all patients who need the earliest 100 percent reliable mothering need also at some point to experience such risk, and to choose unconsciously between life and death. In the most ill this becomes ultimately a matter for the body ego. These are often people who have truly wished to die but could not make the movement to bring it about because to them any movement will bring not death, but annihilation. Drugs (sedatives, tranquilizers, or amphetamine, etc.) are linked with the need for mothering care at a level earlier than the oral, and with delusion they can be important in the transference.

There are patients who behave dangerously to themselves by

taking overdoses or to others, e.g. by leaving the drugs around where children may find them. When the danger is serious, it must be treated seriously, by hospitalization. Analysis must be continued throughout wherever practicable, and when it is impracticable it must be firmly linked psychically with the hospital care (as in somatic illness) when it is resumed. Some patients, in large enough areas, understand the potentialities and dangers of the drugs and use them reasonably, but in other areas behave irrationally.

Violet became anxious if she had forgotten to put into her handbag the vitamin tablets originally prescribed by her family doctor for a mild deficiency, which she now rarely took. On one level they were a magical talisman, and also a mysterious and persecuting danger. On another level they were a transitional object: she would take them out and look at them, play with the bottle, think of taking one, and do so, or not. Ultimately they were lost, or thrown away, "not good any more," or no longer needed. On the surface they carried their original reality significance. In her session she sometimes lay holding the bottle; sometimes they were left across the room in her bag. Sometimes they were handed to me and demanded again at the end of the hour. Then they were left with me overnight and finally left at home and forgotten altogether.

On the deepest, delusional level the tablets *were* me, and I was the healing, life-giving, substance, to be eaten, excreted, breathed in and out, or simply absorbed, by virtue of my presence. When she became afraid of them, "I think they've gone bad by now," I was the poisonous, persecuting substance to be got rid of. Similarly, on this level they *were*, also, both herself and her mother, good and bad.

But the actual bodily life-or-death situation is not enough without its psychic counterpart, the situation in which nothing whatever can be done and there is no choice, a situation which is experienced as annihilation. This is often avoided and rejected by means of some panic move. But when it can be reached and endured and discovery made of the utter release of its corollary, no demand, a very deep integration comes about that is there for life. It is the acceptance of death, and so of life itself. Up to this point there can only be either life-in-death or death-in-life, according to the degree of the illness. At this point the change comes about of which Freud (1914) wrote: "There must be something added to auto-erotism—a new psychical action—in order to bring about narcissism."

In the analysis of psychoneurotic patients countertransference is not often of primary importance. In an overall way, of course, it matters: none of us would do analysis at all but for the presence in us of those things that would form transference elements in other relationships. Our choice is determined by their predominant strength in a particular direction.

In the analysis of psychotic patients and of the psychotic areas of borderline patients, countertransference plays a much greater part. It is all-important to have one's subjective and objective feelings clearly distinguished and to recognize wherever one's reactions or interactions are disproportionate. The possibility of an area of countertransference psychosis (delusion of identity between oneself and one's analysand) has to be considered and analyzed.

I will go back now to *Beatrice.* I have not brought out so far the almost physical sensations I had of being torn, scratched, bitten, and generally knocked about by her. I would end her sessions exhausted, shaking, and unable to move on psychically to my next patient.

She made a great point that everything must always be exactly the same when she arrived. It was useless to point out that the room itself was the same, or that I was. I struggled for months trying to understand why it mattered so much, and then to adapt to her apparent need and fix it so, failing day after day. I tried unsuccessfully to find what it was in myself that was making for difficulty. Finally I gave it up, and just said I *would not* fix it. There was hardly a protest, and that was the end of it! I had defeated my own superego, which had been identified with her, and I had apparently found unconsciously what she really needed.

As time went on I made less and less effort to restrain the feelings she aroused in me, but gave interpretations only after having expressed them. I made it clear that there was a limit to what I would stand, and she began to develop a respect for me and to experience and express real feelings of her own, finding that the relationship with me stood, and that neither of us was annihilated. Differentiation and integration became continuous processes, and she became not only human but also mature. I gained a great deal, too, in these same ways, from her analysis.

Unconscious awareness of what is going on in a patient (empathy) is something that always surprises me. Sometimes we hear a neurotic patient say "It's funny you should say that: I was just thinking about it," and we know that we are in contact with him on an unconscious level. (It is, of course, a two-way thing, and I am equally surprised by my patients' unconscious knowledge of me.)

I have found myself in a silent patch wanting to do something violent to a patient: to shake her, to kick his shins. I have said "I think you were wanting to shake me yesterday," or "Is it my shins you're thinking of kicking?" and found it confirmed exactly.

With one patient much bigger and heavier than I, I have been aware of a wish to murder her and have come to know that I was in actual danger myself. She is so disturbed that it is a relief when she is enraged with her colleagues at work and not with me or with her mother who constantly provokes her.

But it is not always easy to let myself trust to my "psychic antennae." The taboo upon an analyst's emotions has been so great in the past that I can see now where several of my unsuccessful analyses went wrong. My unconscious guilt about such things as "stealing" from a patient, having secret knowledge concerning him, or being (psychically) intimate or identical with him have made analysis impossible.

The delusion of oneness between analysand and analyst, "basic unity," has never been given up in borderline patients as it has in psychoneurotics, though it has been repressed. Even those who, like John, only need momentarily the 100-percent mothering, nevertheless need to make the link with it that is there in any body contact.

Whatever delusion is there must be fully accepted both verbally and nonverbally by the analyst as having absolute reality for the patient; its *factual* unreality must be made plain—this is the point of no choice, or annihilation—and its psychic reality for both must be preserved, as a memory of a primary omnipotent state.

I have described and illustrated some of the technique which I have found useful in analyzing borderline patients. I have laid more emphasis on the analysis of the psychotic areas than on that of neurotic areas for two reasons. First, because unless the psychotic areas are treated no analysis of the neurotic areas will be meaningful. Second, analysis of neurosis has been amply described elsewhere and is familiar to all analysts. The danger in this is that the importance of analysis of the neurotic areas and of verbalization might be over-looked. It is essential, as its omission not only leaves dissatisfaction but actually *prevents* the necessary integration and leaves the way open for continued illness. No analysis will ever be complete, in any case. Ultimate separation will depend on the extent to which the basic unity is established or preserved, and the patient enabled to take over and continue the analysis himself: to take over respon-sibility for his own life and to bear repeated breakdowns, rather than expect never to experience them again.

I will put together the principles which underlie the technique that I use in analyzing areas of delusional transference, where the prob-lems are those of existence, survival, and identity—where reality has to be found, before it can be imaginatively elaborated.

1. Analysis of delusion cannot be carried out except in regression, and regression to 100 percent dependence. Whatever percentage of dependence the patient cannot manage for himself must be managed for him either by the analyst or by others.

2. Those who care for him in factual reality must be allowed to join up with the analyst in some way and so become psychically continuous and identical with him.

3. Where delusion prevails, the patient cannot use inference, deductive thinking, or symbolism. Areas where he can use these are handed over temporarily to the analyst; he needs concrete, actual, and bodily realities. When these have been found, they can be linked with words by the analyst and brought within reach of interpreta-tion, i.e. linking together the body ego and the psychic ego, and they then become eligible for psychic elaboration (i.e. fantasy). The analyst's acceptance of the importance of both verbal and non verbal, psychic and somatic, is made clear in his use of both, in himself as well as in his patient.

4. This brings about an alteration in the patient in the area of autoerotism, and as a result a new area of narcissism develops (Freud 1914). Differentiation begins, and self begins to be sorted out from not-self, both bodily and psychically, as he begins psychically to live in his body, and relationship becomes a possibility.

5. The adaptations which the analyst makes, according to the changing needs or states of his patient, have limits. These lie partly in himself as he experiences himself ("What I do is me; what is not me I don't do") and partly in the patient as the analyst experiences him at

any given moment. ("I do this, here, now, with this patient. I do not do that with him, now or ever. I do not do this with him at another time, I do not do this at all with another patient.")

6. Neither an absolute of analysis, nor of a particular style of technique, nor the work or discoveries of any individual other than the analyst himself can determine the limits. We have good precedent for an empirical approach in Freud himself. Not all analysts have to be willing to make adaptations, but an analyst who is not willing to do so may have to limit either his choice of patients or the expectations of his results. It is a matter of investment.

7. Adaptations (or parameters) serve the limited and specific purpose of the analysis of delusion. The technique of analysis of transference psychosis must be rooted and grounded in the established classical technique of analysis of psychoneurosis (Freud); otherwise it becomes "wild analysis," and truly dangerous.

8. Analysis of these patients is a life-and-death matter, psychically and sometimes somatically as well. The analyst, or some extension of him is all that stands between the patient and death. At some point he has to stand aside and simply be there, while the patient takes his life into his own hands and becomes a living human being—or a corpse.

To sum up, borderline patients have every kind of mental illness, from psychosis to "normality"; they have every kind of symptom from disorders of perception and delusion to ordinary oedipal conflicts; they have patches of thought disorder of every kind and degree; and their anxieties range from survival anxiety through persecutory and depressive anxiety to separation and castration anxiety. The quality of the superego varies, from extremely primitive sadism to benign and ego syntonic ego ideal.

In psychoneurosis survival is already axiomatic; annihilation does not exist and does not have to be considered. In psychosis it *has* happened, totally. The problems of these patients in the areas where psychotic anxieties predominate (annihilation or survival, and persecutory) are those concerning existence itself, and identity. When these are established, the anxieties are neurotic in type, separation, depressive and castration anxiety; the problems are those of concern, mourning, pleasure and pain, and sexuality.

Where psychotic anxieties predominate, ego nuclei are present and are functioning, but are not joined up, and the ego does not function as a whole, the person does not live psychically in his body; id and ego have not fused; basic unity persists as a delusion, and differentiation has not happened, so object relations do not exist (subject and object being the same); love, hate, and ambivalence have yet to be discovered.

In other words the ego has to come into existence and functioning—the distinction between self and not-self has to be found—and all this must be linked with words before imaginative elaboration (fantasy) can be used.

To analyse these areas means to go back to a not-yet-personalized state and to allow time for the psychic work to be done, which means experientially going through annihilation and death and coming forward again, but differently.

All elements of psyche and soma—id, body ego, and psychic ego, and superego, human and nonhuman—have to be worked over, fused, and de-fused, differentiated and integrated, projected and introjected, again and again. The protective shield, or supplementary ego, has first to be supplied by the analyst and then gradually withdrawn again.

> An analytic result depends upon the revival, repetition and mastery of earlier conflicts in current experience of the transference situation with insight an indispensable feature of an analytic goal. [Zetzel 1956]

> A basic human need for security is taken very seriously and will always be respected, though this does not mean satisfied to a greater extent than is necessary for the day by day development of the analysis. [Hoffer, 1956]

Treatment must depend upon whatever is presented at any given moment. Classical analysis is the appropriate thing wherever it is practicable; when it is not, parameters are appropriate, and they must be supplemented and succeeded by it. *Nothing* can ultimately supersede classical analysis, but there is no "canon" or "absolute" of analysis which can determine the limits of adaptation—only the limits of the individual patient and individual analyst.

Success in analysis largely depends upon how far we ourselves, despite our anxiety, can really accept and live by the very things we are trying to get our patients to accept: (1) that the same things are both good and bad, and the whole includes both aspects (whether of emotion, body products, people, things, actions, or analytic inter-pretations)—*everything* has ambivalency; (2) that normal and path-ological phenomena come from the same place; (3) that a patient's illness is a spontaneous attempt at cure, and that, paradoxically, his "well" self may turn out to be the most ill part of him; (4) that psychic reality is as important as factual reality and vice versa.

It comes down to our fundamental honesty or hypocrisy, integrity or the lack of it. We have to admit the limitations of our knowledge, skill, and insight. We may have to act on the principle of the balance-of-good-over-bad; we may be using what we have faute de mieux. Or we may use what we have because it is worth using. What we have is what is in ourselves and in our patients: bodies, sensations, and emotions; movements and actions; words, ideas, thoughts, intel-ligence, and imagination. And that is quite a lot.

9

BORDERLINE STATES

The whole spectrum of borderline phenomena appears in the range of patients whom we see, from the mildly neurotic to the frankly psychotic. But this same spectrum is also seen in each individual, ranging from the areas of least disturbance to those where the disturbance is greatest. In this a borderline patient is like an adolescent—swinging between extremes and often existing at both, and at other levels too, simultaneously. (I think Donald Meltzer called attention to this.)

The chief anxiety found in the areas of greatest disturbance is psychotic in type, i.e. relating to such things as survival, identity, or loss of something which is not perceived as separate from the self or differentiated out from the rest of the self.

In other areas neurotic anxieties predominate, concerned with the loss of something perceived as whole and separate (a person, place or thing) or something differentiated out (a part of the body), recognized as such.

In the earliest, totally undifferentiated state the term *symbiosis* is not appropriate, as in true symbiosis each partner is dependent on the other. An infant could not survive without the mother, though she could survive without him. Psychically, in the infant "I" is a one-body relationship.

In my view the term should be used as referring to a developmental stage where differentiation has already begun. It can be quite early where the environment makes it possible, and in such an environment it will not be prolonged.

Persistence of the undifferentiated state is seen in borderline patients as an area of delusion, whereas a prolonged symbiotic stage may be seen either as delusion, or as illusion, the latter being far more readily resolved than the former. This is partly a matter of it being nearer to the level where verbalization belongs and ordinary interpretation can be used and partly of something that has been repressed versus something that has never yet been in consciousness, and has to be brought there.

In their delusional areas borderline patients make far greater demands on their analysts than do other patients or than they do in their nondelusional areas. They may often be working in both at the same time and be fully aware of the unreasonableness of the demands as well as of their intensity and urgency—i.e. that they are real *needs* which must, somehow, be met. This makes for conflict.

The overriding need is, of course, for the delusion to be made conscious, which in itself shows the patient that there really is a oneness between himself and his analyst; i.e. that at bottom there is a reality. Beyond this the distinction between the *psychic* reality of oneness and fact has to be made clear, and it follows upon what the patient in his nondelusional areas can recognize and accept—that no two people can *actually* be identical.

This provides automatically the ultimate limit to the patient's demands and the point from which relationship can begin.

But it is the point which is both most needed and most feared, and it can be reached only when the patient can risk handing over temporarily the more mature (nondelusional) functioning to his analyst—that is in regression to dependence.

The analyst has to feel his way to it, accepting at every step both limits that he himself sets and limits set by his patient. They may be limits of time, distance, silence, movement, feeling etc. The analyst puts these things at his patient's disposal, in doing so he becomes exposed to his own annihilation anxiety, feeling invaded, merged, swamped, rejected, over and over again. But he must respect the limits set for him, otherwise the patient feels these things. It is a matter of a most delicate balance between active and neutral responses, between trying to go too far or too fast and missing a vitally important moment when it is presented to him.

It is usually better to stop short of the patient's limits, rather than overstep them. But to perceive them is only too often far from easy—the analyst is dependent upon his own capacity for empathy and spontaneity, and his own integrity, but trusting also in those of his patient.

If these are there in both, the delusion can be resolved, the area of psychosis is reduced, and new development or growth can come about; capacity for forming relationships is enlarged, and new relationships not based on delusion (folié à deux) are formed; as well as a new relationship between patient and analyst.

10

BASIC UNITY AND SYMBIOSIS

The concept of basic unity, a state of total absence of differentiation, is a very difficult one for many people to accept. It arouses the most primitive psychotic anxiety of all—annihilation anxiety (not anxiety about death).

The idea of losing one's identity, of being merged in some un-defined homogeneous mass, or lost forever in a bottomless pit is very frightening and disturbing, an idea which we all tend to avoid.

The logical conclusion of the idea is that there is a point at which all separation or difference ceases to be—when *all* polarities and all distinctions vanish; where life and death, pleasure and pain, hope and despair, love, hate, destructiveness and creativity, all persons, places and things are one and the same. There *is* only one—and *no* other.

The old song "Green grow the rushes O" is an expression of this deep anxiety, with its refrain: "One is one and all alone, and ever more shall be so," and its theme of two, three, four etc. bringing reassurance.

Symbiosis, on the other hand, is something that is already recog-nizable in the natural world and therefore easier to accept. Plants and animals are found in symbiotic relatedness. It is a dependent relatedness, for neither partner can live without the other. But however primitive the organisms are, there is always one degree of distinction between them—for each there *is* an other. It is a two-body relationship.

In human life the fetus is parasitic—the mother can live without the fetus, but the fetus cannot live without the mother. The separation at birth means that the mother no longer provides directly all the infant's biological systems—the infant must breathe, and suck for food. But though he remains dependent on his environment he is no longer parasitic; he can become symbiotic and later develop increasingly a relatively high degree of independence.

In ordinary infancy when the "average expectable" or "facilitating" environment is provided, the psychic state of total undifferentiatedness can be very short, and annihilation anxiety is both minimized and readily met where it occurs. But when this does not occur, areas of undifferentiatedness persist as a delusion; unless environmental changes come about that are enough to support the child's biological changes, these areas do not alter. They then form the basis of a psychosis, where the main anxiety is annihilation anxiety. The degree of the psychosis, or its position in the spectrum of mental states, depends on the extent of these areas.

In a relatively few individuals they are enough to determine the development of a parasitic state, where there is permanent dependence. Some psychotic patients can live only in an institution of some kind; others need lifelong "maintenance doses" of drug or therapist.

Symbiosis also appears to be a part of ordinary infancy, and development out of it ordinarily happens. Difficulty comes where the child is fixed in a relationship with a mother who has not been able to emerge enough from her own symbiotic phase.

Here, while there may still be some annihilation anxiety, the difficulty is rather that of establishing a sense of identity, or selfhood and of moving on to both ordinary mature independence and tolerance of interdependence with others.

Infant and child observation and analysis has greatly enlarged awareness and knowledge of symbiosis and of its resolution.

Treatment of adult patients, especially those nearer the psychotic end of the spectrum, has shown me that the (delusional) areas of undifferentiatedness where *actual* identity is demanded can often be reduced, but to do this is rather like trying to separate two pieces of cellophane tape that are stuck together by their adhesive surfaces.

But the psychic reality of both basic unity and symbiosis is surely valuable. Without them there could be neither empathy nor tolerance, mutual understanding, or any real capacity for relationship or coexistence.

11

RECIPROCITY AND MUTUALITY

Reciprocity and mutuality are often regarded as synonymous, that is, as each having the same meaning as the other, implying either an alternating or a reverberating movement of feeling between two people or something shared between them, something they "have in common."

But there is a real psychodynamic difference between them. Reciprocity implies that the same feelings are aroused in each person, *determined* by those in the other, whereas in fact the feelings in one may provoke or arouse quite different feelings in the other.

Mutuality implies that the same feelings toward each other are present in two people, but exist in each *independently* of their existence in the other.

What two or more people have "in common" (like mutuality), each feels or experiences independently, undetermined by any other.

PART III

EXPANSION IN MORE GENERAL AREAS

12

TOWARD MENTAL HEALTH: EARLY MOTHERING CARE

I have called this chapter "Toward Mental Health: Early Mothering Care," and the general sources on which I have drawn are first of all, Freud himself, then Winnicott and Searles, Melanie Klein, Marion Milner, and many others. The particular sources from which the chapter derives are not only infant observation, in which I have not myself taken part, but also regressive states of adults in analysis. My own work has largely been concerned with borderline patients.

Mental health is so often defined by what it isn't, and the definitions that one gets on the basis of what it isn't are usually based on a classification of mental illness according to disease entities: hysteria, schizophrenia, and so on.

For myself, I much prefer to think of it in terms of the type of anxiety that prevails in any individual patient. *Psychotic* anxiety has to do with questions of survival or annihilation, the question of separation from something of which you are a part (or which is a part of you), and problems of identity. *Neurotic* anxiety has to do with separation from an object perceived as whole and separate from you, problems of sexual identity, loss of part of one's body, often castration. In trying to sum up what I mean by mental health, I have arrived at: *emotional and intellectual development appropriate to the chronological age and situation of the person concerned, remembering that what is healthy at one age can be quite unhealthy at another.*

I am starting with a pregnant mother—a very obvious thing, an ordinary woman with an ordinary husband, living in an ordinary world. Of course this is, in any case, to some extent an idealization, and simultaneously it can be the very opposite—it can be intensely dreary. Within her body is a growing organism which will in time become separate from her. She and the fetus constitute a physical entity whose oneness is broken up by the birth process. But up to that time, although the fetal circulation is largely distinct from hers, her respiratory, digestive, and excretory systems are working for both. The fetus could not go on without her, but she could, of course, go on without it. Her needs are met by people and things which exist and are seen by her to exist separately and independently of her.

The infant's first major contact with the outside world comes at birth. For the first time, he breathes air, feeds, digests, and absorbs his food and excretes waste products. And for the first time his body has weight. He is bathed, dressed, handled, and pushed around. He is still dependent on the mother, or on mothering by someone, for a long time, but to a gradually lessening degree.

To preserve stability, there is an urgent need for the reestablishing and maintaining for a time of conditions as much like those of intrauterine life as is humanly possible. This is as much a life-and-death matter for the infant psychically as was earlier, physically, the going-on-living of the actual mother. Without it this massive, total experience of being born cannot be assimilated, that is, joined up with prenatal body experience, and so it remains a disturbance of the order of world catastrophe. All later experiences will tend to join up with these body memories, rather than with prenatal ones.

Where the restoration is brought about, a sense of continuity can be found. Survival of the entity "mother-infant" can be taken for granted, and out of this a sense of identity and a true independence can in time develop. Without it, survival cannot become axiomatic. Annihilation or catastrophe is always expected. All energy is used in the fight to survive, and nothing else can come to have any meaning. I have been talking of two extremes, neither of which perhaps ever happens. Usually there is something between them, and according to which end of the scale the infant's experiences are and according also to later experiences, which can modify things either way, so in greater or smaller areas expectation of catastrophe will persist, and growth of the self and of independence will be helped or hindered.

The entity of mother-infant is at first a physical reality. This entity persists psychically for some time after birth in both mother and infant. Our ordinary mother has, during her pregnancy, developed what Winnicott has called "primary maternal preoccupation." That is to say, throughout her pregnancy she has become progressively more and more centered on the coming child: dreaming, planning, arranging for the care of herself, as herself; of herself in relation to him, of him as an individual; and in relation to the home and the rest of the family and of both in relation to the outside world. By the time he is born, she is deeply committed to him, and experiences him not only as a part of her own body but as a part of her very self, in such a way that his needs are hers, and her needs are for him. For her, as for the infant, there is a one-body relationship.

The puerperium is a time of maximal dependence in the infant and maximal infant-centeredness in the mother. Hence, her vulnerability both during pregnancy and the puerperium. But from the time of birth there is a gradual and progressive separation out from him, so as to allow him to be a person in his own right, a separate individual with whom, nevertheless, there is a deeply felt closeness, rooted in the shared, albeit differently felt, experiences of prenatal and early postnatal life.

In the newly born infant bodily life and body happenings are all-important, and psychic life as we come to know it later is, in the ordinary way, near enough nonexistent. There is no distinction between them, any more than there is, for the infant, any distinction between himself and his mother, or between any two parts of his own body. At one moment, he is all mouth, all breast, scream, chuckle, etc. In fact, he seems to be a state of being rather than a person in such a state and the experiencing person is the mother. We speak of an "infant-in-arms," a "lap" or "knee baby," and later, a "toddler," showing the progression of his changing relationship to his mother, to himself, to the outer world, and his growing independence.

Because of this undifferentiatedness, his earliest memories will be body memories, and the earliest form of remembering will not be recalling but reproducing or reenacting in a concrete bodily way. We see this later, of course, in the repetitive play of young children when they need to assimilate a painful or frightening experience by joining it up with memories of good and reassuring happenings, reliving it in a safe setting. The more good experiences a child has had, the more he has to draw on in times of pain and fear or difficulty, and the greater his inner strength where he has been able to take in, and build up into himself, a predominantly friendly and protective world.

Our ordinary mother actively separates herself out from her infant, while also remaining close to him. His growth and maturation and his lessening dependence on her, as well as the other realities of her life, foster this process. She may experience his birth as a loss within herself, which she can only deal with by caring for him. A pediatrician has told me, and mothers have said the same, that where too great separation happens early in the puerperium the mother loses the sense of contact with her baby, and the reestablishing of it makes for difficulty especially in the early feeding situation.

Workers concerned with adoption find that the baby must be separated from the mother *at birth,* otherwise she cannot stand the pain of it until she and the child have grown away from each other to some extent. For the infant the process is even more difficult.

It is important that alongside the progressive separation there is also a continuity, providing imaginative or psychic continuity from prenatal right up to adult life, through infancy, childhood, and adolescence. Breaks in it are damaging to emotional life and development. This is more obvious at some stages than at others. It is, of course, more obvious once the infant has perceived the mother as a whole and separate person, achieving two-body relationship and later, in adolescence, for instance, when the relationship to the outside world (multi-body) becomes relatively more important. Out of the stability of this continuity new things can safely come. I have spoken of it elsewhere as a "basic unity," a state of the essential self, the basis of all communication and relationships, and a sine qua non for the healthy emotional life and development of every individual.

One difficulty lies in the common feeling that what one *wants* to do must inevitably be wrong! Mothers are often under pressure from outside; in hospital they are often not allowed to have their infants with them, to pick them up or feed them when they cry. After a few days, just long enough to break the continuity, they are sent home to get on with this disrupted state and run the home at the same time.

Incidentally something similar often happens with mentally sick patients, who supposedly for their own good are coerced and regimented into things like occupational therapy, group therapy, and into returning to the status quo ante, quite against their own feelings, and their own need to have an illness; they are made to feel unwelcome if they don't cooperate in the process. Perhaps only a mother who has been able to care for her baby as *she* felt, can really know how important it is for the relationship between them. For this, which is the basis of all the child's future relationships, can be made or marred at this time.

A newly born infant, totally inexperienced, un-understanding and dependent, unaware of either himself or his environment, starts on the journey toward becoming an adult, to gain a whole range of experience of the stages between, and all that these bring in the way of understanding and development, relationship and concern, becoming able to take responsibility for himself and for others. Within the space of twenty-one (or is it now eighteen?) years, the individual, as it were, passes through the history of the race, just as in the nine months of intrauterine life, the fetus has passed through stages comparable to the evolution of man from a "primordial protoplasmic globule." These things ordinarily happen automatically if the setting is right. The changes come about from within the child, as they have come from within the race, and interference or prompting from outside cannot bring them about or even hurry them, except at the cost of disturbing a finely balanced organism with built-in patterns of development.

The foundations of mental health are there from the beginning, and the building is furthered and, so to speak, emotionally financed, by millions of ordinary parents, who are willing to invest in their children the courage and patience needed to watch and wait, and make adaptation to them, providing their own setting for them, responding spontaneously to outward movement, being sensitive to individual needs, and encouraging the finding of individual ways. They do not try to mold their children to any pattern, whether their own or society's.

The parents themselves need to be firmly rooted and grounded, for it is their stability and maturity that provide the milieu in which the child can find himself. An important element in the integrity of the parents is their willingness to enlarge their own boundaries and take full responsibility for their child right from the time of conception, (whether it was consciously intended or not), acknowledging that he did not ask to be conceived or born and therefore has a right to his existence and individuality without demands on him to pay emotionally or otherwise for his keep, or to be grateful. If they can, then, accept what he gives in his own time, they find that his body movements—screaming, biting, hitting, excreting—can become loving things, and if they can allow him to be his age, to be himself and nothing more, abrogating their own rights for long enough and bearing guilt and anxiety for him, he will in time be both able and willing to take over for himself. When he has perceived them as separate from himself and become aware of what they have been doing, he can accord them rights, feel concern for them, and recognize that a shared event is experienced differently by the partners in it.

The idea that "normal" or "mature" people are free from hate, guilt, inhibition, sadness or anxiety, dies very hard. The continued interaction of people with conflicting individual needs and claims, and their equal rights to exist, makes life a precarious and difficult thing at best, and those who carry the greatest responsibility must also carry, and not be overwhelmed by, the considerable burden of all of these. But the demands made must be realistic, that is appropriate to the individual's age and situation, and they can be enriching. The guilt of infancy about imaginatively destroying the mother in an orgy of eating, and the despair at the loss, should be resolved by the discovery that she is not destroyed in fact, nor does she destroy him in retaliation, and by the discovery of the difference between factual and imaginative reality.

It is very rare for an infant not to be born "normal," in the sense of having the potentiality to develop all the ordinary bodily faculties and also capacities for forming relationships and taking responsibility. A "normal" baby is potentially a person from the start and begins to become that person as he moves in response to impulses within himself, which relate both to his own body and to his environment. There is a continual interchange to and fro between him and his environment, and the response of the environment to his movement or expression of feeling will largely determine his next movement or next feeling.

Here I would like to look at something of what happens when an infant moves, remembering that it looks different from the inside (that is, to the infant) from how it looks to an adult, outside.

Some kind of urge turns up—hunger perhaps, or mother. Neither seems at first to belong to the infant, both are apparently alien, and they may apparently be experienced as exactly the same thing, (though one might expect one to feel bad and the other good). The infant's mouth, his whole body, or his whole self, again experienced as one and the same, is excited and is impelled violently, toward or away from the stimulus. He is hurled at it, dragged by it, meets it, fuses with it, and destroys it, or is destroyed by it (again the same thing in this undifferentiated state), as the urge itself is destroyed and is no longer there, being now satisfied.

Separation out is not perceived at first, but when the climax has been reached and the urge vanishes, there is a turning away, a losing, a forgetting, though the body memory remains. This is on the same pattern as that of sexual orgasm. It *is* an orgasm, something in which the whole infant is involved. Many repetitions where the urge is met spontaneously, just right, by the mother, lead to the establishment of the pattern of that movement as valuable. It can come to have meaning, to be emotionally enriched as a loving movement, and to be imaginatively elaborated, to be repeated, or not, at will.

First, the elaboration can be as simple as a headline: "I am," "I eat," "I eat that." Later, ideas of what "I" is, what "eat" can mean, and what "that" may be, go on to ideas of what happens afterward. When teeth come "that" is torn in pieces. The pieces are inside, and products come out, while others are absorbed and built into the child himself or may remain unaltered and act again from within as stimuli. All this is the stuff of the child's inner imaginative life and world.

What I want to underline is the importance of the discovery of first the child's own body, of sensations and movement, and then the sense of being a person who has felt and moved, that lies in that "I am," followed by the discovery of the "not I," the "that" which also feels and moves in response or spontaneously, separately and differently. This is where both self-knowledge (insight) and relationship begin.

If when the infant moves, perhaps in hunger, hallucinating the mother who will satisfy it, the mother is not there or maybe begins by diaper changing or wiping away saliva from the excited mouth, the movement becomes useless. It falls in a vacuum. New discovery is minimal or misleading, and something potentially valuable, that could become a capacity to make assertions of the self and go on to the development of relationships, is lost. If a movement brings pain—an excited hand hits the cot's bars, or is slapped, or the child's excited body is suddenly grabbed and hugged by the equally excited mother, the movement becomes positively dangerous, catastrophic, annihilating, in fact, and becomes one of hate. The sense of self then is only of a hating self, living in an unfriendly not-self world, a world which denies the child existence or personhood.

Walter Menninger (1968) has spoken of "the inevitability of violence when certain types of men and women go unheard or believe that they are not heard." He quoted William James: "No more fiendish torture can be devised than when you speak, no one answers, when you wave, no one turns, but everyone simply cuts you dead. Soon there wells up within you such hostility, you attack those who ignore you, and if that fails to bring recognition, you turn your hostility inward upon yourself in an effort to *prove* you really exist."

The processes of differentiation and integration go on in the child, so that through a building up of his awareness of self and not-self and this sorting out of the various people around him, personalization or individuation becomes a rhythmic and continuing process throughout life. Repetition makes for stability, and variation can make for an increasing capacity to bear surprise, and even shock, without too much difficulty. Anxiety and emotion are found and expressed in body ways and are only later translated into psychic phenomena, largely separated off from these body things and expressed in words or in substitute, symbolic ways. Because of his smallness and total helplessness, the infant needs to feel magically powerful, and the mother's size and her abilities lend a quality of omnipotence to the mother-infant entity. Separation out from the entity involves destruction, guilt, and anxiety, and a gradual giving up of this omnipotence, with growing recognition and acceptance of human helplessness and limitations.

If the mother herself has to keep her own infantile omnipotence because of failure of her early environment, she cannot allow the child his, for she has to feel herself superior to him. She cannot let him create or destroy her imaginatively. She feels his development as a threat to her own existence, and she depends upon him reciprocally. He will then remain in psychic dependence on her, developing the kind of false independence based on pathological omnipotence which we see in mentally ill patients, often delusional in its intensity and fixedness, manifested as arrogance and superiority, maintained to avoid loss and awareness of separation and annihilation.

Where the mother has been able to accept the loss of her own imagined omnipotence and retained it only as part of her world of fantasy, that is, psychically real, not *actual*, she is able to bear her own ambivalence and the child's, and so helps him to bear his. Without this the child is caught in the "double bind" of love and hate and is in the impossible situation where he cannot *but* develop biologically, and yet must remain part of an entity which cannot be dissolved. To become a person means to him literally to destroy the mother and to bear unlimited loss and guilt. In reality, to stay dependent is to be destroyed himself.

Going back to movement, at an early time, of course, the infant's movements are not effective, partly because of his size, but to begin with they are uncontrollable reactions, not voluntary or even coordinated. Induced reflex movements are often not distinguished as such. Automatic bladder or bowel control is only too easy to establish and has to break down before the control can become voluntary. The development of deliberate and intentional movements depends, as I showed earlier, upon the response of the environment to the movements made by the kicking foot, waving fist, clutching fingers, and sucking, biting or yelling mouth. When these movements can be established and elaborated they can also become effective and emotionally motivated, and the ability to choose between immediate and delayed action or expression of emotion can be found.

The ability to experience and recognize emotion and to express it in ways appropriate to a particular situation depends upon the capacity for observing and assessing or evaluating, and the development of this again depends upon the critical faculties of the parents: their ability to distinguish between real and imagined dangers, their scale of values, their degree of insight, their ability to stand anxiety and to bear separateness or fusion.

The building of the child's inner world goes along with his body maturation, and the widening of his outer world, consequent on his increasing motility. His discovery of his father and other members of the household as separate and whole people is important for this, quite apart from the father's importance all the while as a back-ground figure supporting the mother and holding the home. The father's importance as an individual increases as time goes on, until eventually it comes, at times at least, to supplant the mother's.

The survival principle gives way to the pleasure principle and this in turn to the reality principle. It becomes possible to distinguish between personal, inner, imaginative reality, and outer, factual reality shared with others, and to live by both, no longer demanding that truth be absolute or unchanging. Lost omnipotence and omnis-cience, his own and that personified in the mother, can be mourned so that guilt and anger give place to sadness, and the pain of ambivalence to pleasure in contrast. Actual oneness with the mother can give way to an imagined oneness with her and with other people and becomes the basis of empathy and understanding.

In stressing the importance of these early happenings between infant and mother, I have tried to trace those things which foster the tendency to mature. Other factors have to be remembered, of course, such as heredity, and other environmental things which can turn up throughout life. Only uniovular twins are genetically identical, and even they will never have identical environmental experiences. A first child is usually a source of more anxiety to the parents than are subsequent ones. A child may be born when the mother is ill or depressed, when the father is out of work, etc. Other children are born, get ill, have accidents, even die. Often the importance of an event to the child goes unnoticed by everyone else.

I have said very little about pathological conditions. Mostly they seem to have their roots in failures of one kind or another in early life. Those characterized by the prevalence of survival anxiety, that is, psychotic anxiety, in my experience include areas of delusional persistence of the primary undifferentiated state. The earliest experi-ences seem to have set a pattern for later happenings of a fairly consistent kind. A child who has been fortunate in the early experi-ences of complete dependence on the mother and of increasing separation out from her will come to the later stages of childhood, adolescence, and adult life not only able to take survival for granted but also with a growing sense of both personal and sexual identity and of life having meaning and value. He will find his capacity for relationships with himself, with people, and with things. It will not come about without difficulty, for difficulty is inherent in life itself, but he will have something within himself with which to meet it and will not be destroyed by it.

Every relationship involves something of both dependence and independence, and each has meaning only in relation to the other, as with all opposites, but for true relationship they must be mutual and not reciprocal. These are often taken to be synonymous but from a psychodynamic point of view they are different. Reciprocity implies that each person's acts or feelings are determined by those same acts or feelings in the other. Mutuality implies that although two people may act or feel the same way toward each other, those acts or feelings come from each of them independently of the other. The development of any relationship, including both those between analyst and patient and between partners in marriage follows, in a way, the reverse pattern from that seen in the mother-infant development. There is separateness at first, then gradually increasing confluence, which progresses through ambivalence to its resolution and finally to a merging in some kind of oneness. The sequence may be repeated many times, and of course in psychotherapy has to end in actual separation, but with each repetition comes new mutuality in both dependence and independence; new personal maturation in each partner, and new mutual creation.

Clinical material can illustrate something of the consequences of failure in early mothering care. Results of success are more difficult to demonstrate.

Jean, who came to me in 1966, at the age of forty-six, was the second of four children. Elizabeth, the eldest, was mongoloid. Two years after her birth the mother found herself pregnant again, and when the child was born, having "lost all her maternal feelings," she hardly attempted to breast-feed her. Jean and her sister Phoebe, three years younger, are both highly intelligent and sensitive people. The youngest, John, the longed-for son and heir, started life with a year in hospital during which the parents visited him every three months; he has spent most of his life since adolescence in expensive mental hospitals, being unable to live without support, though regarded only as neurotic. Elizabeth, having become unmanageable at home, was put into a "Home" at the age of seven.

All the children were put into the care of nannies and only saw their parents for a short time each day, when they were expected to behave prettily and be a credit to the parents. One, at least, of the nannies was actively sadistic, though with curiously inconsistent patches of kindness. When in adolescence Jean tried to tell her mother about this it was hotly denied as "impossible," for the mother "would, of course, have known and dismissed her."

Her father was still alive, though very old and completely deaf, with the paranoid reactions which so often accompany deafness. He was the son of a well-known musician, ambitious professionally and socially. The relationship between him and his wife was still idealized; they were devoted and inseparable, and the children could not be allowed to disturb this. He confirmed Jean's picture of her early life, and diaries of both parents were still extant.

The mother died after a long and distressing illness, incorrectly diagnosed at first, not long after Jean had returned to her parents' home with her own baby son, having divorced her husband soon after his birth. Jean nursed her mother and looked after her father until she remarried eight years later. There were no children from this marriage.

Jean was referred to me by Phoebe's (woman) psychotherapist. She presented as a depressive, expecting both to be told that no treatment was necessary—she must "pull herself together"—and a "miracle-cure in six sessions." The kind of help she consciously wanted was to have her marriage made successful, but by her husband altering, not herself. The depression had been precipitated by having to have destroyed a much-loved dog when her husband was promoted and had to move to London. A large part of her unconscious sex life had centered around the dog, which on one level represented the lost Elizabeth.

She also wanted (consciously) to alter her relationship to Phoebe. This relationship, according to Barry, her husband, was the cause of the trouble. The two would have hour-long telephone calls daily, and if either bought or was given anything the other would compulsively get the identical thing. The only apparent differences were that Jean had remarried after divorce and Phoebe had not, and that Jean had only one child and Phoebe had two. These were cited as showing how completely different and separate they were. Phoebe apparently behaved as if her elder child were her husband.

At the first interview Jean attributed her difficulties to having been at a progressive ("crank") school where she became involved with one boy after another. It turned out later that in fact she had been sent at age eight to a girls' boarding school, where she was deeply unhappy, later to another where she was less unhappy, but was expelled for "necking" with the garden-boy, and finally to the "crank" school in the hope of "curing" this tendency. She was happy there, but the really important person (unconsciously) was the headmaster, whom she loved and respected as she had never been able to love or respect her father (though he was warmer toward her than was her mother, or than he was to Phoebe). Here was where her repressed oedipal fantasies lay.

After her divorce she became first receptionist, then patient, then mistress, to a gynecologist. She finally sent Phoebe to him as a patient, and he seduced her too.

At the start of her treatment she insisted that I should see Barry; she could not imagine why neither he nor I should suggest or want it. I found that we could get nowhere until I did, and then she became acutely paranoid. She found, by opening the bill that I sent him, that her suspicions of me were unfounded. This was very important and valuable in building up her trust in me.

The analytic work has been mainly concerned with the finding and establishing of her identity, both personal and sexual. This involved first the perception of her own body and its separateness. It was to begin with quite unreal to her—either she was dying of the cardiac condition from which her mother died or she was going deaf like her father. To go to a doctor for the bronchitis from which she actually suffered would be useless: he would misdiagnose, despise her, hurt her, seduce her. She expected, and to some extent sought or provoked, pain and humiliation, believing that all the world thought of women as inferior to men, but was enraged when a man jokingly spoke of her as "Colonel Jean."

The delusions of identity with both her sisters, her brother, and her son (she was infantile, she must be insane or defective); of identity between Elizabeth and her dog (both nonhuman and both dead, as was her mother); and later, after he sustained a fractured skull with extensive frontal-lobe damage, between Barry, Elizabeth, and the dog; between me and the sadistic Nanny, the seducing gynecologist, and the uncaring parents. The delusion of omnipotence in herself, projected onto me and elsewhere (especially all psychiatrists), are gradually being resolved. She is progressively finding me to be a real person existing in my own right and able to let her exist in hers, finding that I am subject to all human emotions, conflict and ambivalence, fallible, limited and often helpless, finding that I am not destroyed by these things nor expecting her to be destroyed by them. Along with this goes her discovery of herself as a person—"I AM"—and that we both survive this self-assertion. Her ego strength (which was always really perceivable) has begun to be real *to her,* and her capacity to organize her own life in a realistic way increases steadily.

An obsession with money characterized all her family and acquaintances and was felt as an obstacle to the formation of relationships. It has been an obstacle to the development of her imaginative life, but she is now able to use money appropriately and to symbolize it. One important element is still undeveloped—the ability to play. The real external circumstances of her life since her husband's accident, which have acted powerfully as a stimulus to her ego development, have not been such as to help her in this way. But working through her mourning over him by caring for him and mourning for her dreams and other losses are helping to build up her inner reality. The ability to play is there, and beginning to emerge, as is her capacity for artistic creativeness.

The other main obstacle is still the folie à deux relationship between Jean and Phoebe. Jean describes it as living "tied to Phoebe by a steel wire," which she cannot break or untie. But as her sense of identity and selfhood strengthen, this grows weaker.

She has, at last, "seen Phoebe with new eyes, as she really is" and has in consequence "come to a decision to alter her own life"—giving up her present unsatisfying job and seriously pursuing her interest in music and painting. She has been able to reach this decision, but still has to carry it out fully and to make it real.

POSTSCRIPT

In England, before World War I, it was thought "sissy" for a man to show much interest in small children. He was *never* seen pushing a pram, and I can remember my mother's horror and embarrassment at coming upon one of my father's colleagues in a railway station waiting room changing his son's diaper!

This altered gradually, but only really in the last ten years has it become fully accepted for the father to take his share in the life and upbringing of his children from the start, and even (sometimes, at least) to be with his wife when she is in labor.

I think this comes largely from the altered standards of living and value of money, which is now spent on cars, freezers, stereos, etc., instead of on domestic help. In many homes both parents are working, often on a part-time basis, which makes the sharing of parenthood both easier and more necessary.

The difference that this can make to an infant in the early stages of his growth and development, and to his ability to deal with the increasingly complex world, is inestimable. Analysts are beginning to recognize and to explore the wide fields it opens up, and I, for one, am more than glad to see it. I believe that it may well help to promote earlier psychic maturation (without loss of the primitive modes of functioning which we need to preserve on a deep level). Such earlier maturation is needed to keep pace with the ever-increasing call for intellectual maturation as modern technology develops and the general body of knowledge grows.

13

WHO IS AN ALCOHOLIC?

A man who drinks too much on occasion is still the same man as he was sober. An alcoholic, a real alcoholic, is not the same man at all. You can't predict anything about him except that he will be someone you never met before.

—Raymond Chandler, *The Long Goodbye*

In most countries of the West it is part of a recognized and accepted social pattern to drink a certain amount of alcohol, on occasion, or even more or less regularly. Drinking too much is not part of our social life; in fact within my memory drunkenness has come to be far less common in England than it used to be.

Among those who do drink to excess, a small proportion come to be known as alcoholics, i.e. alcohol addicts, and the aim of this chapter is to examine what distinguishes them from other people who take too much alcohol, and how the addiction has come about. Our original question leads on to others: Who is not an alcoholic? What is an alcoholic? and Why is an alcoholic what he is?

Two other groups of people help to define the group we are considering. The first is that of "reactive drinkers." These are people who suddenly start drinking too much, changing the pattern of their alcohol consumption to a marked degree, following a loss, accident, shock etc. This change is a temporary one; the earlier pattern is gradually resumed, as the control is reestablished with the working through of the emotional disturbance.

While it lasts, this drunken phase can cause much distress and anxiety to the person's relatives, but it is apparent that it is part of a wider disturbance that he himself recognizes, even if he is not able immediately to know it for something that will pass in time.

The second group is that of "habitually heavy drinkers." These people drink regularly the same large quantities of alcohol; they frequently suffer from such symptoms of chronic intoxication as gastritis, intestinal catarrh, headache, etc., but they are able to exercise a definite control over the amount they drink, and a choice of occasion. Such people are able to accept the need to abstain, either for their own sake or that of others. Though their abstention may be temporary, it will last as long as is necessary, and will recur, if needed again. In other words, their behavior is predictable, and to a large extent realistic.

The drinking is purposive, in each case, though the purpose is different. Reactive drinkers seek relief from mental pain, much as sufferers from a painful somatic illness use analgesics; when the pain is no longer there, the analgesic is discarded. Heavy drinkers seek positive pleasure of an ordinary kind; they find the stimulant effect of the alcohol pleasant, it increases their enjoyment of various aspects of their lives, including social intercourse, and in many cases they enjoy the actual taste of a particular liquor. Each individual has his preference: a whisky drinker does not find the same satisfaction in drinking brandy, for example, nor a beer drinker in drinking wine.

These people, then, are not alcoholics; they may come within the range of so-called "normal" people, or they may have abnormalities, even perhaps serious enough ones to make them seek psychiatric help or to bring them into conflict with their environment, but their main problems do not center around the taking of alcohol.

This is where the alcoholic differs from all other people, except other addicts. To him alcohol is his life, and everything depends for him on being able to obtain it; he will go to any lengths to do so. He differs from other addicts in the matter of drug of addiction and in the mode of intake, for the use of morphine, heroin, hashish etc. call as a rule for some form of parenteral administration.

The outstanding characteristics of an alcoholic are the degree of his dependence on alcohol and the magical qualities with which it is invested for him. A tendency for his illness to progress is commonly found, as he is unable to admit the failure of the thing upon which he depends, and more of it is taken in the unavailing attempt to find the security he needs.

I am here stating that the alcoholic is a sick man, in contrast with the older idea that he is morally at fault. The recognition of the compulsive element in his behavior, the fact that he acts as he does because he cannot act otherwise, gives the greatest hope for the treatment and prevention of alcoholism. Attempts at punishment, or even reformation, based on a moral judgment are bound to fail, for we are dealing with a condition which (as Rado has pointed out) is based on delusional ideas.

Before going on to discuss the content of these delusional ideas and so to seek for their origin, I want to digress into looking at some wider concepts concerning alcoholism. Just as the idea of an alcoholic was associated with a moral judgment, so such things as crime, sexual perversion, prostitution, and other social evils have been associated with alcoholism.

It is of course true that there are many instances where these things are found together with excessive drinking, but it is no more true to attribute them to alcoholism than to label the reactive or the heavy drinker an alcoholic. Alcoholism is not restricted either to any particular social or intellectual class or to any psychiatric category. It may appear in people whose other traits and tendencies are predominantly psychoneurotic, psychotic, or those of character disorder or psychopathy.

Alcoholism then is not a disease entity: it is a symptom, part of a disorder affecting the personality, and the personality may be affected in a larger or a smaller area, in the same degree. There are alcoholics who are, in many areas, mature people, who suffer very greatly by reason of the compulsion, which offends their self-esteem. And there are others who are almost unaware that their alcoholism is anything out of the way; their acceptance of it is facile and naive, for they are immature throughout.

Let us look next at the characteristic behavior of alcoholics. First there is the excessive consumption of alcohol itself. Drinking is often done secretly, especially at first, and it is punctuated by resolutions to stop. The capacity to stop at the time of making the resolution is never doubted, but it is always a thing of the future, and it never becomes an accomplished fact. The alcoholic who "goes on the water wagon" for a time sooner or later feels the need to test out the success of his abstinence, and this always fails, for the "test drink" is invariably the beginning of a resumption of the habit. The lack of insight behind the making of the test is the same as the lack of insight behind the making of the resolution.

The conscious wish to stop drinking can, and often does, result in total abstinence. Unfortunately this is not the cure of the illness; it is the other side of the same coin. Where the wish is only conscious, but not also on a deeper, unconscious level, other symptoms such as compulsive smoking or excessive gain in weight are liable to appear. Real cure implies that drinking or not drinking are equally unimportant in themselves and moderate social drinking may become acceptable.

Recently (c. 1974) an idea appeared, chiefly in the United States, that alcoholism is an allergy. I have never found anything to support this. In my experience it is an addiction, of the same nature as any other addiction such as smoking, drugs, gambling, even analysis, and the underlying psychopathology of all addictions is the same. This does not, of course, rule out variations in the psychology of individuals in areas other than those of the addiction.

When he drinks, the alcoholic does so under a different urge from that of either the reactive or the heavy drinker. It is not either relief of mental pain or ordinary pleasure that is sought, or found. What he seeks is an ability to carry on the everyday things of his life, his work, his relationships with other people, his sexual relations, and so forth. The lack of capacity does not relate to any unusual happenings, although he rationalizes it in that way and although there may have been some specific, precipitating factor in the development of his illness. What he finds is not relief of an ordinary kind. He becomes first elated, euphoric, and omnipotent in his own eyes. Now everything will be all right; now he can work wonders; nothing bad will come to him through his drinking, even though he knows the dangers (there are doctors, nurses and welfare workers among the ranks of alcoholics). The stage of elation is followed by a stage of acute intoxication, culminating in coma. Rado has described the quality of the drinking bout in terms of a body orgasm of a primitive kind.

Drinking alcohol has, then, for the addict, the significance of something magical. But the corollary is that his incapacity is also of a magical order, and here he is near to the delusional ideas, including ideas of annihilation and persecution, which he cannot allow to become conscious, partly because they are too near to the truth that he is himself his own persecutor and destroyer.

The nearest that he can come to this realization is in the pain and guilt that he suffers when he is once more sober. His failure to control his drinking is fresh evidence to him of his incapacity and worthlessness, and it serves to drive him to fresh excesses. And so the vicious circle goes on: depression has to be denied, converted into a manic kind of elation, and guilt is assuaged by self-destruction that masquerades as the salvation which he is genuinely seeking. His efforts at self-cure, which the alcoholism itself represents, fail because they depend upon his delusions.

I must mention in passing as an essential concomitant or constituent of the condition I am discussing (which a psychiatrist has to take into account), i.e. the physical effects of a high concentration of alcohol in the blood. They complicate the underlying psychic condition and contribute very considerably to the development of this vicious circle, and so cannot be ignored. But I cannot discuss this fully here.

The other characteristics are well known to those who have experience with alcoholic patients. One is a marked degree of irritability, and the other a lack of time sense. To an alcoholic the only time that matters is right now; the future means nothing (as we saw in connection with the intention to reform), and to wait is something impossible; what is past is forgotten as if it had never been. It is not difficult to recognize the infantile quality of all these characteristics.

Earlier writers on psycho-analysis have stressed various aspects of these phenomena. Freud, Abraham, Ferenczi, and Jones regarded the condition as a regressive one and a retreat from heterosexuality, under the stress of castration anxiety aroused by the emergence of oedipal ideas. They emphasized the importance of the depressive element and the unconscious tendency to something of suicide, as well as unconscious homosexuality. Glover agreed with the views concerning depression and suicide, but regarded alcoholism as due to a failure of progression rather than as regressive, and he pointed out the importance of the aggression and sadism which appear in the suicidal or destructive component.

In my view, neither the depression, the suicidal tendency, nor the sexual inadequacy with unconscious tendencies toward homosexuality is the primary thing. I agree with Rado in his emphasis on the importance of delusion in these cases and with Glover in regarding them as due to failure of development. An alcoholic patient is someone who in adult life, and with his adult body, is living still events of his own early infancy; this accounts for all the phenomena I have described, including the difficulty concerning time, for he relives, in each bout of drinking, actual happenings of the past. In this sense his life is an anachronism. It is only when he can relive these happenings in a new setting, in relation to a therapist who is not involved in them, to whom he can transfer the feelings which belonged originally to the people in the environment of his infancy, *a human being to whom he can safely become addicted,* that there can be some hope of breaking the vicious circle and of finding new growth and development.

So far I have generalized; of course each patient is an individual, and the psychopathology and the meaning of his symptom is specific to him. His genetic endowment, the circumstances of his infancy, the personalities of his parents together determine the form of his illness and are reflected in his individual version of an illness common to many people with differing backgrounds.

For example, in some alcoholic patients analysis shows that what Rado has called the "alimentary orgasm" is the most important thing, while in others it is the reaching of the stage of coma; in others again it is the presence of the fluid in the mouth. In each separate patient actual, specific bodily events are being shown, and only the detailed unraveling of these events can bring understanding and insight. It may be that feeding experiences were often nearly, but not quite, satisfactory, and in the repetition of the oral ingestion of alcohol repeated attempts are made either to find an experience that will bring satisfaction, or to find the original failure which came before he had become a person.

Drinking may represent an unconscious denial of separateness, or again, a means of communication or of making contact. It may represent an attempt to replace the saliva, by means of which the infant establishes contact with the mother's breast and with the milk, which at the time of actual infancy was repeatedly wiped away, leaving the infant isolated and incommunicado. Weaning may have been carried out too early, too quickly, or without enough care.

The persecutory anxiety of an alcoholic patient may tell the therapist something of the mother's behavior toward her infant. The need to fill his mouth may be his present-day way of showing the still-persisting infantile need to push away a mother who was continually interfering with and impinging upon him by pushing things into his body orifices. His irritability may reflect this, as well as the extreme sensitiveness and vulnerability of the infant.

I can only mention very shortly some of the many ways in which the environment may have failed or been inadequate. Such failure can of course come at any stage of infancy, and the form of mental disturbance that results will depend partly upon when it happened.

We can assume from the oral quality of the symptom (and analytic experience goes to support this assumption) that in people who have become addicts to alcohol there was a failure in the mother at the time of oral primacy and before the mother was perceived as a person, or as separate from the infant, i.e. at the time of normal breast-feeding. I have tried to indicate the kind of failure, but have not related it to what was going on in the environment.

It is a matter of common observation that the early environment of alcoholic patients was in most cases disturbed in some way. Divorce, parental incompatibility, poverty, unreliability of various kinds are obvious predisposing factors. But short of these obviously traumatic things there may have been a mother who was ill, depressed, preoccupied, overanxious about her baby, and so on, any of which can lead to this kind of failure or not-good-enough care.

The mode of dramatizing such failures—acting them out in the pattern of drinking excessively—is an infantile one. It is a way of repeating infancy in an attempt to make it happen over again, but differently. The infant part of the personality knows no other way but this of attracting attention to the suffering and need, so the alcoholic patient makes demands on his environment through his illness, and he treats it as he feels he was treated.

I think that what I have written elsewhere about certain phenomena that I have found in the analysis of some patients whose anxiety is of psychotic, rather than neurotic, type (annihilation anxiety) is relevant also to alcoholic patients.

In analysis addicts develop a transference psychosis, in the form of an addiction to the analyst, with a delusion of absolute identity with him; they attempt to make actual a state of total undifferentiatedness from him. This identity extends so that he is also identical with both the actual parents and with those parents both deified and diabolized, i.e., invested with magical qualities, good and bad. This delusion is a defense against the discovery of a state in the patient of complete undifferentiatedness, the reaching of which is both needed and feared, for it involves depersonalization. It is experienced as chaos, or annihilation.

Only through reaching this state can the delusion be resolved, but it is essential that there should be both recognition of the unreality *in fact* of these ideas, and simultaneously their acceptance and retention *in imaginative or psychic reality*.

I traced the origin of these ideas to the existence of some real unity of the fetus with the mother, in prenatal life, (the totally undifferentiated state of the infant at the time of birth) and showed the necessity of establishing continuity between the body memories of intrauterine life, the total birth experience, and early postnatal life. Without such continuity processes of differentiation and integration cannot proceed normally, and there is interference with the development of narcissism and the capacity for forming object relations.

I regard the existence of unconscious belief in unity with the mother as the basis for mental health; discovery of the factual unreality of the idea, and its preservation in psychic reality, are the normal outcome of the processes of differentiation and integration which go on in an infant, but which can only do so provided there is good enough mothering.

We find in alcoholic patients the delusional belief that survival depends upon the drinking of alcohol (which is in fact absorbed and metabolized, becoming, in a sense, part of the drinker's body); we find a magical quality attributed to the alcohol; we find the ideas attached to something nonpersonal; and we find the compulsion which goes with insistence that the ideas *must* be true. The important difference between alcoholic patients and these others of whom I have written lies in their type of addiction, in the one case to a drug (alcohol) and in the other, often, to another person of the same type (folie á deux). The drug acts ambivalently, both as the thing which brings relief and as a poison. But it cannot *feel* ambivalently as a human being does, and here the alcoholic is attempting to retreat from feeling, but stating at the same time that only his own feelings matter.

In each case the object of addiction has to be replaced by a human being whose own basic unity is established. Only such a person can be of any real help to an alcoholic patient who wants to be cured of his illness. He may feel ambivalence, but he can control his actions; he is predictable, and survival is safe with him. He has to accept the reality *for the patient,* and the *psychic* truth of the delusional ideas, as well as recognizing their *factual untruth.* He has to recognize and act upon the actual truth of the danger to life and of the patient's inability to control his alcohol intake. He must be able to allow the patient to regress to dependence for life, and he must allow himself to become a substitute for the alcohol.

During the stage of substitution hospitalization is likely to become necessary, and even perhaps some degree of restraint.

Only where such substitution is available may it become possible to enable the patient to work through the delusional phase, to find and retain the imaginative reality of unity with a good enough mother, and to give up the unavailing attempt to bring about, and make factual, total identity and undifferentiatedness between himself and the analyst.

Analysis of such patients is both long and difficult, and it cannot be carried out except by an analyst who has had the necessary training. The success of organizations such as A.A. depends upon both total abstinence and the formation of reciprocal identifications between the members of the group and the identification of each member with the leader (Freud 1921). These identifications are essentially delusional and addictive.

Any form of treatment other than analysis is a matter of treating a symptom and not the illness; the danger when the symptom is removed (and this is not such a difficult thing to do) is that some other symptom will take its place. Sometimes the new symptom appears to be more acceptable socially, but it represents a greater limitation of the patient's personality, rather than a freeing of potential.

It is hardly necessary to say that the best results are likely to occur in patients whose area of failure of mothering is relatively small and in those whose lives otherwise show evidence of potential. Young patients, especially adolescents, usually have the advantage of plasticity to offset their immaturity.

To sum up: Who is an alcoholic?

An alcoholic is an individual who seeks by means of the symptom of drinking excessive quantities of alcohol to restore the basic unity between himself and his mother, which was disturbed mainly at an early oral level of development through some failure or inadequacy on the part of his environment. As a result of this disturbance of the basic unity he has been unable to find survival as a psychic reality.

At that level differentiation within himself, between himself and his mother, and recognition either of himself or of her as a person was far from complete. The belief: saliva = milk = mother = self, etc. has remained unaltered in a large area of his personality, and in that area he has remained an infant, with infant needs, infant ideas, and infant modes of action. He suffers from delusions and magical ideas.

His infantile strivings to find adequate mothering and to express the hate aroused by the inadequacies from which he suffered are carried out in his adult world, by means of his adult body, and are inevitably unsuccessful, unsatisfactory, unproductive, and a cause of distress to those around him.

14

NOTES ON IBSEN'S *PEER GYNT*

I

I first became interested in *Peer Gynt* when I saw it staged by the Old Vic Company (London) in 1944; Ralph Richardson, Sybil Thorndike, and Laurence Olivier (as they were then) played Peer, Aase, and the Button Molder. The impact made me read (in translation) almost all of Ibsen's plays (*Emperor and Galilean* defeated me), as much of his poetry as I could find, and many bits of writing about him.

My interest then centered around the personality change in Peer, apparently from pathological liar to psychotic, when his mother died. I came later to regard it rather as the breakdown of a psychopath into psychosis, against which psychopathy was a defense, when I saw this happen both in patients and acquaintances.

I am limiting myself to two main themes: (1) an attempt to relate what the poem tells us of its author to what I know about him otherwise, and (2) to relate it more fully both to things in my own experience and to some things in the outside world.

I am also limiting myself in the matter of quotations, cross-references, or comparison; I can virtually only refer to a few poems, to *Brand,* to Ibsen's last play, *When We Dead Awaken,* and to brief quotations from other authors.

II

Ibsen himself was most insistent that *Peer Gynt* is *poetry* (it is not verse); he also stated that all his poetry came from his own mental states and actual experiences. He denied that *Peer Gynt* was auto-biographical or a self-portrait (he called it a "caprice"), though he acknowledged that both Peer's mother and his father were some-thing like his own parents: the ambivalent and rather helpless woman, taking refuge in a world of dreams, myths, and fairy tales from the difficulties of life with an overambitious, irresponsible, spendthrift husband. He considered what kind of man the child of such a marriage could grow to be.

He wrote many poems, and most of his earliest plays (which were historical and nationalistic in tone) were written in verse. Three of perhaps the most striking poems are one describing the miner, who delves into the caverns of the earth, striking "hammer blow on hammer blow" into the heart of the rock; the second concerns living and writing; "to live is to war with the troll, in caverns of heart and brain; to write—that is to hold doom-session [to sit in judgment] on one's self."

The third—"On the Vidda" (the wide open mountain plateau)— tells how a young man leaves his mother and his betrothed to hunt in the mountains, at the call of a strange hunter—a call to action, not dreams. He stays there through summer and winter and then finds he has grown away from his former love and ways of life. He mourns for their loss, but finds that he is now free and can live a life of action. The "hunter" had been an unknown part of himself.

This was published a few months after Ibsen's marriage, and three years later he toured Norway collecting myths and folklore to use in his later work. Two years after this, in 1864, he left Norway in a mood of despair and disillusionment, having never been successful in his life or work there. He had struggled to establish himself academ-ically, in the theatre, and as a writer (and, moreover, carried for fourteen years the burden of supporting an illegitimate son whom he had begotten at the age of seventeen). He identified himself closely with the struggles of his country to become independent of Denmark (and later, of Sweden, which was only finally achieved in 1905) and to establish the freedom of the Norwegian language.

He was deeply affected by the failure of his country to support Denmark in the war with Prussia when Schleswig-Holstein was annexed. On his journey toward Italy Ibsen saw in Berlin the Victory Parade of the Prussians, where the Danish guns captured at Dybbol were displayed and spat upon by the crowds.

Twenty-seven years later, he returned to Norway to ensure that the son of his marriage would retain Norwegian nationality.

Brand was written a year after he left Norway, and with its publication and performance came success. *Peer Gynt* followed *Brand,* and he described it as if it had written itself, triumphantly. The poem shows all the characteristics of dreams, the apparent inconsequence of changing scenes, hallucinations, recall of memories, condensation, displacements, etc. And as in a dream all the people who appear are aspects of the dreamer, so all the characters in *Peer Gynt,* I believe, represent aspects of Ibsen, whether known or unknown.

But as we follow through *Brand* and *Peer Gynt,* we can see Ibsen's growing self-recognition, maturation, and integration, with the logical development from the omnipotent dreamer, through mourning, to the free man of action, decision, and reality sense.

After *Brand* and *Peer Gynt* he wrote very little more poetry, saying that poetry actually hindered drama. He chose instead to write more directly and realistically, in prose, although he found this far more difficult. His next play, Emperor and Galilean, (which seems long, rambling, and moralistic, though he spoke of it as his "masterpiece") was followed by the series of "great plays," *Pillars of Society, A Doll's House, Ghosts,* etc., dealing with moral or ethical problems of his time, in his country, but gradually tending more and more to return to poetic or lyrical ideas, and ending with *When We Dead Awaken,* which he subtitled *An Epilogue.* This is not about death, but rather the realization "when we dead awaken we find what we have lost. We find that we have never lived," and the inalienable right of every person to live, and to be his true self, which is impossible without love. (Edith Weigert has written of "the horror of non-being.")

III

Brand ("fire" or "sword"), Ibsen says at one point, is his own best self. He is a man of immense courage, strength of will, and trust in his God; but he is a fanatic, without insight, and without compassion. His God's "love" is truly hate (this is said, in as many words). He demands sacrifice, of everything—"All, or nothing," and Brand seeks to force his own will on others as the Will of God, while insisting at the same time that a man must be *himself.* He is, himself, in effect, his "God." He has been deeply scarred by both his "heredity" and his childhood experiences, among which he recalls seeing his mother furiously ransacking his father's bed and his dead body, in search of *all* his money.

He refuses to visit and give the sacraments to his dying mother unless she gives all she has to build a new church. He insists that his wife give away to a beggar all the clothes of their dead child—she may not even keep back one small cap. The child, and later the wife, too, dies because of the demands of Brand's God that he (Brand) and they, should give all or nothing, living and working in a cold, unfriendly, and sunless village on a remote fjord.

After his wife's and his mother's deaths, Brand goes into the mountains, led by a crazy gypsy girl, who is his own illegitimate half-sister, in search of the "Ice Church" of his dreams and visions, only to be swallowed up in an avalanche. A voice proclaims "God is Love."

Brand is what we would now see as a primitive, sadistic "super-ego," showing clearly its roots in the id. Ibsen was to write later a good deal on the subject of conscience and the conflict that is associated with it. Brand is free from inner conflict; his conflict is with the outside world, first with storm and tides when he risks his life to visit a dying man on a distant island hoping to save his soul, and later with his family and his flock.

Peer Gynt is a ne'er-do-well, cowardly and destructive, and an "incurable romancer," telling the deeds of others as his own. He abducts his neighbor's daughter Ingrid at her wedding, and for that he becomes an outlaw, a "wolf's head," with everyman's hand against him and all his goods forfeit. He is, in turn, seduced by three cowgirls who are looking for trolls as mates, and then, after falling on a rock and being concussed, in an hallucinatory episode, by the Troll King's daughter. He is trapped by the trolls, forced to adopt their ways of life, and their motto "To thyself be enough," instead of the human "To thyself be true," but he refuses to let his eyes be cut, which would make him a Troll forever. He escapes after a violent struggle with the trolls, when the church bells are rung by his mother and the little girl, Solveig, with whom he has fallen in love for the first time and idealizes, and who loves him in spite of her fears.

Still dazed, he encounters, fights with, and tries to destroy the invisible troll—the great Boyg—something immovable, unknowable, which will not let him pass—"Go round about"—and answers the question "Who are you?" only with a growl, "I am myself."

Till now Peer has known that he lied, that his dreams of flying, of being emperor, etc., were lies; he is aware of his plight, and that he now has to fend for himself. He builds a hut in the forest. He sees a boy, due for army service, deliberately chop off his right forefinger with a sickle—to dodge the draft—and marvels that he could do it: "to have the idea, the wish, yes—but to *do* it, NO! that is beyond me."

He dreams of living in his hut with Solveig, but finds the Troll King's daughter and her child, malformed and misbegotten, magically by his lust alone, setting up house next door. He flings away, promising himself that Solveig will wait till he comes back.

He flees to his mother, Aase, but finds her dying, and the house stripped of everything but her bed. Ingrid's father and the officers of the law had carried out the sentence. In a most moving scene he comforts Aase by playing the sleigh-ride game that she had played with him, with Blackie the cat as the horse Grane, journeying to heaven's gate, where St. Peter would turn her away but God the Father welcomes her. The journey ends—he closes her eyes and kisses her. "Thank you, dear, for all you gave me, the thrashings and kisses too. But now you must thank me also." His kiss is her "fare for the drive."

From there he *knows* he must get away, and he goes "to sea, and farther still." And from there until the end there is little of reality.

We follow his journey through a long series of fantastic dream scenes, in which comedy predominates at first (Ibsen mocks at his own dreams, his wish to be rich, to be emperor, to live without commitment to family and others, to be promiscuous without the binding responsibility of relationship). In the desert Peer hobnobs with other psychopaths, who leave him in a ship that "miraculously" explodes, which he sees as an act of God on his behalf. He meets the singing statue of Memnon, and the Sphinx (which closely resembles the Boyg); then we see him in an asylum where the "sane" become "mad," crowned with straw as "Emperor of Self." Finally we see him returning, an old man, to Norway, and moving to his death at the hut in the mountains where Solveig waits.

Ibsen's "war with the troll" is very clearly defined in the antithesis between the human who is *true* to himself, and the troll who is *enough* to himself—who lives without commitment or relationship and who may have an idea, but dare not carry it over into action unless he balances it with its opposite, keeping a bridge by which he can go back. Peer sends idols to China, and then missionaries. He offers money to the crew of a sinking ship until he finds that they are married men with families waiting to welcome them. Then he will give only enough to buy drink, to wreck their homecoming, since *he* is alone.

Peer comes to a village where there is a funeral. The Pastor speaks of the dead man, who had come as a stranger among them and who always kept his right hand hidden—the forefinger was missing; he had chopped it off. He had worked and striven; he built a home, and raised a family in spite of endless adversities. He had been *himself,* always, *within his limits,* and now they could pray that God in His mercy would make him no longer a cripple. (How unlike Brand!)

Peer eats wild onions, peeling them and finding them onion all through—"no heart." He reaches the hut, and hearing Solveig sing, he dimly remembers it and her and realizes "My Empire was here."

Out of the mist and darkness he hears "the sound of children weeping, weeping that is half a song," and finds threadballs on the ground at his feet. These are the thoughts he never thought or gave life to, the words he never spoke, the songs he stifled, the tears unwept, the deeds undone.

The Button Molder comes out of the wood looking for Peer, on the Master's orders. Peer's grave is dug and the coffin ready; he is to be melted down in the casting ladle (Peer's own childhood toy) he has "lost his loop" and cannot be what the master intended—a "shining button on the waistcoat of the world." He who had dreamed of being emperor had thrown away his real empire, in a woman's love; he who had prided himself on always being *himself and nothing else* had never been himself. Nor had he even been a great sinner.

Peer cannot believe this, and seeks for witnesses. He finds the Troll

King, now down-at-heels and begging. But the Troll King points out that even though he had refused to let his eyes be cut he had accepted and *lived by* the motto that distinguishes Trolls from human beings; the motto that makes trolls of men: "To thyself be enough."

Again the Button Molder comes, and Peer asks what it means "really to be oneself." "To kill the worst, so as to bring out the best in yourself. . . . To carry out the Master's intention." His "intuition" ("insight" or "instinct") should have told him what this was.

Still unbelieving, Peer looks once more for proof that he *had* been himself. He meets the Devil, in disguise, but is rejected even by him as not having been himself, either in the right, positive way, of commitment and relationship, or in the wrong, negative way, of avoiding *everything* that made demands on him. He had more or less "blotted himself out" with his inconstancies and contradictions. He must now give up the hope of being a real person in his own right, the person he should have been, and be melted down with all the other insignificant people.

And so, at last, having tried every way to avoid his fate he becomes still. "I was dead long before my death."

He knows now the emptiness and poverty of his own spirit, and contrasts it with the richness and generosity of nature; he has wasted the beauty of the sun and the earth in his nothingness, and asks their forgiveness. He thinks of climbing to the top of the highest mountain and looking out long over these things, till he can look no more.

Then the snow shall cover him, and the inscription on his tomb shall read "Here *No one* is buried." After that, "let come what will."

Again the Button Molder comes, and he realizes that the Boyg's "Go round about" is no longer for him; "this time it's straight through no matter how narrow the path."

Once more he hears Solveig singing, and he begs her forgiveness. He asks her "Where has Peer Gynt been all this while since, with the mark of destiny on his brow, he first sprang forth as a thought newly born in the mind of God? Where was I, my real self, my whole self, my true self, with God's seal upon my brow?"

She answers ("as a mother speaks of her child"): "In my faith and in my hope and in my love. But who is his father? He who forgives in answer to a mother's prayers. Sleep and dream, my own dear love."

The Button Molder would have the last word—"to the last crossroads, Peer"; but Solveig sings again. Perhaps, for the first time, in his death, Peer is alive and is, within his limits, his true self.

IV

In a speech to students (1874) Ibsen considered what it means to write; the importance of a special way of *seeing,* as a poet sees, what is actually experienced in life. He goes on to say: "When Emperor Julian reaches the end of his career, and everything is collapsing about him, there is nothing that depresses him so profoundly as the thought that his total achievement was this: to be remembered with respectful acknowledgment by certain cold and clear minds, whilst his opponents were lodged in warm living hearts, rich in love."

In both *Brand* and *Peer Gynt* the mother's death is a point of climax, after which there is a lasting loss of contact with reality. This differs from previous episodes, such as Peer's hallucinatory meeting with the trolls, from which the thoughts of his mother and of Solveig recalled him, like the sound of church bells.

Ibsen's mother was still alive until two years after *Peer Gynt* was published; his father lived another twenty-five years. He remained estranged from them, though he wrote affectionately of both after their deaths.

He shows us the importance of the loss of the mother (e.g. through weaning, the birth of a younger child, neglect, or disillusionment), the lack of a strong and loving father, and the cold hatred that is aroused. Ibsen himself was the eldest of five children, and he left home at the age of fifteen, henceforth to support and educate himself entirely, but he never "lost his loop."

Ibsen knew a great deal about mental processes and mental illness, and although this comes out in all his poems and plays, I think, it is shown perhaps most clearly in *Peer Gynt.* There are trolls in many of his other plays: *Hedda Gabler, Gregers Werle, Hilda Wangel, the Rat Wife, Rubek,* and even *Brand.* Through lack of love they wreck the lives of those around them; there are also many like Peer, whose proper fate is to reach the casting ladle.

In Rome Ibsen found himself more in touch with earlier sculptors such as Michelangelo or Bernini—"the kind of men with the courage to do something crazy now and then"—than with the more conventional sculptors of his own day. He had spoken of Peer Gynt as a "caprice," and wrote to Grieg that he wanted "some devilment" in the music.

But the more serious aspects are there too. Ibsen was far ahead of his time in his recognition and understanding of delusion and its relation to conflict, and in *seeing* the search for the self with which psychoanalysts and others have become so familiar, and which he himself had experienced.

In the years when he was writing his poems, *Brand, Peer Gynt,* and *Emperor and Galilean,* Ibsen resolved these clashes and conflicts in his own life and found himself. His marriage and the close and warm relationships between himself and his wife and son (his real "Empire") were fully developed, although this was a time of great hardship, poverty, and isolation. He *might* have become Brand, Peer, or Julian, but neither would have been his "real, whole, true self, with God's seal upon his brow." His love saved him from becoming a troll.

In Peer we see the conflict and search; we see his growing loss of ability to distinguish "truth" from "lies," (i.e. between dreams, psychic or poetic, and factual, truth) and his intolerance of the separation between them. At the same time, we watch the struggle of the psychotic to remain "true to himself" in face of the impossibility of being "enough" to himself.

Ibsen's own ability to distinguish was in him to the last. When he was dying, after his last "stroke," his wife saw him open his eyes and said "Look he is better." He said: "Not at all," and he died. He could *assert* his death because he was alive and was himself—if within his own limits.

Struggles such as Peer's are those seen by psychoanalysts who treat psychotic and borderline psychotic patients whom Freud would have considered inaccessible because of their failure to develop a transference neurosis; transference psychosis was only recognized later. In the histories of these patients we often find elements such as those shown in Peer's. I quote four:

Patient A

On an Atlantic crossing aboard a freighter I was called to see a young engineer who had broken down. He was threatening to damage the steering gear and had to be restrained. This was his second voyage, and we were approaching his homeland.

His first voyage had been very long, and on returning he had found that his mother had died more than a year before, soon after he had left home, no one had told him. Now he feared that he would find his sister dead.

His father had left the mother when he was a child; at fifteen he had had to identify the body of his elder brother, killed in a motorcycle crash.

When I first saw him, he was plainly psychotic, paranoid, and out of contact with all reality. I told him that on landing he should be admitted to hospital. Within a few days he became, instead, an aggressive psychopath—defying authority, denying his fears, unloving, and unlovable; still out of touch with his feelings, but sane.

Patient B

I was asked to see a man who was in trouble, threatened with law proceedings, and suspended from his job. He was a psychotherapist who had seduced (or been seduced by) an adolescent boy, one of his patients. He was said to be depressed.

At consultation I could find no depression. Again, what I saw was a psychotic patient with flight of ideas, talking incoherently, and with no reality sense. It seemed impossible to establish contact. I offered analysis, which he would accept only if his wife were willing. He spoke so extravagantly of her, and of his enormous love for her and for his children, that I feared he might commit multiple murder and suicide.

He and his wife finally agreed to hospitalization and analysis for him, and I visited him. The acute psychotic state lasted only a few days and did not recur during the year that I attempted analysis with him. He demanded arrogantly to be allowed to practice as a psychotherapist again; he pursued both his former patient and other boys, and some of his seductions were actually incestuous. He asserted that only as a psychotherapist and an active homosexual could he be truly "himself." He played incessantly records of Mahler's Kindertotenlieder.

Both parents were alive, but apparently ineffectual. His elder sister had died when he was six, and his elder brother when he was fifteen; he felt that his parents had cared only for them.

He broke off treatment when told that he would not be prosecuted and when I made it clear that I would not treat him if he were practicing as a psychotherapist. I was not attempting to "cure" his homosexuality or to prevent its consequences, except insofar as the ethical aspect of the therapist-patient relationship was involved, which he rejected.

Patient C

After some years of psychoanalysis, in the course of which (owing to the extent and degree of the disturbance) modifications of classical technique had been necessary, in the delusional areas, a borderline patient needed short hospitalization during a psychotic episode, and I visited her in hospital and continued the analysis. This proved to be the beginning of the terminal phase of her analysis, which still lasted another two years, but ended quite dramatically.

The material throughout this time was concerned with her search for her identity and separation of herself from me. I could have been the BOYG. She screamed repeatedly: "Who are you?" and no obvious response or "interpretation" brought relief. What did was a whole series of answers such as: "I am your pain; your unhappiness; I am your love; your hate; your headache; I am the tree you bashed your head on. I am the parents who could only let you be an extension of them; the person who has hurt you; who has listened to you, cared for you, held you"—and so on, "and you are *my* headache, *my* love, *my* hate" etc. (I had to allow myself to *be* these things, not represent them, i.e. to accept her delusion as true.)

Later her question was: "Who am I?" and she answered herself—"I am your patient, for whom you have cared; and you are my analyst, *not me*." After that came the real sorting out, intensely painful and difficult for us both. "You breathe. I didn't know. And you have *your own* feelings, which I don't feel."

Eventually she fixed a date for ending which I felt unsuitable, but she insisted on it. She would sit facing me and move her chair till she was nearly touching me, at which point I moved mine back. She was furious: "Why? why? why?" I would point out our separateness and that I had a right to refuse something I did not want. I had allowed her her rights, including the choice of date for finishing.

Finally, on the day before we were to finish, she announced that we would go on, and I firmly said "No." This precipitated a violent temper tantrum, in which she behaved like a child of three or four. I sat and said nothing, even though she screamed and threw herself on the floor, and clutched my legs, *imploring* me to say yes. At the end of the hour I said only that it was time for her to go and that she had been reliving an actual experience from childhood. Next day, she came, calm and friendly. She thanked me for all the years of our work together, and said goodbye.

Her recovery has been complete. She is a whole person in her own right, and knows it. And she is free, as never before; she has known loss, and mourned for it; she has accepted both her limitations, and her troll self, and is able to love and to create.

Patient D

The pattern of "wandering" in the patient described in chapter 1 was defensive. She moved whenever psychotic anxiety threatened to overwhelm her, if she could no longer contain her true ambivalence. When I drove her to admit that she *knew* that she loved and was loved by me she found that we both survived her love, and the hate that she had acknowledged in herself and believed to be all that was in me. Then she could give up her paranoid view of the world, and at last find a home where she could live happily without magic, among human beings, not devils, being now human herself. Her acceptance of analysis followed the death of her mother, and there was eventually a real change in her personality.

All four of these patients showed in their early histories failures in early environment leading to lack of belief in survival, and in inability to develop a true sense of identity, with capacity to mourn and for concern. In patients A and B these failures were so massive as to result in the use of psychopathy as defense against psychotic breakdown. Their anxieties could not be relieved, and the defense was maintained. Patients C and D were both manifestly borderline psychotics. In them the relatively less massive failures allowed for the development, through analysis, of increasing belief in survival and successful search for their true selves, with consequent integration and maturation.

V

Ibsen's relevance for today is shown again in *Peer Gynt*.

What the trolls demanded of Peer, under pressure and threats, was that he should support their lies; it was their lies that divided him from "his real self, his true self" and from the world of men. The lie that he could be "enough" to himself—not "true to himself"—drove him to give up involvement with, or commitment to, all that is human, and so avoid conflict and conscience.

The tyranny of totalitarianism (arising out of earlier tyrannies) with increasing bureaucracy, indoctrination, secrecy, censorship, and denial of the importance of individual human beings with their right to be true to themselves, is of the essence of the trolls' ideology and ways of life.

In a speech in 1885 Ibsen said "An element of nobility must find its way into our public life, into our government, among our representatives and into our press. Of course I am not thinking of nobility of birth, nor of money, nor even of ability or talent. What I am thinking of is a nobility of character, of mind, and of will. That alone can liberate us. This aristocracy ... will come to us from ... [those] which so far have not suffered any irreparable damage under party pressure."

Commenting on "Rosmersholm" Strindberg (c. 1887) wrote of "modern mind murder." He said: "In previous ages one killed one's opponent without having changed his convictions; now one creates a majority against him, 'persuades' him . . . ascribes to him different intentions from those that he has, deprives him of his livelihood, denies him social respect, makes him look ridiculous, in a word tortures him to death by lies or drives him insane instead of killing him."

Here again is a reference to the power of the lie—the trolls' chief weapon—"brainwashing". And today even in the world of psychiatry we are seeing this very use of the lie for mind murder and destruction of the true selves of those who dissent or resist it.

Other authors writing of more recent happenings support Ibsen implicitly in his clear distinction between trolls, whose motto is "to thyself be enough," and humans whose motto is "To thyself be true."

In his book *Licensed Mass Murder,* H. V. Dicks portrays one of the Nazis he interviewed as "A Norm-Setter." "He still wanted some powerful daddy to come and tell the world he was a good chap. I have seldom, if ever, experienced such pain at the depth of degradation of, or non-arrival at, a human level as with this man. This may be the nature of fiends; that they, needing to love, must needs love those like themselves—the fellowship of the damned who hate lucky sissies and softies who can love and create."

Hannah Arendt, in *Eichmann in Jerusalem,* writes of "the banality of evil," describing people like Dicks' "Norm-Setter" and comments "how few people have the resources needed to resist authority."

The Dean of Johannesburg (The Very Rev. Gonville ffrench-Beytagh), in *Encountering Darkness,* has written of his discovery that the root of apartheid is the "real belief that 'blacks' are animals, *not* men."

Some time ago Alexander Solzhenitsyn's oration to be given in Sweden, on receiving the Nobel prize for Literature, was read (in translation) over the radio, and next day similar words of Mikos Theodorakis were quoted in the *Observer* (London). "Violence cannot continue to exist without the lie. Violence does not take people by the throat and strangle them; it demands only that they support the lie. . . . A lie can resist many things, but it cannot resist art. . . . There is a special relation between art, especially that of the writer, and truth. It is the only real force which can unite men and not divide them."

Ibsen's spectrum is far richer and wider than I could hope to show. I will end just by wondering if it is not significant that, while Solzhenitsyn has been honored in Sweden, it was the Society of Norwegian Writers and Artists that offered him a home, if he were exiled by force, as has, in fact, happened.

PART IV

PERSONAL EXPERIENCE

15

FIFTEEN POEMS 1945–1977

. . . . demoniac frenzy,
Moping melancholy and moonstruck madness.
                                    —Milton, *Paradise Lost* xi:485

These are but a few of the poems I wrote during these years. I don't
mind people analyzing or interpreting their *content* so long as they
don't tell me about it! In other words, please keep it to yourself, or
wait till I'm dead before you publicize it. Criticism of them *as poems*
is another matter. C'est à vous.

RESTLESSNESS

I must be "doing," all the time;
The wind itself is not more purposeless.
I walk, daub, scribble—cannot rest.

What for?
To keep a hold on time!
The silver seconds slip away
And I am left, bereft,
Silver is turned to grey,
Grey rocks, grey sea, grey sky.

A memory comes
Of such another day, long past;
Grey flooded fields, grey sky and trees;
Two swans,
Their wings outspread,
Drop slowly down to breast the stream.

Today,
The gulls fly by,
And distant ships,
With far-off trails of smoke;
And cormorants air their wings;
The sea itself grows silveréd.

The sun
Filt'ring thro' misty air,
Turns grey to blue and green,
The cliffs to rusty gold and red,
And then reveals among the rocks
A raven's nest.

(St. Just-in-Penwith,
April 1945)

QUESTIONING

Gorse, sea, and sky;
And I,
Mean spirited as they are generous,
Miserly, clutch fast
To what I have
And grasp all I can get.

How can I loose my grip
Lest I lose all?
Let slip
That which I have
Lest it should fall
Shattered, to the ground.
The golden bubble,
Evanescent,
Misty as a wraith,
Thin, brittle, frail,
Break,
Vanish, pass from me?
In exchange?
Reality.
Abstract or solid
So it is—
Thus, thus, and thus.

Waves, rolling to the shore,
Throw back a cloud of spray
Catching the sun,
Falling in rainbow veil.
They're real!
So are the wren
Singing above me in the gorse,
The prickles—and the sun!

And I? myself?
Earth? Water? Air?
How shall I know?

My hand, holding the pen,
Making these marks
By which, through devious paths,
Another's mind
Perhaps may grasp my thoughts,
What does it mean?
How shall I understand
This senseless phantasy?

Yet—*is* it phantasy?
Or something real?
And while bewilderment
Clouds my mind
The wren sings on;
The rainbow foam still blows
From the oncoming waves.

My thoughts,
My words, my tears—
Their worth?
No less, no more
Than is the worth of that wren-song.
For whom, then, sings the wren?
For whom is blown the spray?
Who knows, or cares,
If all were blotted out,
Wren, sea, and I?
Where goes the song?
And where the rainbow light?

Who knows? Who cares?
The bird has sung
And is content.
The wave, breaking inshore,
Its strength has spent
And still another comes.
But I. . . ?

(St. Just-in-Penwith,
          April 1945)

EARTH CHILDREN

Not for us the clouds of glory
Trailing as we go;
Not for us the doves appearing,
Loud acclaiming "Be it so";
Not for us the Father's pleasure,
We are *not* His heavenly treasure.
Dust we are, to dust we go.

(1950)

THE COLD LOVER

Loneliness was my bed-fellow,
His child I bear.
His chilly arms enfolded me;
His icy hand played with my breast.
His clay-cold lips sought mine;
His frozen breath stirred in my hair
Played on my cheek, and pierced my heart.
So the soul's death is born, that solitary child,
By Loneliness, out of Despair.

(July/September 1950)

MOURNING

I

The sullen furnaces of hidden hate
Erode, destroy. Create
A desert land, limitless waste,
A wilderness wherein may grow
No blade of grass, no leaf.
With bitterness of brackish pools
And twisted rocks—
Dead Sea—Remorse, not grief.

II

Pain is an ungracious thing,
Unlovely in its crudity.
Yet, out of pain is born life,
And grace, and love.
Life without pain—
Can it *be* life? or love?

III

The bitterness of tears is healing salt
That gathers up torn flesh,
Cleanses, and makes whole, and fresh.
The open crucibles of rage
That scorch the earth leave smouldering
A soft and silvery ash. A covering.

IV

So, underneath, when time has passed
And coolness comes, and rain,
New life has birth.
Seeds there have lain
Unknown, unseen, beneath the earth,
Or, borne on the wind,
Have reached the plain,
And germinate.

(1951)

DESOLATION

All love is lost
That in me lay;
Love, in the living world,
By night or day.

Sorrow is left me
And grief, alone.
All is destroyed.
How, then, atone?

Harsh, bitter tears,
Heartache, despair;
None can bring back
What no more is there.

Darkness still covers
Living and dead
With star-piercèd shroud.
So, cold, to bed.

(November 1952)

LIFE-IN-DEATH, or DEATH-IN-LIFE.

I live among shadows
Unseeing, unhearing,
Unknowing, unthinking
Unfeeling, uncaring.
All is unreal,
Chaos, deceit
I have no focus
No mainspring, no God.

Had I a framework,
A structure, a holding,
A scaffold, or cross,
There might thorns pierce me,
Thrust inward, infiltrate,
There might the chaos
Cling, focus, and form.

(April/August 1953)

MENTAL HOSPITAL

This place is
So full of faces;
They come too near—
I long to flee.

They come and peer,
They come and leer,
They come and jeer—
Or—is it me?

There's Dr. Prosy
And Sister Cozy,
And Mrs. Dozy—
And then—there's me.

There's Mrs. Bit,
And Mr. Spit,
And old Miss Hit,
And—then there's me.

This place is
Full of faces
And I can't flee,
For they're *all* me!

(August/September 1953)

WORDS

My words were stolen, years ago.
Now, behind bars, I cannot find
What is my own.

Henceforward I am dumb—
Dumbfounded,
Dumbly, doubly dumb.

Words that *should* rise
Swell in my throat and choke
In salt and bitter tears I cannot shed.

Between my words and me,
Between my thoughts and words
Cold bars, unshakeable, are fixed.

Beyond the bars an iron will,
A will that none can fight,
Strong as my life itself.
So am I dumb, undone.
I have no speech, no words,
No mother tongue.

(January 1949/October 1953)

THE GOLDFISH

What does the goldfish dream,
Alone, in his glass bowl
Revolving aimlessly,
Fixing the outer world with fishy eye?

What does he see through that curved glass
That magnifies, distorts, reflects?
What does he hear? Taste?
Feel? Experience?

How long for him is Time?
What reaches him
From that strange world outside?

Like him, I am alone, enclosed,
Within a glass through which I see the world;
That world, to me, seen through my past,
So different from the worlds of other men.

How can I leave the enclosing bowl?
How learn to live where I must breathe,
To move among strange things,
Distortion gone,
All altered, all things new?
And I, alone, a child again,
Bewildered and confused.

(1954)

IN SHORT—"THE DEPRESSIVE POSITION"

Love would be meaningless mockery
Life just a stupid sham,
If death had *no* sting
If grave had *no* victory,
If it were *always* "I AM."

(1961?)

ENOUGH IS ENOUGH IS ENOUGH!

The truth is
I'm a bore—
No less
No more,
And that's enough!

(October 1961)

RELATIONSHIP

"There was a man of Babylon
And he was wondrous wise
He jumped into a quickset hedge
And scratched out both his eyes

And when he saw his eyes were out,
With all his might and main
He jumped into the quickset hedge,
And scratched them in again."

We need each other, you and I,
Though but with a fraction of our beings.
The key cannot turn of itself;
A hand must hold it,
And beyond the hand
A person, and a will.
The lock will not open
Save it be set in a door;
The door within its frame.

So, you and I, by natures long determinate,
And circumstance,
Meet with each other, and can do
That we *can* do;
Bring to each other what we have,
We can, no more.

Our needs, our hopes, our wants
Are all our own.
Our rhythms of love and hate
Are incoordinate
So each the other troubles, whilst we love.
Blindly we feel our way,
And mingle deep, while yet we jar.

So, here and there, the two are one,
And here and there each one is two;

An alternating frenzy,
Shifting in its feel,
Its focus, and its emphasis.

But where we meet, fuse, and are satisfied,
(Or part in wrath, with bitter words and blows,
Failure of love, or cold indifference),
From action, interaction, and reaction,
New forces spring and flow;
New fire is born, laughter and tears,
Birth and creation new.

Let us go on then
Together, and apart;
Not seeking fear, nor yet denying it,
But travel through our fears and pains
To Zion—Babylon—World's End.

"How many miles to Babylon?
Three score and ten.
Can I get there by candlelight?
Yes—and back again."

(1949/1966)

27 SEPTEMBER 1977:
"MY LORD! WHAT A MORNING!"

—old song

A falling leaf,
A little stream,
And sunlight, filt'ring thro' the leaves;
Robin on branch, and bee
Perching to drink.
Good earthy smell of mould,
Death *and* fertility.

Up on the hill
(A stiffish climb)
A seat, set in full sun.

A distant gleam from reservoir,
Where ducks, and swans, and geese
And all the other birds
Float, swim and feed,
Puddling in squdgy mud,
Build nests, and breed.

Further—the forest, open heath and trees;
Beyond it lies the fruitful Weald,
Further again, the Downs, and sea.

"There go the ships, and that Leviathan. . . ."
I take *my* pleasure in *all* these.

(Ide Hill)

OUR BRITISH WEATHER!

Yesterday was Indian Summer.
The rest
You've guessed;
Today's a right come-down!

Skies grey,
More bills to pay,
And Income Tax,
A visit to the dentist. . . .

Ah well!
"Tomorrow is another day"
The sun might shine,
I daresay I'll survive!

(28 September 1977)

16

ACQUAINTANCE WITH DEATH:
A PERSONAL RECORD

Acquaintance: Knowledge of a person or thing which is more than
mere recognition, and less than intimacy.
—*Oxford English Dictionary*

It began, in childhood, with unfledged baby birds that had fallen
from their nests and squashed frogs, that someone had trodden on.
The birds weren't yet birds, but the frogs had been frogs.

Then, vaguely, it was my grandmother, whom I had known as a
kindly, but faintly disapproving person. My father went to her
funeral one day, wearing unfamiliar clothes, and she didn't come to
see us any more, but nobody seemed to mind very much.

One day, when school began again, my best friend—indeed my
only real friend, who had chosen *me* to be *her* friend—wasn't there.
She went on not being there, and I was told that she was ill, and her
brother was too. They were in a sanatorium, and I "ought" to write to
her. I *couldn't*; there was nothing I could say. Sometime, I was told
she was dead, but it didn't seem important to anyone else, and as I
had (apparently) been so uncaring as not to have written it was taken
for granted that it didn't matter to me either.

After that came the first War: long casualty lists every day in the paper; my father's former pupils killed, wounded, missing, or P.O.W.; young Highlanders billeted in the town dying of measles and scarlet fever, on stretchers in the streets, waiting for ambulances. Other girls missed school for a day or two and then came back dressed in black. Father or brother had been killed, and their sadness showed, but one couldn't speak of it. What *was* said about any of these things carried overtones of a sentimental kind of solemnity, and again it was assumed that I was unfeeling and selfish, and "understood nothing about the war," as I was told later.

Then I became a medical student. The dissecting room shocked me into a breakdown. Some of the bodies were slung from the ceiling, as if crucified. (Had these ever been people?) I gave up anatomy for a year and then went to another medical school. The corpses there were laid on tables, and I managed to carry on in spite of the smell, and the grease stains that soaked everything, and the hostility of those men students who thought nothing of throwing an odd bit of bone or flesh across the room at one of the women as she went by.

Work in the wards followed. Patients would be there one day and gone the next, some home, others to the mortuary. One Saturday afternoon I had gone in for some reason, and screens were around the bed of one of "my" patients. He was dying, in delirium, shouting out "Won't someone give me a bit of paper, to wipe my bottom?" The other twenty-nine patients were silent, hidden behind newspapers, or under the bedclothes, and answered in whispers if spoken to.

Finding myself qualified—a doctor, now, with responsibility for life or death—was terrifying, and although I applied for house jobs it was a relief *not* to get them. Once again I put off taking that responsibility for a year on the excuse of working for another exam, which I managed to fail. A friend's illness finally pushed me into taking it up, and in a kind of desperation I went into general practice, without having had any hospital experience at all.

Three nights after I had "put up my plate," I was called to attend to a woman whose husband had knocked her about, and had to stitch up a scalp wound which covered my surgery in blood, as only scalp wounds can. Two hours later a distraught father called me: "Come at once. My wife took the baby into bed, as we only moved yesterday, and the house was cold; we think it's dead." It was. The coroner's officer took it away for postmortem examination, and then came my first experience of giving evidence at an inquest. (Eleven years later, during my last surgery attendance, a baby was brought in dead, but this was for my successor to meet, as she had been seeing it.)

In between, there had been many deaths: twins, in a filthy, slummy flat, both with measles and whooping cough; a man in his fifties who prided himself on knowing he had cancer (I now see him as defending himself with that pride against the *real* knowledge that he would die); a suicide who had gassed himself, believing he had cancer when he had not; another, who cut his throat but did not die; and a woman whom both my partner and I had been seeing without being able to reach a diagnosis, and who was finally sent into hospital when her condition worsened, as probably having appendicitis (the operation was delayed until too late, and her family blamed us for her death). There were others, where blame *was* justified, for misdiagnosis, or even some lack of care.

But during those years my younger sister died. She had been ill for many weeks with an infection, starting in her ear and spreading— pneumonia, pericarditis, peritonitis, and finally multiple pyemic abcesses. I was only recently qualified then and had not the courage to do as I would have done later—turn my practice over to a locum and go to be with her. Only in the last week did I do this, before that taking turns with my elder sister to go at weekends.

She was dying on a stormy February night, and the wind howled and shrieked among the pinnacles and crockets of York Minster, right near, as I took turns with a night nurse in sitting with her. Suddenly she sat up and said to me: "You know I'm dying, don't you?" I couldn't take it. I said: "Oh no, Joan! You'll get better, and we'll go away and have a holiday and some fun together." She was very downright; "Margaret," she said, *"don't be silly.* I *know* I'm dying, AND IT'S ALL RIGHT!" A few hours later she went into coma and died.

For the first time, then, I learnt that when death becomes a reality it is no longer feared, or fearsome. What is dreaded is the *imagining* of death, or rather, perhaps, of annihilation. What she taught me that night has stood me in good stead ever since. It has fallen to me to meet and mourn the deaths of many people I have cared about and to meet it with others for themselves or for those they cared about.

One well-loved patient who had been under my care for twenty years I had virtually to give permission to die, in spite of a friend who would have forbidden it if she could ("She *must* go on"). The patient had had two mastectomies, had earlier nursed a sister with an inoperable carcinoma, and knew well when she herself was dying. I went to see her, and we talked and said goodbye, and I told her that I would miss her. I could do nothing to help her friend; I could only say that everyone has a right to die in his own time.

Once I came near to death myself and again found the truth of what my sister had said. I had had too much barium run in too quickly, for a barium enema; my colon was overstretched, and I went into surgical shock. I lay on a trolley, and I knew that whoever came to fetch me might find me alive or dead, and it couldn't have mattered less which it would be.

A few years ago my husband died after a year of illness. I had known for nine months that he had a lung cancer, and he gradually reached the recognition himself; this was after the chest specialist had pointed out that at his age such a serious operation as would be needed to find out for certain whether this was cancer or not would not make much sense.

I heard the recognition develop in the months that followed. He would tell friends "I've had an X ray, and they aren't very satisfied with what's there"; then, "You know I've got some serious trouble in my chest"; and a few months later: "You know I've got cancer, don't you?" Then we could begin to talk freely together about it, and that helped us both, all the rest of the way.

He had known death before, from the First World War and from many tragedies among his family and friends. Now it was no longer an "acquaintance" but something "known intimately." He dreamed that he was going to Liverpool. (He had been there just before the outbreak of the Second World War, en route for Canada to look for somewhere to take his first wife and young son, coming back on the last available boat.)

Next night he dreamed that he was going on a long journey—he didn't know where. I *didn't* say "perhaps you are," but reminded him of the previous night's dream.

The third night, he looked around at the room, and said in a tone of surprise: "We're *still* in our own place, then," and I asked: "Where did you expect to be?" but he didn't know.

He died next day, peacefully, in sleep. He *had* been a living man.

All the events surrounding his death were closely linked unconsciously with the anniversaries of his only son's death and the boy's mother's, and he died on the day before that of his son's birth. The details were very striking, and I was reminded of how Sir Winston Churchill died without regaining consciousness on the anniversary of his father's death, after being in coma for many days.

These experiences, and many others, of losing loved people have been my progressive "acquaintance" with death—knowing it, more than merely recognizing it. Intimacy is yet to come, though I will not remember that.

In the last of his *Letters to Georgian Friends* Boris Pasternak wrote: "Everywhere in the world one has to pay for the right to live on one's own naked spiritual reserves."

Perhaps that is what being alive is about.

17

THE JOURNEY FROM SICKNESS TO HEALTH: ILLNESS, CONVALESCENCE, RECOVERY

We all know two different kinds of recovery from illness or operation. There are the people who for months, or even years, bore everyone with the detailed and embroidered story of "my operation," and there are those whom everyone admires for the plucky way in which they make light of pains and difficulties and seem almost miraculous in the speed with which they are on their feet again. Sometimes *their* first illness is followed by a second, and even a third, from which recovery happens in the same way. (A similar thing is often seen after a holiday, when return to work is followed at once by an illness.)

A third type is less obvious than either of these, but probably in fact more common than both together. With these people recovery is slow and painful, having no quality of miracle, either good or bad, but a quality of reality which the first plainly lacks and the second can be shown to lack.

These notes are an attempt to look at the process of recovery in this third group and to understand in what ways failure (as seen in the others) comes about.

I am taking as my prototypes such a "journey" which I myself had to make (studying as objectively as I can a subjective experience), and one made by a patient of mine.

MY JOURNEY

Many other people have had similar experiences, and this personal version of the boring tale is unique only in being mine.

At the age of sixty I underwent cholecystectomy. The medical history was one of long-standing attacks of gastroenteritis (a generic term used to cover a variety of symptoms), occurring mainly when I was away from home and eating unfamiliar food. Two of the severest attacks had been associated with emotional stress, others not, and there had been periods of great stress not associated with attacks of this kind or with other illness. There had been various other illnesses both with, and without, coincidental emotional disturbances.

It is worthwhile considering the kind of disturbance which accompanied these attacks and that which turned up in relation to other illnesses. There seemed to be a certain specificity, in that conditions affecting the musculoskeletal systems, e.g. fractured fibula, acute lumbago, and osteoarthritis, chiefly affecting the legs and limiting mobility, were associated mainly with depression; whereas visceral conditions, hyperchlorhydria, gastroenteritis, and gallstone dyspepsia were accompanied by paranoid anxiety and guilt about being ill, needing attention, and not working.

There was apparently no specificity of the *emotional stimuli* associated with the various illnesses. Loss of one relative, incidentally involving absence from home, was followed by an endocrine disturbance. One particularly severe "bilious attack" followed another relative's death not involving either absence from home or change of diet, while the loss of a third was followed by acute bronchitis and cachexia.

In 1961 I had a mild gastroenteritis, which did not clear up in a few days with antispasmodics and alkalis. At the end of six weeks of nausea and anorexia, with alternating diarrhea and constipation, I sought help from my doctor. To my surprise he found marked tenderness over the gall bladder; I was x-rayed within a few days, and a gallstone was found. I consulted a surgeon, who arranged there and then the details of admission to a nursing home and fixed the date of the operation for three weeks later. I then remembered that I had once had a mild biliary colic which did not last long, being relieved by belladonna, and I had not seen a doctor at that time. The operation now suggested seemed to me to make sense.

I worked until a few days before the operation. During this time I was forced to look at a whole range of violent and destructive fantasies concerning my illness which appeared in my patients. With one accord they imagined me torn to pieces by sadistic surgeons, the subject of postmortem examinations, rape, murder, burglary with violence, mutilation, crucifixion, dying of carcinoma, obstructed labor, hemorrhage, sepsis, starvation, poisoning etc. One patient, a Jewish doctor, dreamed of playing bridge with his former professor of surgery, whom he loathed. The professor had a large vulture perched on his shoulder and he said to my patient "Mazel tov!" (Good luck!)

I had to know that these were somewhere my own sadomasochistic fantasies and wishes, about which I felt profound guilt and apprehension. To have died seemed easier than to have to live with these ideas, and I found a melancholy satisfaction in the knowledge that the operation carried a 2 percent mortality rate, in spite of my seeing the unlikelihood of my falling within that 2 percent and my doctors' reasoned assurance that I would be cured.

Preoperative preparation was simplicity itself—I just remember being on a trolley in the lift and then seeing the surgeon's suspenders, as he scrubbed up in the theatre. The anesthetic removed me immediately, and when I came round a few hours later I was convinced that twenty-four hours had passed. (I experienced disorientation in time after subsequent operations, being then convinced that I was still waiting for the operation.)

Postoperative pain and vomiting were negligible and easily relieved, but then began a spell of acute anxiety over micturition. It subsided when I had *vomited,* and I realized later that I had been unable to distinguish between the need to vomit and the need to urinate. This inability to distinguish between one bodily need and another lasted for several days, and took various forms.

Within forty-eight hours of the operation I was free from pain, I had been out of bed, and my alimentary tract was functioning ordinarily. For a fortnight I was cared for and maximally protected from outside impingement, but when this support vanished on my return home I had to fend for myself, and this became almost unendurably difficult.

The difficulties were external, having to make arrangements for convalescence, and also internal, and there was constant interplay between them. Among the most painful things was finding myself unstable, irritable, peevish, and unreasonable. I felt utterly useless, being wholly concentrated on myself, valetudinarian, and totally lacking in humor. Once I could laugh at myself again, I knew I was really recovering.

I went away to convalesce for three weeks, during which time both paranoid anxiety and depression returned and faded again many times.

After another week at home I began to work again, eight weeks after the operation. But it was another three months before I was able to build up any reserve of energy, and I found a pull backward toward remaining ill that took some accounting for. It seemed difficult to commit myself to recovery as I had committed myself to illness, and I had to fight against the tendency to fall ill again, and at the same time to *allow* psychic regression.

After three months of mild but increasing illness, in the space of forty-eight hours I had undergone a regression to dependence for life in both factual and imaginative reality. The process of rehabilitation—the working over of the experience—was not complete several years later (and is being repeated in writing this paper).

The clichè "your life in their hands" is more than a mere sentimentality, though the time of actual total dependence may be, as then with me, quite short.

Psychic regression is to the wholly dependent state of infancy—with lack of orientation in time and space and confusion of body image; paranoid anxieties and sadomasochistic fantasies come to the surface, linked with repressed memories, many of which are body memories reactivated by the immediate body happenings.

The pattern of recovery is in general determined by the original pattern of mothering in the infancy to which regression imaginatively occurs, i.e. the infancy that was *actual*. The memories of later, usable experiences, especially experiences in analysis, fuse with the earlier ones and gradually modify their pressure.

MY PATIENT'S JOURNEY

Laura underwent radical mastectomy. Excellent doctoring and nursing care at and after the time of the operation greatly contributed not only to her somatic recovery but also to the psychic recovery which she achieved.

Her regression was to infancy in the arms of a chaotic and extremely paranoid mother, whose own infancy had evidently been disastrous. Laura had been under my care in a mental hospital twenty years before, having been committed, nude, wet, dirty, and suicidal. Her long and difficult analysis had provided many of the necessary usable experiences, which were followed by postanalytic experiences of living and working successfully in the world of ordinary men and women.

Sadomasochistic fantasies were conscious throughout Laura's mental illness and related largely to her father's work (he was a butcher, and as a young girl she had assisted in his shop). In the analysis they had been worked over repeatedly but were reactivated by the operation, and it was not until six months after it that we were able to approach her fear of death—not simply of dying, or of being dead, but of a violent dismemberment, dissolution, and annihilation which (like hell fire) would be eternal and endless. These fantasies had to be related to the fact that in neither hospital nor my consulting room had she been torn to pieces, dismembered, or destroyed, though she had *felt* torn and destroyed by her own violent love and hate.

She had previously nursed an elder sister who was dying of breast cancer which had been left too late for operation. She described vividly her sister's two breasts, one whole, the other diseased, "like two eyes looking at me, one livid, and fungating." This sister had cared for and fed innumerable stray cats, which Laura had had to get destroyed when her sister was moved to a terminal hospital.

The actual loss of the breast, the presence of the scar, and edema of her hand caused her lasting grief, from which she did not shrink. She could not bring herself to ask for a prosthesis, but made one for herself as best she could. This served not only to rebuild her self-esteem but also to correct the disturbances in her body image and to establish her identification with herself and her separateness from her sister, the cats, and the slaughtered animals in her father's shop.

The surgeon told me that he would have had no idea that she had ever been mentally disturbed—she had shown courage, fortitude, and composure (for she knew the nature of her illness), and she had cooperated throughout with those who were looking after her, as indeed she had with me. Only she and I knew of the intensity of her terror, its origin, and its delusional nature.

She lived for two years after the operation, and in the manner of her life and of her death she showed clearly the depth and extent of her psychic recovery.

When she conveyed to me that she knew she could not live much longer, I went to see her. We talked about this and about our long and close relationship, and our work together. She spoke gratefully, and I thanked her, and we said goodbye. Within a week she died, peacefully, in her sleep.

The disability involved in illness or operation, the somatic need for immobilization and for rest, as well as the psychic regression, have highly important effects. They interfere with, and largely prevent, much activity of a "sublimatory" kind (one cannot, for instance, dig the garden, or even tie up plants, for some considerable time after a cholecystectomy), but the psychic regression *promotes,* as well as seriously handicaps, moves toward creative activities, whether artistic or intellectual.

Anxiety is then secondarily increased, for not only is there a large amount of free-floating anxiety left unresolved, but the self-assertion required for the reestablishment of activity arouses, temporarily at least, an access of fresh paranoid anxiety. The greater the interference, the greater are both the need for activities and the difficulty in getting them going again, and the more there is a tendency toward fresh illness and fresh regression. Only persevering *insistence* on resumption of activity brings relief and full recovery, and small setbacks have quite disproportionate repercussions.

Convalescence is notoriously more difficult and painful than illness as such. This pain can be recognized as very much like the pain of mourning (which, in fact, it is), that of the symptoms accompanying withdrawal of a drug of addiction or dependence, and also feelings found in old age. The pain of convalescence is compounded of the savage, helpless, cosmic rage of infancy manically believed to be omnipotently destructive, and the corresponding overwhelming guilt and despair. It resembles adolescence in the instability, and simultaneous or alternating bouts of progression and regression.

The tendency to become ill again repeatedly, and the persistent retelling of the saga of "my operation" imply something of *addiction* to illness and to the regressed, dependent state. Withdrawal of support from outside is reflected in the development of both fresh physical symptoms and their psychic counterparts.

Recovery, or renewal, comes, as in analysis, when paranoid feelings give way to depression, and this is finally resolved by working through once more to the depressive position—i.e. when there is ego development in a new area. It may involve acceptance of less than total cure (as with Laura) but is to the person's own greatest capacity. Some psychic wounds never heal and may be reflected in recurrent or lifelong somatic illness.

Here, then, are the processes which go on below the surface in the large majority of those who suffer and recover from illness, injury, or operation.

In those who make "miraculous" recoveries, regression is too much feared, and the sadomasochistic fantasies are manically denied. Infancy was altogether too painful to be endured again, for there have not since been the necessary restorative experiences, and cure cannot be accepted from outside—it depends upon the imagined magical, omnipotent self.

In these people sublimations etc. were apparent, rather than real, with a preponderance of defensive (ego/superego) over gratificatory (ego/id) aspects—a precarious state in which the need to rebuild defenses and avoid breakdown is paramount, by reason of failure in the outside world in the original situation, where the mother did not provide an effective "supplementary ego" or "protective shield."

In those who relive perpetually "my operation," infancy was not bad enough to make regression impossible, nor good enough to make it possible to leave it behind, and again, enough restorative experiences have not been found. There are perseverative attempts to make the outside world provide the cure, rather than to find it within.

The story of "my operation," like a neurotic symptom, is an attempt, of a kind, at artistic creation, i.e. sublimation of the content of the regression itself, which has a creative aspect. As such, it is a necessary part of the process, but it fails. The superego is overstrong, and the ego is weakly organized and not sufficiently integrated with the id.

The journey is not an easy one, and those who make it on a magic carpet or those who forever retread the same bit of the path, rather than move on, are the victims of their psychotic anxieties.

For those who make it successfully, it becomes part of their journey to maturity, and illness or operation can then become paradoxically, like childhood, the "tide," the "full sea" which must be "taken at the flood, or all the voyage will be bound in shallows and in miseries."

18

SOME MISTAKES AND FAILURES IN ANALYTIC PRACTICE: HINDSIGHT

We all make mistakes and have our failures, and because they are painful to us, as well as to our patients, we tend to avoid talking about them.

Through reviewing my own work recently, I have come to feel that it is time to look at my failures and consider why they happened and what are perhaps the commonest causes of failure. I will list them as they come to me, though the items cannot be clear-cut—they often overlap, and more than one factor may contribute to the failure in any one case.

I should add that I am not talking here about the many patients we find who cannot manage without what I have called "maintenance therapy"—i.e. those fixed in an infantile dependent state which cannot be resolved. With them we may have to decide whether to go on providing the "maintenance doses," on the grounds that we have undertaken a responsibility in regard to them, or whether to reserve our skills for those who can make more profitable use of them. This would mean finding some other ways for these patients to get their needs met, which is not an easy matter. And as many of the more seriously disturbed patients are now being treated, the number of permanently dependent ones seems to grow, while facilities for them do not increase at the same rate.

Incidentally we can often learn a lot from long contact with these very dependent people, which is useful in treating others.

Unsuitable choice of patient

This may be a matter of faulty assessment in the first instance. Diagnosis is not always easy; a patient may present a very different appearance at first from what comes out as the analysis develops. What is known in medicine as "clinical sense" plays an important part in one's assessment of a prospective patient, and if one goes against one's clinical sense, or intuition, for any reason, one is liable to run into trouble.

I once agreed rashly to undertake an analysis without having first seen the woman, on the recommendation of a colleague. She presented an appearance of great assurance and balance. She had been working with considerable success in a psychiatric clinic and had published her results. Toward the end of the first interview I expressed my lack of understanding of her wish for further analysis (she had already been in analysis elsewhere for some years). She took off her rather heavy horn-rimmed glasses before answering, and I suddenly saw a totally different person—very immature, childish, and very brash.

I had already committed myself and had to go on, but it was only a few weeks before I found the analysis quite impossible because of the violent anger she aroused in me. I referred her for an opinion to another colleague, who advised me against trying to go on. He told me that she apparently had no real wish to be analyzed and that her interest in psychiatric work lay in having the illness or disturbance in others—never in herself. Where she did not find it already, she would provoke it.

Certainly she nearly drove me crazy, and I found later that this woman had been to many analysts and that she was a pathological liar.

Incompatibility

This is not always easy to recognize at first. One does not necessarily refuse to undertake the analysis of a patient because of a feeling of dislike. Beneath this feeling there may well be an unconscious liking, and again, as the analysis goes on, respect, regard, and liking may develop too.

But the opposite may happen. An initial dislike may persist and grow, or an initial liking may fade.

It does not mean that this patient could not be analyzed successfully by someone else. I have taken over and carried on the analysis of patients referred to me by colleagues, and I know that more than one patient with whom I failed has worked successfully with another analyst, whom he found more compatible.

Failure to recognize a need at a critical point

One patient was taking large doses of sedative drugs. Her husband had found her in stupor on several occasions and finally found her unconscious. He called in the family doctor, and she was hospitalized at once.

I had persisted in attempting to analyze the anxieties, but failed to recognize their full intensity or the dangers in the situation. It could have led to "suicide," which she did not really want.

Overanxiety and excessive zeal

These may lead to either prolongation of the analysis into something that can never end or to premature ending, through repeatedly giving ill-timed or wrong interpretations, or using inappropriate words. Doing so occasionally does not always matter; the patient usually gives one a second chance.

In trying to convey to an adolescent, at the start of a holiday break, that this did not mean that I was abandoning her, I emphasized "You are my patient—you belong to me." If, instead, I had said "I am your analyst" or "You belong with me," it is just possible that she might have come back. As it was, she made it very clear that she would not return in any circumstances. The only real way to make return possible for her would have been to leave the matter apparently very casual and the choice entirely up to her.

The problem can be trying to do too much at once—to go too far, or too fast, not allowing the patient to set the pace, or, equally, failing to take the initiative when the patient shows in some way that he cannot do so will bring about failure.

Working through is the important thing here. Sometimes the patient has to do it, but sometimes it is the analyst who must do the greater part of it.

A patient's false reason for terminating

A patient who has formed a new and apparently successful sexual relationship, and marries, or has found an important new job which makes coming for analysis difficult will often break off the analysis.

With one patient who broke off his analysis on marrying, I was aware that this was his defense against his homosexuality, but there was nothing I could do. The choice between his wife, who could not tolerate the analysis, and me was too much for him.

I heard some years later from a consultant psychiatrist at a hospital that the marriage was in danger of breaking down. The question of further analysis was not raised.

Not understanding the way in which a patient resolves his anxiety

In the previous instance I was aware of the defensive element; in the following I was not.

One patient had recurrent anxiety dreams, but they always ended in her finding some magical way of escape—a door which she found in the enclosing paneling, a switch, or handle that released her. I did not see that I should have put to her the question "What would have happened if you had *not* found it?"

She released herself from the analysis by asking me to admit that it had failed, which I did. But I pointed out that this was once more the magical mechanism, and that the fear had been that the analysis might succeed.

She had never been able to win in any struggle with her mother.

I heard later that she was now happily married, which hitherto had been impossible. So perhaps my admission had a therapeutic effect—I still don't know.

Too rigid technique

This links closely with the question of diagnosis, and recognition of psychotic anxieties.

In chapter 3 I have described the analysis of a patient where for seven years I went on using the classical technique which I had been taught and had experienced myself in my training. Altering my way of responding and using a far more flexible technique enabled this patient to reach a satisfactory and successful ending to a long and difficult analysis.

She became a different person; her marriage, and other relationships, altered materially, and for many years now she has made a valuable contribution to society.

Being out of one's depth

Hearing by chance from an outside source of an important change in the life of a former analysand triggered off a fresh, deep and painful piece of self-analysis.

His analysis had begun while I was in analysis myself, but extended long beyond my own termination. I continued from time to time afterward to discuss it with my former analyst, and he was consistently encouraging: "You're doing very well with a difficult psychotic patient." But after the first few years I felt doubtful. In spite of continuous efforts I could not understand why I persistently reacted to and interacted with the patient as I did or why my feelings were so deeply involved that the matter became something of an obsession.

The patient continued to come, and my analyst continued to reassure me, and so we went on. I was well aware of ambivalence on both sides, and it was a relief when we finally agreed to stop.

Some very tragic happenings in this patient's life were attributed to me. I knew that while some of the blame might be justified, he had never considered that they might still have come about either in the course of analysis with someone else (which I had suggested, and he had refused) or even independently of any analysis.

Suddenly years later when I heard this news, I found myself deeply disturbed. I became manic and paranoid by turns, with intervals of depression and anxiety. I recognized at long last that both his transference and my countertransference had been psychotic, and that my former analyst had failed to see this.

Now I was faced with a new question. I had to understand, without my analyst's help, why he had so failed me. Had there been, perhaps, an area in him of countertransference psychosis?

The answer gradually became plain. He had, as I had (and as indeed all analysts do), been working in an area beyond that which he had yet reached himself. I remembered that, when early in my analysis with him I had expressed the wish that I could have come to him years before, he had answered that it would not have helped. He could not have done my analysis sooner; he would have been out of his depth, as, in fact, my previous analyst had been. (One might think of Newton knowing nothing of the theory of relativity or Einstein not knowing of catastrophe theory.)

I had been far out of my depth with this patient, and now, at last, omnipotent sadomasochistic id and superego demands could give way to reality and to ego recognition. I became free of my obsession and was able to disentangle the patient's transference psychosis from my own. In other words, I could discard my hitherto unconscious delusions about the patient and about our relationship.

I could do nothing more about the patient's transference psychosis. I could only hope that it had been resolved in some way, perhaps through further analysis with someone else or through his own ego development; increased insight and decreased omnipotence might have brought resolution.

Without complacency, guilt, or anxiety I am content now to leave it there and to accept that my failure here was not due to lack of integrity, as I had feared, but to lack of knowledge, understanding, development, and experience.

So—for what it is worth—I put this account of some of my failures and mistakes there for others, in the hope that they may find something helpful in it. Putting it down has been useful to me in sorting out my own ideas.

19

TRANSFERENCE/ COUNTERTRANSFERENCE IN POST-THERAPEUTIC SELF-ANALYSIS

INTRODUCTION

The original version of this paper was written in 1964, when I was about to visit the United States. I sent it, together with a paper on transference in borderline states, to the Washington Psychoanalytic Society for them to choose which they would prefer to discuss—they chose this one.

I said then that it was experimental and I felt it to be incomplete. It was well received, and the discussion, led by Dr. Searles, was very generous and friendly, though it seemed to me that the topic was anxiety provoking.

In 1967 I read it again in the British Society, quoting something of what had emerged in Washington and adding to it an account of some personal experiences. Again it was generously discussed, and many colleagues made helpful and valuable contributions—and still I could not seem to find what was missing. At last, in 1978, I think I have found it and have finished the paper accordingly.

Because of its long history it may feel rough and disjointed. But because so much more is understood now about psychosis and so much has been written about self-analysis since those earlier times, it is unlikely to arouse anxiety. It may also be of so much less interest and even trite, perhaps.

It has been very important to me, as part of a series of papers, and I am still not altogether happy with it, but I have to leave it there. In his *Diaries 1898-1918* Paul Klee writes "there can be no more critical situation than to have reached the goal." So perhaps it is just as well!

*   *   *

There is an old saying among analysts: "The difficulty in self-analysis is with the countertransference." For myself I changed this round long ago to "the difficulty in self-analysis is with the transference."

Now I want to look at the proposition that self-analysis consists of analysis of the transference/countertransference phenomena, the splits within oneself, the tensions between one's own polarities which will inevitably be carried on largely on the basis and patterns of the original therapeutic analysis (in which I am including training analysis, for it has long been recognized as essentially therapeutic), but also on those of one's own analytic work with patients. Transferences between ourselves and others come in too.

Such a discussion could become subjective, too personal, and embarrassing; my aim is to keep it as objective as possible. I am writing from a clinical, rather than a metapsychological angle. Some of what I have to say at the beginning is rather obvious and not very interesting, but it cannot be left out of a serious study of self-analysis. I will put it as simply and shortly as I can.

Let us look first at self-analysis where the transference phenomena are essentially those of a transference neurosis. The anxieties will be neurotic in type, castration anxiety, and separation, or depressive anxiety; the fears will be those of loss of a part of one's body, loss of an object, loss of an object's love, loss of self-esteem, where self and object are recognized as whole, real, and separate. The original transference will be resolved by means of reality-testing and secondary identification; symbolization and metaphor are both available; the channels of communication both between the self and the environment and those within the self are blocked only in limited extent, and in the degree of *illusion,* or fantasy, not *delusion.* The main defense mechanisms involved will be the more sophisticated ones of repression, displacement, etc., rather than denial, splitting, projection, introjection, or primary identification.

The kind of thing that happens is that in some situation one finds oneself reacting disproportionately or inappropriately, and it is usually not long before it is possible to recognize a transference, either positive or negative (or both), to some individual concerned, which links in memory with a particular episode or episodes from early childhood and with something remembered from earlier analyses. Often the analyst's comments or interpretations are recalled, or there may be conscious imitation or repetition of the way in which such material was dealt with then.

The situation is perhaps most often one in which the (unconscious) primitive superego is involved. The content of the material may even be directly sexual or aggressive, and provided we allow the ideas and emotions to become conscious we can recognize them as infantile, and resolution can follow when insight is reached.

We are all meeting something of this sort much of the time in our analytic work, and a large proportion of it goes on without ever becoming conscious, or, for instance, may appear only in our dreams.

When we are dealing with neurosis, only neurotic anxieties are aroused as a rule, and anything more disturbing (psychotic anxiety) will arise only in situations in the outside world or in our private and personal relationships; neurotic anxieties of course may be stimulated there too.

What I have been describing are the ordinary day-to-day "leftovers" from the analysis of transference neurosis which has gone far enough for all ordinary purposes. It is the kind of thing we see in our patients usually in the terminal phases of their analyses, and it is one of the signs by which we recognize that termination is nearly due.

In analytic work of course we are most often struggling with a counterresistance, and it is the analysis of this that makes possible the analysis of the patient's resistance. In this instance our own transference is externalized and becomes a transference to the patient (countertransference in the literal and restricted sense of the term); a few words or a piece of behavior on the part of the patient can often be very helpful to us in recognizing what is happening, if also sometimes unpleasant.

In these days, when training analysis is generally adequate for the handling of neurotic patients, countertransference neurosis does not usually make much difficulty except for an inexperienced analyst. We have gone a long way since it was thought that if patient appeared in the manifest content of an analyst's dream he should give up the analysis forthwith and seek further analysis for himself from a colleague. But where we are dealing mainly with psychotic anxieties and transference psychosis, we are up against something very different and often groping in the dark.

Perhaps I should say here that I think it is unlikely that many of us ever attempt to carry out regular analytic sessions with ourselves. (This is partly, of course, because training and therapeutic analyses tend to be much longer than they used to be. The lengthening began when Freud realized that intellectual recognition is not enough and that working through is needed for changes to take place. New discoveries meant that there was more to be analyzed in most patients, and the changing type of patient particularly over the last forty years has also contributed to this tendency.)

Nor, in general, I think, do analysts return for further analysis. Some do so, and a few start all over again, usually with an analyst of a different orientation, but these are not what I am trying to discuss.

A piece of conscious self-analysis usually happens because of some specific strain or stress either in analytic work or in daily life, and if the earlier analysis has gone far enough, life situations can be used for self-analysis and therapy.

But where, in all this, are transference and countertransference?

I think it is well recognized now that in the analysis of transference psychosis what goes on in the analyst is very much more important than it is in the case of transference neurosis, where the more important thing is what goes on in the patient. This is not to say that what goes on in the patient in transference psychosis is unimportant, but rather that it depends on the analyst in a way that it does not in neurosis, and the *interplay* between the two matters more.

It has been widely known for some time that analysis of patients whose anxieties are psychotic in type, i.e. annihilation and persecutory anxiety (using the term in the sense of a phenomenon of ordinary psychic development, not a clinical manifestation of paranoia) can only be done through regression to dependence. Whether the patient's dependence ("management") should be actually carried by the analyst in any given case is a matter of opinion, or sometimes of circumstances, and I will not go into it here. But it is inevitable in self-analysis.

I am indebted to Dr. Clifford Scott for a saying. "How long is schizophrenia?"—how long is regression? It may be a matter of a ten-minute interval between two patients, a weekend, or part of a long holiday. My point is that it can't be done without, wherever psychotic anxiety is stimulated, whether in analytic work or in life situations. Just as we need to enable psychotic or borderline patients to tolerate repeated temporary breakdowns, rather than encouraging them to expect to reach a stage where breakdown does not happen again, so we need to allow ourselves to regress, or break down.

George Santayana wrote of "the suppressed madness in a sane man." And like Palinurus' (Connolly's) fat man, who has "a thin man inside trying to get out," our sane selves have "the lunatic, the lover, and the poet" inside them, trying to get out. We have to find ways of allowing them to be there.

Self-analysis then, in the case of psychotic anxiety, requires regression to dependence, the dependence here being dependence of one part of the self upon another—call it, if you like, dependence of the id upon the ego, the ego being both body ego and psychic ego. Since one cannot exist or have any psychic activity whatever without bodily existence, the final dependence is upon body ego, and the person who is both his own analyst and analysand has to provide and accept whatever "management" is needed.

What makes for most difficulty—resistance—is that psychic structure which shows the most primitive characteristics, the earliest superego. It tends to be paranoid, to view the whole proceeding with mistrust and suspicion, as having superstitious and magical elements, and to rationalize every possible defense against it. (I find I cannot write without "personalizing" these parts of the self. There is a good precedent for it, in Freud's writings.) I am using the word *self* in its most popular and generally understood sense and not equating it with *ego*.

As regression goes on, the tensions are progressively experienced more somatically and less psychically. Pregenital conversion symptoms may be developed, or psychosomatic illness, or important psychic accompaniment to somatic illness, and they may be extremely difficult to unravel in self-analysis where there is any delusional element, *because recognition of delusion in oneself is so very difficult.*

One can become sensitized to the presence of delusion in someone else, and it is possible to see one's own reactions as *like* those of a deluded person, and so deduce that a delusion must be present. Its content, and its unreality, are usually much more difficult to reach, but it is essential that they be reached, and this recognition is the first step in that direction.

These things, of course, are of precisely the same nature when occurring in self-analysis as when they come in analysis of patients; they contain the same kind of transference references, are resistant to analysis in the same way, and stimulate the same kind of counter-transference responses. And they have to be dealt with in the same ways.

Fortunately we are not alone in this, and I am grateful to Dr. Harold Searles for emphasizing it in his discussion of this paper when I read it in Washington D.C. in 1964.

As I have said, implicitly at least, in two of my earlier papers, "Counter-Transference and the Patient's Response to It" and "On Basic Unity," we can have and should be willing to accept and acknowledge a good deal of help from our patients. Their behavior and their words can often have interpretive effect for us, but we may also even depend on them at times, to some extent, much as they depend upon us, but without this dependence necessarily becoming explicit. The acknowledgment can usually come later.

Counterresistance can take many forms, and it is worthwhile looking at some of them, as they become the resistances met with in self-analysis.

In analyzing a transference psychosis an analyst may resent many things—the invasion of his personal life, both inner and outer, as a patient endeavors (often successfully) to take possession; making use of his emotions, invading his dreams, and stimulating especially his depressive, paranoid, and even annihilation anxiety to an intolerable degree.

If the analysis is to succeed at all, it is useless trying to hold these things at arm's length. Since both analyst and analysand are human, there will inevitably be failures; and no analysis can ever be "complete," as no one individual can ever know the whole of any other. That would be, by definition, actually to *be* the other. All that one can do is to enter into the closest psychic unity that one can find and that the analysand can allow.

But this entry into close psychic unity can involve one, by entering into the patient's inner world, in madness that is painful and frightening. It can sometimes be difficult to see *whose* madness it was in the first place; to accept it even temporarily for one's own arouses annihilation anxiety that is far back beyond persecutory anxiety—losing one's boundaries and merging with another, or even becoming someone else (psychically) for a while.

And so it is in self-analysis—reaching the closest possible psychic unity with oneself, exploring one's own persecutory and annihilation anxieties, and merging together parts of oneself which have hitherto been separate.

In persecutory anxiety the fears are of destruction by something outside of and distinguished from the self, which may yet be recognized as a projection of part of the self, the object perceived being a part-object, and the main defenses used being those of projection and introjection, splitting and denial. Magical omnipotence is used as a defense against helplessness and passivity.

In the areas concerned there may be both illusion and delusion; primary process thinking predominates; there are symbolic equation, concrete thinking, and inability to make correct inference or deduction or to use analogy or metaphor; there may also be disturbances of perception.

Resolution comes about through primary identification on the pattern of eating, digesting, and absorbing (not magical introjection); verbalization or some other form of rendering accessible to consciousness, e.g. visualization, is essential.

Persecutory anxiety is experienced when the security of one's inner world is disturbed or threatened, and the most common stimuli are the presence of persecutory anxiety in someone else and somatic illness or injury. It chiefly concerns one's bodily state and bodily reactions to excitation.

The fragmented images of the eaten and destroyed parents, former analyst and others, represented by bodily manifestations of excitement and invested with destructive and magical qualities, are perceived as persecutors by the analysand-self and are transferred to the analyst-self. The anxiety may be manifested in the form of somatic symptoms or hypochondriacal ideas and valetudinarianism.

A history of actual illness or injury early in the first year of life may contribute to the condition, and the illness itself is then transferred. I have analyzed a patient who behaved toward me as if I were *actually* the infantile eczema from which she had suffered, denying me all other existence. She would respond to remarks or interpretations, or to anything new or unfamiliar about my house, my clothes, or my consulting room by becoming restless, scratching and tearing indiscriminately at herself, the couch and the wall; she tore at me verbally or with aggressive silence.

Where such experiences have not been reached in therapeutic analysis, they may come later in self-analysis, and the analysand-self transfers to the analyst-self the persecuting, magical, and uncontrollable features of such a condition. The analyst-self may react also in a paranoid way, and the anxiety is, as it were, bandied to and fro, repeatedly projected and reintrojected both into the outside world and between the parts of the self until the memory of the internalized (eaten and absorbed) person comes into play strongly enough for resolution to take place, by breakup of something which is in part illusion and in part delusion.

This may either coincide with or (more often) follow recovery from the somatic condition, which can then become memory, instead of something to be lived in the present.

The resulting intrapsychic state might be perceived as in the words of W.S. Gilbert's sailor:

> I am the cook and the captain bold
> And the mate of the Nancy Brig,
> And the bo's'n tight and the midshipmite
> And the crew of the captain's gig.

A cannibalistic eating having taken place, the integration of the ingredients results in one whole person having all these aspects or attributes and bearing the guilt and anxiety, or feeling satisfaction.

The greatest difficulty encountered is usually the destructive so-called narcissistic element, which sets out to make all attempts at analysis useless. It is manifested in the conversion symptom and hypochondriasis (being now a superego manifestation), and just as this becomes a sadomasochistic attack on the analysand-self, it also becomes a sadomasochistic attack on the internalized (original) part-imagos and on the analyst-self. It arouses hostility and destructiveness in the analyst-self, in countertransference; the factual reality of the oneness of analyst-and analysand-selves is used *against* the self-analysis.

Recognition of any delusional element is essential for the breaking of the deadlock and recognition of the transference to the internalized part-imagos. Working through is a long slow business, but gradual improvement of the symptom becomes undeniable and heartening. Again, it depends upon modification of the superego, which appears as a destructive biting, sucking, grinding, not-self, force.

Differentiation here is between self-analyst, self-analysand, and analyst- and patient-imagos; it is a valuable stage in the evolution of one's own analytic ideas and recognition of points of agreement, and of difference, between them and those of others, especially perhaps one's former analyst.

Analysis of one's own persecutory anxiety concerns areas where psyche and soma are at least partly differentiated, ego and id partly fused, ideas of self and not-self, of inside and outside, of separateness and fusion, of subject and object are already developed to some extent. But areas exist in us all, all our lives, where these conditions do not obtain (Freud called them "the id") and to reach these deepest layers involves depersonalization, disintegration, the experiencing of annihilation anxiety, and the analysis of delusional ideas, against all of which most people's defenses are extremely strongly organized. The defense against recognition of a delusion, which is perhaps the strongest of all, is the use of factual reality; this is very clearly seen in the case of somatic illness with a psychic component or concomitant, when the fact of infection, injury, etc. ("somatic compliance" Freud 1905) is used to deny absolutely the presence of any psychic element, and yet its very use is part of that element, and what is faulty there is perception itself.

In the chapter "On Basic Unity" I described a condition found in regression to dependence in which the patient allows himself to reach the primary unintegrated state and hands over the ego functions of experiencing and observing to the analyst, becoming "a state of being," a rage, a mess, a scream, etc. It is experienced as disintegration and depersonalization with total loss of contact, as chaos and annihilation. It is a state of frenzy. I described how resolution out of this state comes about when the analysand, being owned by the analyst as *his* rage, scream, mess etc., which is himself, is impelled to a specific *movement,* and through making it finds a contact, usually of some bodily kind, with the analyst, and so discovers himself and the analyst each to be in fact a whole and separate person.

Such a movement becomes a statement, or assertion, of the self. It is experienced as an aggressive act, taking up more room in the world, and is followed by a paranoid phase, the very separateness making everything else seem retaliatory and persecuting, until the movement and all its consequences are assimilated and integrated into the patient himself.

The "unity" of the patient's and the analyst's psychic reality is limited, as is also the unity of their factual reality. Their lives and experiences overlap, but do not coincide, otherwise there would be one person, not two, and separation could never happen.

Such separation has, in certain cases, to be enforced in some way, sometimes by the analyst's initiative, sometimes by the analysand's; otherwise the analysis would go on until one or the other died, leaving an impossible mourning situation.

In self-analysis the proposition is different. There *is* only one person, but he has to develop the ability to split (so that one part of him can observe the rest, but also so that at the same time he can relate to a variety of other people) and also to reunite (so as to remain whole and unfragmented).

Let us assume that such a regression and disintegration have occurred in self-analysis, and the primary state of unintegratedness has been reached.

In one part of the self there is a state of being: for the sake of argument I will say a state of muddle, or of unknowingness, which has its roots in the original infantile state of total unknowingness and links with a present-day adult state-of-not-knowing, via childhood experiences (of muddle, confusion, loss of contact, of uncontrolled defecation, helplessness in face of bodily excitation, inability to understand words or situations, adolescent disturbances of various kinds, etc.). Many of them are of course guilt-laden, though others may be pleasurable, but toned with anxiety.

The rest of the self is concerned with the experience, observing, watching and waiting, suspending comment, criticism, or intervention, allowing whatever is there simply to *be* there. Resolution comes through some kind of climax; body tension rises and joins with mounting psychic anxiety or excitement until an intolerable point, or frenzy, is reached, and discharge can only come by some body movement, excreting, stretching, taking a deep breath, etc., or engaging in some activity. It is a primitive orgasm, in fact. The situation changes with the coming together again of the whole self in, as it were, an altered molecular pattern. A paranoid phase often follows, until the episode is assimilated and accepted through the recognition of the links between this episode and its preceding stimuli, of memory links with experiences in earlier analysis, and in early life, going back to infancy, and ultimately to the birth experience itself where (as Freud pointed out), the prototype of anxiety is to be found in the body experiences of the fetus and neonate.

After this there comes an access of energy, which usually finds expression in some creative activity—a kind of *psychic* stretching. The writing of this chapter is a case in point.

I want to distinguish between what I have been describing and either a trance or a catatonic state, of which it is the antithesis. A trance or a catatonic state can also occur where there is absence of integration and loss of cohesion within the ego; in these states everything, both psychic and somatic (not only ego functions) is surrendered to the other colluding, interacting, or reciprocating person (whether real, imagined, hallucinated, or split off). Awareness, memory, emotion, muscle tone, flaccidity or rigidity are put at the disposal of someone else, or of the split-off part of the ego. Body movement and resolution can be initiated only by suggestion from outside, or through undoing the split. In trance states induced from outside (e.g. hypnosis) repetition is needed to avoid or relieve anxiety, and when the colluding or suggesting agent is not actually present, the recall of an agreed specific word or phrase acts "magically" as a substitute. But no real change comes from this, only a restoration of the status quo ante.

It seems to me that the important difference lies exactly as it does in the ordinary analytic situation, (where analyst and patient are two different people), in the nature of the transference and countertransference; the essential condition for reaching and resolving the frenzy seems to be that which I have described as "basic unity."

The regression in this instance is regression to the state of unity in prenatal life, where the fetus is not only dependent upon, but also continuous with, and inseparable from the mother, as analyst and analysand in self-analysis are continuous and inseparable, and the analysand part of the self is dependent upon the analyst part.

In the prenatal state nothing is "known," and yet nothing "unknown" is recognized (except possibly in post maturity). Birth itself introduces the first "not-known" of all, and a very complicated thing it is. (I am including all elements of the experience, from the first uterine contraction up to the time when the infant, put to the breast, handled by the mother, then bathed, weighed, dressed etc. is laid down for sleep). Not only anxiety is triggered off or at least stimulated by it, nor the bodily activities of breathing, sucking for food etc., but also much psychic development (including such things as development of the ego and superego). Bonding plays an important part in preserving psychically the basic unity.

Recent research seems to show that memories from prenatal life can later be found and used, especially those of sounds heard both from the mother's body (her voice, heartbeat, breathing, intestinal movements etc.) and those penetrating from outside ("Music that is heard so deeply that it is not music at all because you are the music" T. S. Eliot). But birth itself, the bodily separation, is the earliest experience with which we have yet been able to make useful contact in analytic work, and I am working from there.

So what is there to be transferred, then, is ultimately the primordial birth process itself, and yet the very transferring is a direct reexperiencing of it—repeated rising tension, climax, and release— by the experiencing self. The release experienced is not only that of delivery but also psychically a restoration of the prenatal state of absence of tension. (This homoeostasis may be experienced by the adult as positively pleasurable, but it is unlikely that the neonate, any more than the fetus, could find it so consciously immediately.)

I have described this so far from the angle of the analysand part of the self. In the analyst part of the self something different is happening, but at the moment of discharge a contact is made between the two—that is to say that in the moment of differentiation within the self integration happens simultaneously, when analyst-self and analysand-self join up and become continuous, inseparable and indistinguishable, for only the self-born-of-self or the self-absorbed-in-self, which is the same thing, now exists.

This is perhaps what Andrew Lang is saying in his verse:

> If the wild bowler thinks he bowls,
> Or the batsman thinks he's bowled,

> They know not, poor misguided souls,
> They too shall perish unconsoled.
> I am the batsman and the bat,
> I am the bowler and the ball,
> The umpire, the pavilion cat,
> The roller, pitch and stumps and all.

In other words, without basic unity there can be no survival, but it is in a human context, with no hint of magic.

In the intrapsychic state where this has been reached the totally helpless and inadequate self is indissolubly fused in a new area with the humanly adequate self, having unconscious memories of the experience of normal infantile omnipotence (not magical omnipotent defense against annihilation). Then comes increased mastery of a human world, but with ordinary humanly limited capabilities and human emotions.

The delusion of oneness would be difficult to sustain, but once recognized it gives rise to little anxiety in its breakup and in the relinquishing of the no longer maintainable omnipotence. It can become a dream, from which one wakes.

What I am trying to show is that a central "state of being" is the important thing. In this instance it is a state of well-being and creativity, in contrast to the depersonalized state of chaos, destruction, and annihilation. It is a state in which id and ego are fused, and while psyche and soma are differentiated they are nevertheless continuous and, practically speaking, inseparable. Analysis itself has here become almost a state of being. On the basis of such a state being present, an enormous and increasing amount of internal rearrangement and psychic interchange can be tolerated without undue disturbance. Continuous self-analysis can go on, a cycle of return to unintegration and reintegration (comparable to the physiological catabolic and anabolic processes), and these become conscious only from time to time, when a threshold is reached.

When that happens of course there is another breakdown, and the process is repeated, but on a level more readily made conscious, as described earlier.

Both of these, and many other intermediate but less clearly defined states, will be present simultaneously, on different levels or in different areas, and there will be continual shifting and changing between them to maintain the lowest pressure of anxiety possible at any given moment.

All that is manifest of the subliminal is a discovery every now and then "I have done something which six months (or two years) ago I could not have done." This is exactly parallel to the discovery of a child. "Now I can reach the things on the mantelpiece, or I can jump over that wall, which I could not do before."

The original analyst and analysand have melted in the mists of prepsychic memory and become homogeneous with the self, part of the basic unity, in the stillness at the center.

The greatest obstacle to reaching the basic unity, and of course paradoxically the most powerful stimulus, is the most primitive superego element of all, deriving both from the actual labor pains (the contractions of the uterine muscle acting upon the whole fetal body), and from prenatal disturbances, and relieved by delivery, screaming, and the start of breathing.

Once again there is exactly the same process as that involved in analysis of a transference neurosis, the difference being that in transference neurosis the superego is at the developmental level of the classical oedipus complex, linking back to the depressive position.

Transference neurosis has been described as projection of the superego on to the analyst; modification comes about by a therapeutic split and identification with the analyst, who makes a therapeutic alliance with the less ill part of the patient's ego, depending upon the existence of a degree of mature ego functioning.

A high degree of mature ego functioning is needed for self-analysis, but splitting and fusion within the ego are repeatedly used therapeutically by means of *intrapsychic* alliances, projections, introjections, and identifications to bring about changes in oneself.

Another intrapsychic state from which basic unity should be distinguished is the state of union achieved by the mystic.

Here I am not on very good ground as I know very little about mysticism. As I understand it, in Christian mysticism the finite helplessness of man is united once and for all with the Absolute, Infinite Reality, or God, the Wholly Other, the external source of all goodness. This union does not protect him in the here-and-now against assaults of evil (again external), but promises ultimate freedom from all ills in a life after death. This promise makes bearable the trials and difficulties of present human life and the human condition, where the supernatural takes over, intervenes unpredictably, and can be known, being both immanent and transcendent.

(Existentialism, Zen Buddhism, and Taoism I believe all contain large mystical elements, but I have not tried to go into these; for the purposes of this paper it isn't necessary.)

In experiences of basic unity in analysis, through repeated and alternating defusion and fusion, the infinite helplessness of infancy is united with finite, relative and human adult. In self-analysis, of course, this is telescoped into a very short space of time because of the biological and psychic growth and maturation which have already come about.

One comes to own and take responsibility for all one's acts, words, thoughts, and psychic processes, and for one's whole life. Life, which began as the responsibility of others, in begetting, conceiving, and giving birth, will end predictably in death, which meanwhile has been accepted, having been experienced imaginatively in these deep regressions and distinguished from annihilation. Immortality is limited, depends ultimately upon one's own creations, and is different from the "eternal life" of the "hereafter." Factual reality is common to us all, however differently we may experience it, and the differences depend upon our own personal, inner, and psychic realities. We live by *both*.

To sum up: I have been describing the *process* of self-analysis, what happens and how and why it happens—i.e. what it is for and what is achieved by it.

It is not simply to bring about a more comfortable state, but for important changes in the ego (that is, as Freud described it, the area or layer of the person capable of meeting reality, or of organizing and coordinating activity in response to it), enlarging it progressively.

Psychotic anxieties (as distinct from neurotic ones) are concerned with survival and with identity. Before the "depressive position" can be reached (after which neurotic anxieties predominate) survival *must* be assured, and identity found. Both separateness and oneness must be accepted, and whole objects perceived.

This can only come about starting from the part-real, part-delusional state of basic unity, through the abandonment of the belief in factual unity or identity, and the preservation of its psychic reality. Sir Peter Medawar writes, "We are all individuals—the only thing that really unites us, makes us one, is that difference between us and any other known species of being able to develop the *psychic* awareness of this. The somatic awareness is inborn in every individual of every species, as immunologists and geneticists have shown. It's up to each individual to develop it."

This means, of course, the acceptance of the complement, or converse of identity—diversity, the separateness without which, in fact, identity or oneness would be meaningless. And this, in turn, leads on to the shifting relations between psychic and factual reality, neither of which can be the whole reality, and only sometimes can the two together.

This acceptance is the essential factor in the development of the ability to tolerate those excruciatingly painful dilemmas of ambivalence and paradox, whose horns we cannot evade: the fact that the same thing can, at the same time, be both best and worst, loved and hated, true and false, "Catch 22," or the ancient Greek problem about Epimenides the Cretan, who says that all Cretans are liars.

It is in that central state of being that I have called "basic unity" that we can come nearest to the resolutions of these things.

From it comes the ability to *use* processes of differentiation and integration. It follows, then, that any person who is willing to bear frenzy, temporarily, to the point of losing his sense of identity and certainty of survival—in other words to "break down," or reach chaos or catastrophe (the point of tension where he *has* to bear *not being able* to bear it)—will emerge from it with heightened abilities. These will include greater capacity for sensitivity and perception, capacities for abstraction, and creativity. Along with these will come the ability to bear sadness and joy, and isolation, a greater willingness for mutuality (as distinct from reciprocity), and hence increased ability to form relationships.

It does *not* follow, of course, that everyone has to break down, or "go mad." But those people whose earliest experiences were such that they could not take survival for granted nor distinguish between self and not-self, between psyche and soma, factual and psychic reality etc. will be less able to understand the psychotic anxieties of others (except as identical with their own), to tolerate their own and others' ambivalence, and to withstand the many and increasing pressures of life—in short, to mature.

Many analysts have pointed out that patches of psychosis are there in all of us. It is through analysis of our own psychotic transferences and countertransferences, wherever these are stimulated, that we can come to deal with ever greater degrees of ambivalence, confusion, and so forth, in ourselves and in our analysands, and with greater degrees of complexity of life. We will widen our horizons and live more fully as real people, able to enjoy the challenge of stress rather than defending against it, and accept both success and failure.

To quote Klee again: "The deep pleasure that comes with artistic development may well be described some day as a manifestation of energy, but only because this liberation is at times crowned with thorns." This surely can also be said of psychic development.

20

DONALD WINNICOTT: A NOTE

In September 1971 I was asked: "A summary of the place of Dr. Winnicott's work and its relation to the total field is much needed. Can you be persuaded to write it?"

I said that I would try, but that it could not be done quickly. By the time I had written what I could, it was already too late and could not then be published, but surely it is still relevant.

These terms of reference, of course, would set any writer an impossible task, and I do not take them too seriously, but I have considered what is called for—not an obituary, eulogy, or memoir, but some kind of assessment—an objective recognition and statement.

It is simply not possible for *anyone* to make something that takes D.W.W. only as an "objective object." Some element of perceiving him as a "subjective object" (his own expressions) inevitably comes in, in anyone who was in any way associated with him, especially for those who (like myself) were his analysands, and our assessment must depend on the degree to which we have become able to perceive both him and ourselves objectively.

Regarding him, then, as an objective object does not rule out a personal element. If it did, we would end up with something fossilized or mummified, nonbeing, to which *no* feeling could attach, and this would automatically destroy the very assessment that we are trying to make.

Winnicott once referred to himself as "an isolated phenomenon" (an historical reference in his paper on his relation to Melanie Klein and her work). He developed the concept of an individual that is implicit in this, speaking (in his paper "On Communicating," etc.) of "the individual's use and enjoyment of modes of communication, and the individual's non-communicating self, or the personal core of the self that is a true isolate."

We have, then, to consider him both as communicating and noncommunicating, and the interplay between these two aspects of him, of his readers, fellow-workers, analysands etc., and to recognize that anyone as much an individual as he could not but strike sparks of one kind or another.

It follows that he is easily both idealized and seen as bedeviling whatever he touched—psychiatry, psychoanalysis, pediatrics and so forth.

Either attitude does him a gross injustice; in fact those of us who mainly approve or agree also have serious points of difference with him, while those who mainly disagree or disapprove often find themselves, however reluctantly, accepting what has hitherto seemed to them outrageous. Perhaps the chief outcome of this is the very width of his impact on the "total field," where ideas which he first put forward have been quietly appropriated and accepted without being attributed to him, and often attributed elsewhere. Things which he reached without tub thumping or ostentation often fall into place, suddenly "clicking" somewhere, and references to his sayings turn up in all kinds of unexpected places, (like a reference in an article on school architecture in one of our national Sunday newspapers). He had quite a special ability to make himself understood by all kinds of people, to say things which could not be put into words, and to get in touch with the creative elements in people, i.e. with the really well part of a personality below the surface.

But where what he has been saying has not "clicked" (often because it has not yet been fully developed, often because it is really obscure, or because he assumed that people understood when they didn't) it is, of course, experienced as puzzling and frustrating. This will go on for a long time yet, and anyway he never claimed to have said the last word on anything.

Attempting to test his work, his discoveries, or his idiosyncrasies, or to make comparisons with other workers—Freud, Klein, Séchehaye, Hartmann, etc.—would be fruitless at this point, but I want to consider some particular topics which seem to me outstanding, apart from some of the more obvious ones such as "primary maternal preoccupation," "transitional objects," "squiggle technique" etc.

First of all is his capacity to stand paradox and ambivalence, knowing them to be inherent in life itself, without seeking ways around, defenses against, or avoidance of them. This capacity grew and developed in him, an ongoing process throughout his professional and personal life, not steadily continuous, but varying in scope and speed ("Human beings are jerky"), and people have speculated how one could *live* with so few defenses.

Out of this came such things as his recognition of the importance of being able to refuse; the need (whether for child or adult) for "no" as well as "yes" and for frustration at the right time as growth promoting, where at the wrong time it is growth inhibiting; the importance of "confrontation" on occasion; the value of destructiveness and of the parent's or therapist's ability to survive it; and many other truths about men, women, children, and adolescents *as real people.*

Not long before his death he began to develop completely new ideas on the origin of creative activity in the earliest, two-sided, undifferentiated, preambivalent, preobject-related stage of development in which, paradoxically, destruction is creative of both self and object. This is the stage of "being," and of nothing-else-at-all, which depends upon survival being guaranteed by the environment, so that annihilation anxiety can safely be ignored and the self *come into being* as a "true isolate".

There have been many former postulates, e.g. Aquinas's "I am psyche-soma," Descartes' "cogito ergo sum." But these are surpassed by the importance of "I am" (long known as the forbidden holy name of the Omnipotent Creator) and finally of the still simpler statement "I," which postulates and includes, but does not state, "not I."

Even this is not new; it is the "Ancient of Days," the "Spirit brooding over the face of the waters"—"One is one and all alone, and ever more shall be so." What *is* new is Winnicott's recognition and use of it, and it is not only new but individual and personal to him, as expressed in his understanding of Hamlet's "To be, . . . or. . . ." (pause) "not to be? *That* is the question."

Somewhere about here he died, in a way, although he was still exploring, writing, lecturing, seeing patients etc. But for him dying was an essential part of his life, which would have been meaningless and incomplete without it, something which he had to reach at the right time.

He failed us, of course, by not knowing everything, or not communicating all he knew; but how awful if he had!

Many different people have described Winnicott as "a genius," and I think their meanings are as varied as the people themselves. Ralph Vaughan Williams defined a genius as "the right person in the right place at the right time," and I think this fits Winnicott. But here it is left to others, especially the many who will come later, to discover him and his work *for themselves* (see his statement to the effect that others before him had found the same things, including Freud, but that what mattered was that *he* had found them for himself).

Lastly—I am indebted to a colleague whose only direct contact with Winnicott had been at a colloquium in Paris. She told of his informal conduct of it—in shirt-sleeves, talking a little, sitting back tilting his chair, everyone else talking, and he finally gathering together, summing up all the contributions, commenting, and expressing personal thanks. Later, in a teaching session, one of her own students stumblingly told her how much she had helped him. To her this was the direct outcome of her sensation of Winnicott's living, ongoing quality. "He was a *yeasty* person," she said.

21

DIALOGUE:
MARGARET LITTLE/ROBERT LANGS

LANGS: Well, I'm especially interested in sharing ideas with you. Let me say it this way. I began to study the analytic interaction after having written a rather straightforward book on the technique of psychoanalytic psychotherapy (Langs 1973, 1974). But even there I was more interactionally oriented, adaptively oriented, than the usual classical analyst. I soon began to use certain Kleinian concepts. For example, the Barangers (1966), who are from Argentina, had a concept of the bipersonal field, a view of the analytic situation as a twosome. And I was very drawn to this; it seemed to fit so much with what I was finding. In the course of writing a book on technique from that point of view, I went to the literature. I went for a very simple reason. When I wrote the technique book, I didn't study the literature very carefully because it was a big book and it was very practical and empirical. But I felt that I could do that only once; I felt that I *should* do it only once.

So I started to delve into the literature. And I must say in all honesty, I have tried to remember whether I had actually read some of your papers as a psychoanalytic candidate or not. I'm not entirely clear; they certainly—and unfortunately—were not part of the core curriculum. But when I went back to your work, I found or dis-covered that of all the analysts that I read, your work—and that of Searles—was in touch with what I was discovering, more than any. To me it was just a beautiful experience.

Perhaps the height of it—I'll mention it right off—was this. I had seen that patients were very sensitive to their therapist's errors. This was discovered mainly in supervision and then I confirmed it in my own clinical work. And I noticed that when the therapist is in difficulty, if you listen to the material in that context, the patient was actually, unconsciously, not directly . . .

LITTLE: No, mostly unconsciously . . .

LANGS: Quite indirectly, he would be making interpretations to his therapist.

LITTLE: Yes. (Rickman had pointed out the two-person situation in analysis—dyadic was his word for it—years before.)

LANGS: And then I discovered in your 1950 . . .

LITTLE: I wrote it in 1950; it was published in 1951. "Counter Transference and the Patient's Response to It."

LANGS: Yes, it was presented verbally first. And there I found exactly the same concept, stated so beautifully. I mean, to me it was a poignant moment. I felt sort of sad that you had said it first, yet so pleased that you had done so—and so long ago.

LITTLE: You should have heard the fuss at the time, but chiefly about my reformulation of the "analytic rule," and the idea that an analyst might acknowledge having made a mistake, rather than about the rest of the paper.

LANGS: Well let's start there. Tell me about that.

LITTLE: Well, that one didn't arouse rage, but the next one did, "R"—The Analyst's Total Response to His Patient's Needs. That provoked Mrs. Klein to saying, in the scientific meeting at which analysands of mine were present: "All that this paper shows is that Dr. Little needs further analysis." Winnicott was in the Chair, and he didn't let me answer that. He said she had no business to say this of anyone; and I believe she had said it of somebody else before that.

LANGS: She was very outspoken, I gather.

LITTLE: She *was,* very outspoken. But so was he, and angry. He said: "We *all* need more analysis. None of us can get more than a certain amount, and the same could be said of anybody: they need more analysis."

LANGS: Yes, how true. Let me ask you this. As I say for me it was a very poignant moment because here I had made what I thought was such an original discovery and then I discovered . . .

LITTLE: Yes! Terribly disappointing. But let me quote Winnicott to you again. He said at some point, something like this: "I know that Freud discovered this in—whatever date it was—1908 or something. The important thing for me is that I discovered it for myself."

LANGS: Yes, that's very beautiful. Winnicott had a way of saying such beautiful things. I find there's a certain beauty and imagination in the English analytic literature that I don't find in the American literature.

LITTLE: Well, it varies. A touch of Raymond Chandler would help sometimes!

LANGS: Yes.

LITTLE: You find some of the more stereotyped analysts in all orientations, associates of Miss Freud, associates of Mrs. Klein, or what we call "independents." They are afraid to speak directly, and they use stilted, meaningless jargon, with no rhythm. But fortunately there are other analysts (for instance Winnicott) who put things very plainly and simply.

LANGS: Yes, this is what I like about your writing.

LITTLE: Plain English. One thing about my writing is that I tend to write what can be spoken, or read aloud. This means using shorter and simpler words and sentences, and then careful pruning, cutting out anything that isn't needed. You get much nearer to people that way. But I had learned a lot from my mother reading to me; she read very well; and then I had to read to a blind uncle, (her brother, to whom *she* had read, as a child), and he read to me too. All these were *very* valuable. And then I learned something about words long before I came to psychoanalysis, which has stood me in a very good stead over my own writing.

There's a Victorian author, Charles Reade, who wrote one of the first novels about madness and the treatment of "lunatics" in his time—*Hard Cash.* In another of his books—*The Cloister and the Hearth*—he points out that Anglo-Saxon words carry much more punch than words derived from either Latin or French. He wrote one paragraph, first entirely in Anglo-Saxon words and then exactly the same paragraph, using only Latin derivatives. And the difference hits you.

LANGS: You can see it immediately. Yes, that's well put. Because that's exactly the point. There are certain papers—by writers like yourself and Winnicott—where there is a direct feeling, a direct communication, a direct punch. Not something you have to cogitate about. It is immediately evocative; there's also a sense of warmth, of being held well by someone who cares.

LITTLE: We owe it largely to our Anglo-Saxon roots. Some of the Latin words of course come indirectly through the Normans, but we owe those to them rather than to the earlier Roman occupation. Our real richness lies in having them *all;* Scots, Gaelic, Manx, Cornish, Celtic, and Norse words, as well!

LANGS: I see, that's interesting. I was going to ask you about the setting of the times when you gave this paper. I want to cover some of that, but can you tell me first—you started to talk a little bit about your background—can you just tell me something of it, what your training was, and how you came to analysis?

LITTLE: Yes. It's a long story.

LANGS: Take your time, please.

LITTLE: I was a general practitioner, and I had never wanted to study medicine at all. I was ill in my first year at college, where I had gone wanting to read chemistry and botany, so I failed my intermediate B.Sc. in pure mathematics. (My father was a mathematician.) Then no Honors School would take me for anything except physiology and biochemistry. My parents said: "No. You wouldn't ever be able to earn a living at that. Come and live at home." My mother had always wanted me to be a doctor, and I had an absolute horror of it. But at that point I had a greater horror of living at home! So I said: "No. I'll go back and start again, and do medicine." I had a couple of breakdowns on the way, not needing hospitalization, but incapacitating.

LANGS: Did you have therapy at that time?

LITTLE: Oh no. There wasn't any ordinarily available at that time—1920–1930.

LANGS: So you worked it out within yourself.

LITTLE: I worked it out for myself as well as I could, and then later I sought help. I had a friend living with me who had a very bad breakdown. For three months she just lay out in my garden and cried; she drove her car furiously on the motorway; she threatened suicide repeatedly. Finally, the local vicar persuaded her to have some therapy, which *was* available by then, and at that point I realized that *I* needed it.

I went first of all to a Jungian, who did help me quite a lot, but he didn't realize how ill I was; I didn't show it. And when the war came, he went into the Emergency Medical Service. Soon I got very deeply involved with a patient and realized that I had got to get some more help. So I went to Ella Sharpe, whom I had met through him. I had six years with her, in the course of which I trained and qualified as an analyst and learned something about analysis, some very valuable things. But when she died, I knew that none of my real problems had been touched, and I thought, "Well, here we're back on the same old grind again."

Then I was very fortunate in Winnicott having a vacancy. I was with him—(I was already by this time a training analyst)—from 1949 to 1955, during which time I had two real breakdowns and just had to let myself be as ill as I had known I was. The second included a short spell in hospital, to prevent me killing myself while he was away on holiday. I had broken an ankle the year before. I had told Ella Sharpe that I was more ill than she recognized; she called me an hysteric. But I'd been working before that in a mental hospital and knew a bit more about it, and she, of course, had not had any actual psychiatric experience and was not medically qualified. (She wrote about King Lear as an obsessional neurotic, with no reference to his paranoia.) So when I got to Winnicott I knew where I was, because he recognized my psychotic anxieties and provided the "facilitating environment," and the "good enough" holding that I needed.

LANGS: Now you wrote the first countertransference paper and presented it in 1950 and then published it in 1951. Can you say something of the climate at that time and what prompted you to write it. I guess you would see these two papers (Little 1951, 1957) as companion pieces to some extent, wouldn't you?

LITTLE: Well, the second one, "R," came directly out of the first one, and I always think of that second one as the cornerstone of my work. At the time that I wrote the first one, the acute phase of disagreement in the British Society wasn't yet over. When I was a student, there were a series of controversial discussions between Anna Freud and her close associates and Melanie Klein and hers, and they got at times very acrimonious. And it was quite difficult not to get involved. I was a student, and going to scientific meetings where these things were raging. And I, of course, trained by Ella Sharpe, was what we would now call an "independent." Then it was called the "Middle Group."

LANGS: Yes, I would think so from what I've read of her work. She too had a sensitive pen and a kind of openness—as, for example, in her fine work on dream analysis (Sharpe 1949).

LITTLE: In fact, she made many of the same discoveries as Mrs. Klein made, but she couldn't acknowledge that they were the same, in a way that is difficult to define. She disowned Mrs. Klein and stuck to Miss Freud. My two supervisors were Miss Freud herself and Willie Hoffer, both of whom encouraged me to find my own way of working. I found it really very difficult, so it was a relief when the tension between the two sides lessened, mainly as a result of the work of Sylvia Payne, who was president of the Society at that time. She managed to hold the Society together, instead of *letting* it split.

LANGS: Yes, which it would otherwise have done.

LITTLE: Then various arrangements were made so that people could move between the two extreme groups without necessarily attaching closely to either, and that meant that it was possible to be "independent."

LANGS: There were a lot of pressures on the students then during those years.

LITTLE: Oh, the pressures were appalling. But the worst thing, which has since been remedied, was that each of the two groups, Mrs. Klein's and Miss Freud's, had regular meetings for newly qualified analysts, and there were none arranged for the others. They felt very much out on a limb, and very much abandoned. Either you committed yourself to one or the other, or you were left up in the air.

LANGS: Now, what was Winnicott's position at this point?

LITTLE: Winnicott was a very independent person—*so* independent that he absolutely refused to join the group of "Independent Analysts," which was formed later and still exists.

LANGS: Oh, I see. Certainly in his early writings he indicates that he had worked with Mrs. Klein and one sees her influence in his writings.

LITTLE: He admired Mrs. Klein *enormously,* and he understood her, in fact, better than many of her fellow workers. But she never really fully accepted him, and neither have many of her followers. Toward the end of her life, Mrs. Klein put forward the dogma of "inborn envy," which Winnicott could not tolerate at all. It postulated something in newly born infants which is *far* too sophisticated. He was very outspoken about it, both directly to Mrs. Klein herself and in meetings of various kinds; and he wrote in 1962 (after her death) "A Personal View of the Kleinian Contribution," (1965) making his position clear.

In 1952 a small group of analysts got together and formed "The 1952 Club," which is still running.

LANGS: And who did this include? Who formed it?

LITTLE: I believe the people who started it were Jim Armstrong Harris, Barbara Woodhead, Pearl King, Charles Rycroft, and Masud Khan. They had worked together as students, and then formed it as a group of newly qualified people. They kept it for some years without inviting more experienced analysts to become members, although they were invited occasionally to come and speak at the meetings. The idea was that if they had too many of the older ones, it would be taken over by them. (Several similar groups have been formed since.) Later they invited some others to join, including me, much later. Now Clare Winnicott belongs to it, and Marion Milner, Martin James, and John Klauber. It's not specifically "independent." There is now, as well, the "Independent Group" in the Society, but that is open for anyone to join, whereas membership in the 1952 Club is a matter of invitation; though, as I say, its *orientation* is not restricted.

The question is always being asked, what is this Independent Group? Has it developed out of the old original British Society before all our continental colleagues came here before and during the Hitler régime and Second World War? Or is it something that evolved? Is it a group of people who think alike about theory or technique? What had happened was that most of our members (this was before my time) were either in the Forces or the Emergency Medical Service, or were evacuated from London during the war, and we had taken in a very large number of colleagues from abroad. They made an *enormous* contribution, of course; but it altered the character of the Society, and it was out of that influx that this tremendous split developed. Because it was mainly between colleagues from abroad and their analysands, both from here and abroad.

LANGS: So they brought it over and battled it out here. Two

things: How did it influence you personally, and what did you feel were some determinants of this extreme division?

LITTLE: This is rather difficult to say. You see, the two dominant people were Anna Freud and Melanie Klein, and both were very distinguished people already, very experienced and highly influential. I always felt there could be some understandable personal rivalry between them, and also between individuals associated with them.

LANGS: Yes, inevitably. This comes up so much among analysts; it thrives on their unanalyzed residues.

LITTLE: It has been transmitted to some extent to Mrs. Klein's followers, rather more rigidly than to Miss Freud's, though, as you say, it happens everywhere, all the time. But at one point I was seeing Mrs. Klein about something, and she said to me: "Look, you're attached to Miss Freud's group."

LANGS: Was that your position?

LITTLE: Both my supervisors were with that group, you see, and my training analyst too: to some extent she had chosen the supervisors for me. Ella Sharpe herself was less close to Anna Freud than Willi Hoffer was. She tended to be isolated.

Then Mrs. Klein asked "What is the setup? What is Miss Freud's organization?" And I said: "I'm *not* attached to it; I'm as much outside their group as I am outside yours, and", I said, "from my outside standpoint, the two look exactly the same." Which she didn't like very much.

LANGS: In what sense did you mean it?

LITTLE: Well, each had a closely organized, close-knit group and held its own meetings, and if you didn't belong to one or the other you were outside.

LANGS: Yes, how do you think it influenced creativity? Do you think some creative things came from it; do you think there were constricting aspects?

LITTLE: I think it had a very constricting and anxiety-arousing effect. You were always liable to be offending one or the other—or even both!

LANGS: I see. It forced loyalties and agreement rather than imagination and innovation.

LITTLE: Yes. But I suppose it also stimulated that, and some creativity.

LANGS: But you yourself had some training from the Kleinian viewpoint as well as from the classical one?

LITTLE: Oh, well, the lectures and seminars that we went to as students were both. They had worked out that much, so that there was a balance. But if you went to the *group* meetings of one, you could not go to the group meetings of the other. And if your analyst and first supervisor were members of either, officially you had to have a "Middle Group" second supervisor. A lot of people would have liked to have a supervisor from each of the two groups. But neither Miss Freud nor Mrs. Klein really liked supervising a student who was in analysis with a member of the other group, and eventually, owing chiefly to pressure by Mrs. Klein, analysands in her group had to have both their supervisors from that group. I believe they still do, but there is much more mixing now, particularly in postgraduate seminars etc.

LANGS: So there were strong constricting factors. There is far too much in analysis in general that stifles creativity. Much that is innovative derives from having to defend and clarify one's own position in the face of unscientific, prejudicial attack.

In any case then, this was the climate. It was beginning to be resolved. Now what prompted you, then, to turn to the analytic interaction, especially to countertransference, at this time?

LITTLE: The story that I quote at the beginning of my 1950 paper was out of my experience with Ella Sharpe. I was very aware of some of her unresolved problems and felt them as obstacles. She was inclined to be authoritarian, and she idealized her own mother, which made it difficult for her to admit that I might be objective either about her or about *my* mother.

LANGS: Yes, I can see that. I want to say something now based on your comment that Ella Sharpe had discovered what Mrs. Klein had discovered, but didn't crystallize it. That statement is really similar to what you said about her approach to you yourself, as I'm sure you realize. You're saying then that there was a pulling back from more primitive parts of the mind.

LITTLE: Yes, a defensive thing.

LANGS: Which is something that, by the way, I believe is reflected in the writings of classical analysts in general.

LITTLE: Ella Sharpe didn't recognize psychotic anxiety or transference psychosis. They were beyond her limits. That wasn't her "fault," and it wasn't due to any lack of integrity in her; analysis had not developed that far yet. She carried out good, classical analysis of her time, of straightforward psychoneurosis, based on the oedipus complex, but nothing more. Like all our pioneers she had had very little analysis herself and must have carried an enormous weight of anxiety. Those of us who came later owe them a lot for that.

She came quite independently to much the same *theoretical* ideas about mourning as Mrs. Klein did, but was not able to carry them through into practice. She could write of Shakespeare's mourning and its outcome in fresh creative work, but twice she effectively disrupted my mourning processes without any realization of what she was doing. The story in my first countertransference paper (Little 1951) is a disguised account of her persuading me to read my Wanderer paper (see chapter 1) for full membership of the Society a week after my father's death, implying (as I understood it) that postponing it for that reason would be held against me. I took this, because of my psychotic transference to her. The paper itself was no part of working through the mourning; it had been finished before my father became ill. So I was not well equipped to mourn when she died suddenly in 1947.

But later Mrs. Klein's development of her formulation of the concept of the "depressive position" (1934, 1940) as a necessary stage in emotional development, together with the work of analysts in mental hospitals, helped greatly toward the recognition of psychotic anxiety, and later of borderline psychosis, where the depressive position has not been fully established, if it has been reached at all.

LANGS: That touches upon one of the things I've wondered about after studying the literature on the analytic interaction written by the Kleinians and the classical analysts—mainly the British and the Americans. I have had a feeling about American analysts that they too don't know the really sick parts of their patients, that they shy away from the psychotic parts of the personality.

LITTLE: I think what they don't know is that the *apparently* sick part of the patient is, in fact, very often the most well part, and the apparently "well" part is really most sick.

LANGS: I sense what you're saying, but I'd like you to elaborate a bit.

LITTLE: I will speak about one particular patient. She appeared to the outside world a well-adjusted, very able, and competent person.

She said of herself: "There is something in me that I *know* is there, that nothing can touch." And she also said: "I know that I am very ill, and I have put up the defense that I can cope with everything." And *I* had to help her to find that "core" of herself and get it to work *with* me instead of being used *defensively* against the analysis—as it tended to be. It was really there.

LANGS: You're really saying that the positive potential, the creativity, is contained in that "sick" part. The other is a facade.

LITTLE: What Winnicott (1956) has called "a false self" (1960). I would like to quote the Russian dissident who has recently come out of the Soviet Union, Bukovsky. I can't quote him accurately; I can only paraphrase—but people ask him: "How could you survive the prison camps and psychiatric prisons? How could you live through that, and come out sane?" And he said: "If there is that core in you, *nothing* can touch it."

If it was protected enough in earliest life, there is no need for a "false" self. This again I *felt* in myself, and quite early on I had really also felt it about certain things in my work, and *then* I had the protection and support from Winnicott.

Of course he, too, let me down, often quite badly. The worst thing was not recognizing my psychotic countertransference to a patient, when I asked for help, and reassuring me that all was going well. This in turn meant my going on failing that patient, and others as well, until I was able to see it for myself some years later. But *all* analysts fail their patients, at times—thank goodness—they can't be omnipotent and don't have to be, and no analysis is 100 percent successful. But for me, broadly speaking, what mattered was that he knew a sick patient when he saw one, and yet could see the healthy part too.

I sometimes wonder whether the proliferation of jargon words, and the ever-growing number of "developmental phases," etc., isn't part of the defensive attempt to be omnipotent, denying the uniqueness of every man, and trying to avoid those bugaboos ambivalence and paradox, which make us all feel helpless anyway.

LANGS: So, much of what you have written obviously has a very personal touch to it, but it also avoids jargon.

LITTLE: Yes. When I went to the States in 1958, my first contact with interns and students was in Oklahoma City. They began by asking me, "How do you come to know such a lot about mental illness?" And I said: "Chiefly through being very ill myself and getting well through my analysis."

LANGS: I think it makes a tremendous difference. Again I think that it contains a creativity you cannot get any other way; it's inconceivable, really. You can't achieve this *from the outside* at all.

Well, again, coming to this period in terms of what interested you in writing on the subject of countertransference. What do you recall of the climate of the times and the place of your first paper?

LITTLE: Well, as I said in that first paper, countertransference was regarded as something to be deplored, as unresolved resistance in the analyst. I had found that for me it was something different from what other analysts meant by it, except Winnicott (1947), who had written on "Hate in the Countertransference." In fact, there's Paula Heimann's paper on countertransference, and when I was going to read what I had already written at that time, I found that I had made the same discoveries that she had. And this made my paper of no use to me, you see. I had completely to rewrite it, to start again.

LANGS: You mean, to expand it? Because your paper is certainly much more comprehensive than hers, though her study was a major breakthrough.

LITTLE: Yes. But I then started from the standpoint that Paula Heimann had reached.

LANGS: Yes, that was in her 1950 paper.

LITTLE: Yes, that's it, 1950. I never told her; in fact, I don't know that I've ever said it to anybody, but it is true. I borrowed the script of the paper from her, that she had read at the Zurich Congress in 1949, which I hadn't been at. And what I had gotten to was already there, no longer new.

LANGS: So you had that experience too, of having discovered something personally, only to find it already stated in her paper. Still, it seemed to push you into some really remarkable insight.

LITTLE: Well, of course, the first was Freud himself (1910, 1925, Strachey 1961), and Ferenczi (1919, 1929), and the next one I think was Ella Sharpe.

LANGS: Right, they had all written something on this topic. It turns out that if you look carefully, there are a series of contributions to the study of countertransference, none of them very original. Paula Heimann came along and really said something quite new; she changed the attitude of analysts toward countertransference—and you did too.

LITTLE: Well, Paula Heimann had arrived at the idea of countertransference as a signal. And having had this other experience in my own analysis, I then was able to use it to point out that countertransference was more than that.

LANGS: Now, Ella Sharpe, what had she said? I know she had written on the subject of the analyst and his work—the satisfactions and, in general, the dangers.

LITTLE: Well, she referred to countertransference in her Collected Papers (1950), in the section on technique.

LANGS: And had she spoken of the constructive use of countertransference?

LITTLE: No. But through realizing that she had by so far missed everything about me that mattered I reacted very much against her, and my paper on countertransference reflects that.

LANGS: I see. So at the time you were really working over a very original area, which had emerged from your own personal experiences. Of course, Freud (1910, 1912, 1915) had set the tone: he saw both transference and countertransference mainly as resistances, and countertransference as an obstacle.

LITTLE: Yes, but you see in the old days, if an analyst had a dream about a patient, he promptly handed that patient over to somebody else and went into further analysis himself.

LANGS: Yes. Gitelson (1952), I believe, wrote something about that. And you're saying this was a basic attitude at the time?

LITTLE: Oh, yes it was one of the basic attitudes. Not by the time I came to write my paper. But earlier it was, about 1937, when I trained as a psychotherapist at the Tavistock Clinic, before I trained as a psychoanalyst. When I applied for training as a psychoanalyst in 1941, Edward Glover, who was chairman then, interviewed me, and he said in so many words: "You have to choose between the two. If you want to go on at Tavistock, you can't train here." Of course, that's all gone since. But at that time, it was either, or.

LANGS: Now, what choice was involved?

LITTLE: The Tavistock or psychoanalysis. The Tavistock was "eclectic"; all sorts of things—Freud, Jung, Adler, Stekel, "Reductive Analysis," hypnosis etc.

LANGS: Oh, I see. I didn't realize that too existed.

LITTLE: It was founded after World War I. And I had already realized that to me the Tavistock attitude was inadequate. I had a discussion with one very senior therapist there about what to do with a patient when you have analyzed his symptoms, and analyzed and analyzed, till you both know all about them, and still they persist. Her solution was hypnosis and *strong* suggestion! At that point I knew this wasn't for me, and I said to her: "No, it's a matter of transference and countertransference." So I left the Tavistock, and taking Freud as the founder of all we know, I chose psychoanalysis. The Tavistock of course has altered a lot since then, but at that time that's how it was.

LANGS: So your inclination was to always understand, and to understand in terms of transference and countertransference. So, what then was the prevailing attitude toward countertransference in the time of your training, in the years before your paper—the forties?

LITTLE: It was something that you were ashamed of, and denied, and got somebody else to analyze in you.

LANGS: So there would be transfers of patients and things of this sort.

LITTLE: Yes. You handed your patient over if you found countertransference there at all.

LANGS: Now, had there been some teachers who had begun to hint at other possibilities, or did this come just really out of your own experience?

LITTLE: I think it came straight out of my experience. I mean, I hate to make such an enormous claim . . .

LANGS: Oh, I understand. But there weren't any obvious revolutionaries so to speak at that time.

LITTLE: Well, of course the obvious revolutionary was Ferenczi, but much earlier, and he had written about countertransference. Balint was tremendously involved with Ferenczi, and he asked me to help him with the translation of Ferenczi's work. He would give me the papers in German, with his own rough translation into English. (I don't speak, or even read, German.) He gave me an enormous German dictionary, and I translated the German/English or Hungarian/English into English/English, so, in fact, I'm credited, in the bibliography, with part of the translation of Ferenczi's work, particularly the third volume. I was asked to review that for the *International Journal,* and I came across my review of it the other day; I'd forgotten about that. But the work was very important to me.

LANGS: So, the other thing too is that you took a very sensitive, interactional approach. That was quite unique, especially at the time. Your statement, for example—some of my favorite writings are in this paper (Little 1951); some of the things I quote again and again. I'm thinking of where you ask: Speaking of the dynamic aspects brings us to the question, what is the driving force in any analysis? What is it that urges a patient on to get well? The answer, you go on to say, surely is that it is the combined id urges of both patient and analyst. So you very soon came to think of the interaction in terms of the duality of everything in analysis.

LITTLE: My answer is that it is the sum total of the transference and countertransference, which is not only id urges, though they are at the bottom of it, of course. But not just the duality, for they are psychically one and the same. You see, I want to go on here to my Basic Unity paper (Little 1960b).

LANGS: Yes, go ahead.

LITTLE: I'm not a "dualist"; I'm very firmly monistic. Essentially everything is one, but paradoxically that would mean nothing if there were not also duality or diversity. So I suppose one *has* to be dualistic, but the monism is important as being primary. Very complicated! But it doesn't have to be "either/or"—it surely must be "one *and* other, *and* all." Perhaps most important of all is the uniqueness of every individual.

LANGS: Yes, I understand. Perhaps I'm not careful enough with my language. The unity of everything you would accept.

LITTLE: Yes, at least as primary, but needing to be preserved *psychically*.

LANGS: Yes, I see. I was separating it.

LITTLE: There again, I've been chasing through the most horrible collection of little bits of paper each with three or four sentences, or even only a few words written on it. And I came across one the other day in which I had written: "Every individual comes essentially from one cell, which already has been formed by the fusion of two. Nevertheless it is one. Each of the other two has come through division from one; they fuse and then divide into two again."

LANGS: Yes. So your emphasis is on the union, the unity. The unity of all that occurs in the analytic experience. Now, where did that idea come from? Because I think it is a very important concept. I don't see very much in the way of antecedents, although I think it's reflected in Balint, whom you mention, and Winnicott. But do you have some perspective on how your thinking developed?

LITTLE: There again, those five papers that were published in the *International Journal* [*of Psycho-Analysis*] really form a sequence (Little 1951, 1957, 1958, 1960b, 1966). There's one more that hasn't been published but it belongs to the sequence. But out of the countertransference paper came "R," and again out of "R" the paper on delusional transference, and out of that that the delusion is of being one. That if you and I were not in fact unconsciously one *somewhere,* we couldn't understand each other. We could have no interchange at all. I found that same idea quite recently in Jean Renoir's book, *My Life and My Films,* in which he speaks of the communication between the artist and his public. But it is based on this fundamental unity, which I have put into words in the paper "On Basic Unity," and the preservation of the delusion in *inner* reality is valuable. Renoir is very strong on this, which is interesting as coming from such a different source. And Marion Milner's "Overlapping Circles" (1977) contains the same idea—which is where she and I "overlap" or are "one."

LANGS: Yes, I think much of it is also related to the study of narcissism and narcissistic disorders.

LITTLE: Then again, in "On Basic Unity" I have quoted Freud where he says that *something must be added to the primary state of autoerotism before narcissism can develop* (1914). He meant first primary narcissism, and then secondary narcissism, though Balint maintains that they are the same.

LANGS: Yes. I think these writings are important not only for the study of borderline and psychotic states but for much of what is being said now about narcissism. What is the fifth paper? You mentioned four, I believe; is the fifth the one on borderline patients?

LITTLE: "Direct Presentation of Reality in Areas of Delusion," and later "Transference in Borderline States" (Little 1966).

LANGS: Yes, I think that they make a very important unity. And I'm still interested in the fact that you began with this study of countertransference, which I think is so important. I'd like to come back to this paper now and get some of your further thoughts on it. Anything more then about what prompted you to write it? You had been studying countertransference, you then discovered Heimann's paper (1950), which sort of prompted you to go back and dig deeper.

LITTLE: It confirmed what I'd already found, but I had to go further. There was a real drive there to use that experience as fully as

I could. And that paper came out of the mourning for both my father and Ella Sharpe.

LANGS: Yes, so what evolved then? I mean, how do you view this paper now in retrospect?

LITTLE: Well, I think it *has* gone further. It hasn't contradicted Heimann's work at all or discredited it in the slightest.

LANGS: Yes. That's true: the two papers complement each other. But there's one area of disagreement. We might as well get to it.

LITTLE: Well, at one time there was a big area of disagreement between Paula Heimann and myself, and it was very important. She maintained at that time that nothing but verbal interpretations of transference brought about any alteration. She qualified this by saying that theoretically it should be so, but in practice it wasn't always that way. We really had a running battle for some years over this. I said that if this *were* so, then she would need to modify her theory.

Again, I came across something I had read in the 1952 Club, in which I had criticized this very strongly. You see, I had *got* to find out whether *she* was right or whether I was! I thought at first that perhaps we were not speaking the same language, but then I found that we were not talking about the same things. I was talking about people who could not use symbols or metaphor etc., deductive thinking or inference, whereas she assumed their use. I realized this fully when, in a personal letter to me after the 1960 symposium, Dr. Heimann wrote that she, too, used nonverbal interpretations. If a patient said that he felt her as "cold", she would switch on another bar of the electric heater.

In my view only a patient who could make use of symbolism or deductive thinking could find an interpretation in this; to one who could not it would seem nonsense. Then I could feel that we were *both* right, in different areas, and after that I could be friendly! and we could be comfortable with one another.

LANGS: Yes, you had to resolve something there. That's a very important issue. Of course you take it up in several of your papers. It has seemed to me, again from a rather naive American perspective, that American analysts have incredibly overvalued verbal interpretations.

LITTLE: That's my point: it was so overvalued here for so many years, and this was a thoery my "R" paper challenged because so much of what happened with that patient was nonverbal. It was not what was considered to be "interpretation," or "analysis," but it had definite interpretive effect. But the nonverbal things have ultimately to be linked with words.

LANGS: Yes, yes.

LITTLE: In the short paper which was a contribution to a symposium on countertransference in 1960.

LANGS: Yes, to the symposium at the Medical Section of the British Psychological Society with Winnicott, Heimann, and two Jungian analysts, Michael Fordham and Ruth Strauss.

LITTLE: When I described how a patient came in in a very aggressive mood and said: "I *must* smash something! What about your sham mink pot?" I had no time to think; I said: "I'll just about kill you if you smash my pot!" She was shocked, and we were both silent for some minutes. Then I said: "I think you thought I really might kill you." I then reminded her of an earlier happening when she had heard my volatile daily help having a row with the laundryman. After listening to them, she had asked: "What are you thinking? I've often seen you look like that, and I didn't know what it meant." I said: "I was just thinking that I would like to bang their two heads together and throw them down the stairs." We both laughed, and the tension eased. Then I showed her that it was possible to have such thoughts and feelings, but not to *act* on them. This was a new idea to her; she was a very impulsive person.

Finally I showed her the "sham mink pot," which (although not sham Ming) was antique, and beautiful, and had a value for me. This led to her understanding that I would protect what I valued; and that even if, at times, I had *felt* I could kill her, nevertheless I had not *done* so; that I valued her, and would protect her from my own aggression. She learnt a great deal about reality and the difference between psychic and factual reality in that session.

LANGS: Yes, that whole sphere, your great sensitivity to the nonverbal sphere, to the influence of the interaction, to the silent introjective identification . . .

LITTLE: Well, I will go right back to my analysis with Ella Sharpe. She had to use a room belonging to somebody else, and she had a terribly heavy couch that had to be dragged out at the beginning of a session and put back again afterward, and she wouldn't let me put a hand to it. It was painful and frustrating, and frightening to watch her. I knew from my own observation that she had a bad heart; she was cyanosed and her fingers were clubbed, and she was over seventy. She would lug this couch to the other end of the room; then she would sit behind me, and on the wall facing me was a photograph with glass in front of it. She would light a cigarette, and I could see the smoke reflected in the glass. Sometimes I would hear her take the pack, deliberately take a cigarette out, fit it into her holder, get a match out of the box, and then wait; and I would scream at her: "For god's sake, *strike* that match and *light* your cigarette!" She would say: "I didn't want it to fuse with what was going on in you." And I said: "It fuses with it *anyway*."

LANGS: You can't avoid that.

LITTLE: It was *frightful* and it emphasized the importance of both nonverbal and personal things. But I couldn't say it then.

LANGS: What you experienced. I'm sure. I think you're aware that not only was there a dispute with Paula Heimann, but also with Annie Reich (1951). In her paper on countertransference, she was critical of your self-revelations.

LITTLE: Yes, her paper and mine appeared in the same number of the *International Journal* [*of Psycho-Analysis*].

LANGS: Right, her original paper. Yes. And then she wrote an overview, a critique, around 1960, I believe.

LITTLE: I don't think I read that. I'm afraid I read very, very little, especially lately.

LANGS: Oh. So you're not aware of her direct comments. See, the criticism had to do with—this is all interrelated—the criticism had to do with two questions she raised. Two areas, which I think are very important, and I want to hear much of your thinking on it. One has to do with what one does in terms of responding to the patient, once the patient has consciously or unconsciously detected a coun-tertransference problem, in terms of your suggestion of directly acknowledging and sharing some of it. The second has to do with the issues of holding the hand of the patient, showing a vase, telling of your own feelings, and things of this kind. Both of these have been questioned, and I'm sure you're aware of that.

LITTLE: Oh, I know. It has to do with both analyst and patient being *real* people, and right for one another. Going back to Ella Sharpe her behavior over the couch, and her attitude toward my perception of her heart condition, which she wanted to duck, nothing could have been more different than Winnicott's attitude.

For example, on arriving for one session, I was told that he would be a little late, as he was not well. He came in after twenty minutes, looking grey in the face and terribly ill. He said: "I'm sorry—I've got laryngitis," to which I replied: "My good man, you haven't got laryngitis—you've got a coronary! *Go home.*" "No," he said, "it's just laryngitis," but twenty minutes later he asked me to go; he couldn't carry on. And that evening he called me and said: "You were quite right. I *have* got a coronary." Two or three years later, after he'd had two more coronaries, I was in his waiting room one day, and I just sat there. Every now and then I went and asked the receptionist, "Is he still not here?" After forty-five minutes I couldn't stand it any longer. I went up to his room, expecting to find him either with another coronary or dead. I went in and found him just waking up! He'd taken off his collar and tie and gone to sleep on the couch.

All this was so right for me; it allowed me to find a real person as well as to have my own perceptions. One has to find out whether one has the right analyst or not.

At an earlier time it was assumed (and I think there may still be some people who believe it), that any analyst should be able to treat any patient provided the technique was right. There was no question of "fitting"; if a patient disagreed with what the analyst said or wanted to change to another analyst, this was understood as "resistance" and "interpreted" interminably.

The *technique* was what mattered, not compatibility. Nowadays changing over is much easier and happens quite often but not for the earlier reason of countertransference. When one prospective student came to see me, he told me that he had been for a short time in analysis with Armstrong Harris, who was at that time Training Secretary. They didn't fit with each other, and Jim had said to him: "You go and see Maggie Little; she's got a lot of bees in her bonnet, but you might find you get on with her." Well, we did get on. He told me about this in the first interview, and we both laughed about it. (This was about ten years ago.) But, there are the people who say: "Margaret Little is talking nonsense; she's absolutely wrong." And there are the ones who could say: "Well, she's got some bees in her bonnet." And there are other people who have said to me: "My work will never be the same again since I read your papers, or since I worked with you."

LANGS: Oh, it definitely can have that kind of influence. I'm going to want to hear more on this, but let me bring in one other thing. This is, I think, a very basic area in terms of the kinds of things that you recommended technically. Now, as far as handling countertransference, let's take that first. Let me introduce one other point. This paper, the 1951 paper, and, I would even say, the whole series, but I'm particularly, for whatever reason—we could be talking about your work with borderlines too—but for the moment I'm interested in what you have to say about *countertransference.* This paper now is more than twenty-five years old, and in the United States, at least, I don't see it having the impact that I feel that it should have. In other words, it seems to me—I'm being candid and perhaps you have a different impression—that many American analysts have yet to discover this paper and what's in it. That the twenty-five years have gone by—and why haven't they gotten to it?

LITTLE: Well, whether we say they have to discover the *paper* or whether we say they have to discover *what I discovered,* it's the same thing.

LANGS: Yes, it's the same thing. But hopefully in our field certain papers—and I consider this series a landmark series for many reasons, and I think this paper is an extremely important paper in the history of analysis—a paper with this level of creativity and clinical importance should be known as classic.

LITTLE: This of course is where Dr. Ramana comes in, at the University of Oklahoma; he's so very valuable because he made one island where this *is* being used. He was using the "R" paper for teaching as long ago as 1958; and René de Monchy and Stefi Pedersen both used the 1951 and other papers in Sweden. Other people who I know are using my work are Dr. Peña in Lima; Marjorie Rowe, Ph.D., Associate Professor in the Department of Psychiatry at Kent State University; and Dr. Virginia Suttenfield, in Connecticut, who told me that it was mentioned in a group of psychiatrists to which she belongs. But Gitelson was the first to mention me at all, and later, Douglas W. Orr.

LANGS: What I started to say is that I feel that analysts, of course, have to learn from their own experience.

LITTLE: Of course they do. And they learn largely from their own experience as analysands. I learnt so much, positively, from the things that Winnicott did, and negatively by what Ella Sharpe *didn't* do.

But she did do *some* things. She lent, and gave, me books, and I remember her fixing a cushion at my back once when I was in pain. She was essentially a very kind and generous person; Edward Glover spoke of her as being "much too kind to her patients." But her kindness wasn't used *as part of the analysis,* and like many of her contemporaries she was a benevolent tyrant.

Again, I learnt from Winnicott about the patient showing the analyst how to do his analysis, as a baby shows the mother how to handle it, and this was such a contrast with Ella Sharpe's authoritarian way of "mother (or analyst) knows best," and giving stereotyped interpretations.

LANGS: But certain key papers should alert you to look in certain directions. Or certain clinical experiences should create a need for a particular literature. You brought many dimensions of countertransference into focus in a very sensitive way. Are analysts too blocked to be open even now to such truths?

Why hasn't this become a key paper; maybe it is. I'm sure that there are many institutes that use it.

LITTLE: Well I'm surprised. You see, over here it's not been a key paper until now. I mean, over here I think only a few odd people thought very much of my work. Now both this paper (Little, 1951) and "On Delusional Transference" (1958) are listed for the European Psycho-Analytic Federation as key papers from members of the British Society.

LANGS: Oh, I didn't know that. I thought perhaps it would be different here. I mean, this work on countertransference is so basic and perceptive.

LITTLE: I mean, I've not been particularly important. Well, a few people would say: "Oh yes." Marion Milner, for instance. It took quite a long while for me to find for myself that we were really on the same wave length; we write so very differently. I find some of her writing difficult to understand, but at one point I had to say: "Look, I've been saying this too," and she agreed. There are, as I say, a few odd people who will say: "My work will not be the same as it would have been without yours." But Sandler and Dare and . . .

LANGS: Holder. I know their book (1973).

LITTLE: Yes, well, I was very surprised to find the references to me in their book. I mean, in large areas, it's been a dead duck.

LANGS: Well, why is that; what's your impression about it?

LITTLE: Well, I suppose I disturbed some people too much at the time, shaking their defenses and going against their ideas and their teaching.

LANGS: So you're saying that even your countertransference paper, which I believe is absolutely fundamental, is still too disturbing for the average British analyst to take as a basic paper?

LITTLE: Yes, until now, I'll tell you; but who was I in 1950? Nobody. I'd been qualified as an analyst five years, and I was in analysis again. And I was just being bumptious, I think.

LANGS: In writing this. And young people weren't supposed to write such revolutionary papers?

LITTLE: No, young people weren't supposed to write revolutionary papers! But it wasn't only that: it was a curiously ambivalent attitude which simultaneously denied that it *was* revolutionary or that there was anything even remotely original about it, and condemned it as being heretical.

LANGS: And you feel that that attitude persisted so long?

LITTLE: Persisted, yes. To some extent still, in some quarters.

LANGS: It's interesting, because I've had that impression too, as I said, in the United States about new ideas, especially as they touch upon the subject of countertransference. The paper is either ignored or condemned as unoriginal by one group, while another faction attacks it as wild or undisciplined writing and analysis.

LITTLE: And then here, if I read a paper or wrote anything, it seemed to be just "Margaret Little at it again." Perhaps I'm being a bit paranoid?

I was unlucky in not being able to get the teaching work I would have liked and could have done, which might have helped. In 1950, under great pressure from Sylvia Payne, I became involved in administration and got fixed there by the sudden death of my predecessor, under whom I was to have "tried it out." I was made Hon. Business Secretary of *both* the British Psycho-Analytical Society and the Institute of Psycho-Analysis, the latter being a job which really needed a specially trained person with a knowledge of Company Law, not a psychoanalyst! My successor managed (where I had failed) to persuade the Board of the Institute of this and got a trained Company Secretary appointed within a year of my giving up.

By the time I had disentangled myself from that (in 1952), not only my contemporaries, but also people more recently qualified than I, were already established as lecturers and seminar leaders and were the people from amongst whom students chose their supervisors. I couldn't get my toe in the door, no matter how I tried.

I have been told that I was "provocative," and "an irritant," and that I was "sticking my neck out." Although I never set out to provoke or irritate people, I have had to recognize that my *manner* when putting my own views could do that, and so I was working against myself.

This was always when I was unsure of myself, (though other people didn't recognize it), and it joined up with both my old childhood pattern of having literally to fight to exist at all and with the struggle with Ella Sharpe for my own reality so it became a chip on my shoulder.

Once I could be sure of the validity of my own observations, of my *right* to find things for myself and to put something forward, I could ease up, take myself a bit less seriously, and behave differently.

It was all very traumatic, and I went on feeling sore about it for a long while, but if things hadn't been like that I might never have made my journeys to the States—which were worth so much to me.

It was not until years later, quite some time after my first visit to the States, that I was able to take clinical seminars with advanced students, and they are the ones mostly who have followed up my work. And then a small group of newly qualified people asked me to lead clinical seminars with them. I enjoyed this a lot and made new friends through it, and also through the work on the review for the *International Journal* of Searles's book (Little 1967) and the contacts with them have stayed alive, as has my membership of the 1952 Club.

After my first paper was published in 1951, I was invited to go as a training analyst to Topeka. But at that time it was impossible, as I was deeply involved in my analysis with Winnicott, without which neither that paper nor any of the others could have been written, anyway.

But later, in 1958 and again in 1964, I went on lecture tours all over the States—Oklahoma City (twice); Topeka; Chicago; Washington, D.C., and Chestnut Lodge (twice); Austen Riggs; Stamford, Connecticut; Los Angeles; St. Louis; New York; and New Orleans. So those people who were interested had a chance to get to know my work.

One obstacle, I think, is the huge quantity of stuff that is being written. Nobody could keep up with it all, and here I am, adding to it!

I think one of the reasons why my work is not thought of very much in the States has to do with Mahler having introduced the concept of symbiosis, which was taken up tremendously and is preferred because it does not arouse the analyst's annihilation anxiety so much; it avoids real merging, or fusing, as there's still a degree of differentiation. It's a two-body, not a one-body relationship, which is what I am postulating in "basic unity."

LANGS: Yes, and you think again to the neglect of this other type of thing. How do you think that influences technique and the work with patients? Do you think something's being left out?

LITTLE: I think it's working from quite a different basis, isn't it? After all, in the symbiotic relationship each of two is dependent on the other. In basic unity there *isn't* an "other."

LANGS: And you feel that if one doesn't get back to that point, then something . . .

LITTLE: With borderline psychotics, if you don't get back to that at all you miss the bus. Psychoneurotics rarely need it—only if patches of psychosis turn up that have to be dealt with. They've mostly got it there already, and one is working from the classical oedipus complex and the depressive position, which borderline psychotics have never fully reached. They have to come to it, and then work through by ordinary psychoanalysis later.

In 1964, when I went to Los Angeles, I read "Transference in Borderline States" to the Los Angeles Psychoanalytic Society, and in the discussion only one person spoke agreeing with me—Ralph Greenson. Everyone else spoke against it. The chairman said: "We all see these patients, but we don't treat them as Dr. Little does." Then at two other meetings there I read other papers, "The Basis of Mental Health: Early Mothering Care," and one illustrated by slides of a patient's paintings; these were both quite well received, but then they were not controversial.

LANGS: It's really very interesting to me. It all seems so typical now—these responses to innovation—and even in analysts! Some day *The Therapeutic Interaction* (Langs 1976) may get around; you have a very prominent place in it. So, don't you feel then that what you're saying is tantamount to stating that there is still a lot of resistance toward understanding countertransference, toward using it constructively, toward not being, as you say, phobic or paranoid about it.

LITTLE: There's an enormous resistance, and I think people are phobic or paranoid about their own feelings, and so about both countertransference, nonverbal happenings, and other variations of standard technique, although they are beginning more and more to take it up. Not because of *me,* but because of Winnicott.

LANGS: Oh, you mean because of what he has written in this area?

LITTLE: You see, what has happened to him is what happens to every great writer. There's enormous enthusiasm aroused while he is alive, and when he dies he vanishes. Then he is rediscovered and resurrected some years later. I think that is happening to Winnicott now.

LANGS: What about your recommendations in regard to countertransference, in terms of sharing aspects of your direct subjective reaction with the patient, which of course has stirred up tremendous controversy.

LITTLE: Countertransference used never to be mentioned in analysis, and I feel now (as I felt in 1951), that if it is not referred to at all, no patient, except perhaps the least ill psychoneurotic, is going to believe in the *reality of transference* or the way that it can enter into and distort any and every relationship.

But I said quite clearly both in that paper and in others that it would not be appropriate to go into detail—only to *acknowledge* that it could or did come in.

But it does depend on the patient. If you have a borderline patient, you have to do far more of the kind of thing we are talking about than you do with a psychoneurotic. You practically don't have to at all with a psychoneurotic, unless areas of psychosis turn up.

LANGS: And how have people reacted to your recommendations in this area? What sort of response did you have?

LITTLE: I think they're really now beginning to recognize the existence of what I have been saying or to find the things for themselves. But you see, they have for so many years accepted Freud's view that only psychoneurotics are accessible to psychoanalysis, *that only psychoneurotics form a transference* of any kind. And the idea of psychotic transference is a very difficult one. Herbert Rosenfeld actually put it in so many words before I did: "transference psychosis." But it is only—since that paper was written, in 1958.

LANGS: "The Delusional Transference."

LITTLE: It was only since then that *borderline* psychosis has been recognized to any extent. Rosenfeld and I, actually, were both working at the Tavistock at the same time (about 1940), and we both changed over to psychoanalysis. I did so first. Now we both had treated psychotic patients, not only borderline ones but full-blown psychotics, and he of course works a very great deal with schizophrenics. I don't reckon I can treat schizophrenics; my experience there is very limited. I had one woman patient who was committed and certified, who made a good recovery after long analysis, and I had one man who was quite definitely psychotic, though he never broke down or was hospitalized. He went on functioning; he was basically stable and he did extremely well with very little treatment. But I wouldn't ordinarily take on a frank schizophrenic, where Herbert Rosenfeld would. Winnicott did. So would Meltzer, or Hanna Segal. And you will find a great deal of disagreement between Hanna Segal's views and mine, though we have a regard for one another.

LANGS: I see, in what sense?

LITTLE: She is a dedicated Kleinian, accepted as such by Mrs. Klein, who would only recognize chosen people.

LANGS: But does she disagree with aspects of your technique?

LITTLE: Oh yes.

LANGS: Such as?

LITTLE: Everything beyond verbal interpretation, I should think. But the point is this. They ignore the importance of nonverbal things. At one meeting Herbert Rosenfeld quoted his treatment of a patient in which the girl got up to go before the end of the session, and he put his arm across the door, stopped her, and "gave her an interpretation." Then he attributed the outcome of that happening entirely to what he *said* and not at all to what he *did*.

LANGS: Well, see, that's interesting. Because again, I don't have enough experience to really judge. But I have questions about the repercussions for example of physical contact with a patient, or feeding a patient and such things, which I would share with you candidly. But to ignore the nonverbal sphere, that's a different issue entirely. Because there's so much that goes on nonverbally throughout an analysis.

LITTLE: Well, I remember one Kleinian analyst describing how he treated a psychotic patient. All the interviews had to be carried out in the patient's car, and on one occasion the patient actually ran upstairs in the analyst's house and hid in a closet. But they don't seem to pay any attention to these really very important things; they are regarded only as "conditions which make analysis possible," not as having, in themselves, any value or interpretive effect, or as being part of the analysis.

LANGS: That's interesting because the Kleinians have a literature that shows great sensitivity to interaction. I think that they do tend to have some blind spots—important ones—about counter-transference; but so do classical analysts. Many evident countertransference expressions are rationalized away or simply overlooked.

LITTLE: Well, I think there are some who do really resent that anybody could have a different idea. The personal rivalry again—it's two-sided, of course.

LANGS: You find that they don't readily take to your ideas?

LITTLE: They insist that Mrs. Klein is right about everything.

LANGS: Do you feel that the Anna Freud group has opened themselves a bit more than that?

LITTLE: Yes, indeed: as individuals, perhaps, more than as a group, but I don't really know. But to be fair to both groups I should say that I have been largely out of contact for some years now.

LANGS: Have you studied the repercussions of the nonverbal contacts that you make with patients on occasion? And I think that's what you're saying, that you do this just on occasion, at very special moments, or am I mistaken?

LITTLE: I'm doing it all the time at special moments, and all the time *not* doing it and I *do* follow it up, of course. But one has to have some idea about when it is appropriate and when not. This is the theme of my paper called "Direct Presentation of Reality in Areas of Delusion," which I mentioned earlier. But patients have told me of things which were important landmarks for them, such as my turning my chair so that they could see me or saying what I felt, losing my temper, for instance. They have interpretive and sometimes "mutative" effect, as in the episode of the "sham mink pot," and also a time when I had to prohibit a patient parking her car dangerously.

LANGS: I see. This is a constant part of your work with borderline patients.

LITTLE: It is a constant, ongoing thing, but limited in its use and its usefulness. One morning, I had a phone call from a patient. My neighbor had told me that this woman had twice parked her car in a very dangerous position and had not only done that, but when she came to go away, she had turned the car around, having to reverse in a terribly dangerous stretch of road. After we'd finished talking about some troubles that she was having in her personal life otherwise, I said to her: "Now when you come next time, I have to say, you must not park in this road; you must park your car up that side turning." She felt very persecuted; she'd been "spied upon" by my neighbors, and so on. And I said: "I forbid you to park your car there. And most particularly, in *no* circumstances whatsoever are you to turn in that stretch of road." I said: "You have the right to kill yourself, but you have no right to endanger other people. Cars just come tearing down there, and it's a frightfully dangerous bit of road."

LANGS: Now, did you expect in the next session to have some repercussions?

LITTLE: I got repercussions straightaway, over the phone. So then I reminded her that at the age of three, she had told me, she went out of her Sunday school and walked home alone, a couple of miles, crossing main roads, without the slightest idea of the dangers involved. And I was in fact talking to her about the situation at her work with her employer and his wife. She was emotionally involved with him, and the wife was very antagonistic, and said "Everything would be all right if it weren't for you." I said: "I'm quite sure that this comes out of your childhood experience, and it doesn't belong rightly to today." This was the point at which I could add the thing about the parking. I had been absolutely shocked when my neighbor told me what she'd seen happening—that she could act so irresponsibly.

LANGS: How do your patients react to such direct intervention?

LITTLE: She was angry and said: "I feel like a naughty little girl that's being scolded, and I don't like it at all." And I said: "No, I know you don't and I'm sorry, but this is the way it is." I went on: "It may *feel* to you as if I were behaving like your parents, but I am not." Her parents had said: "Everything would be all right if it weren't for you." Which is exactly what her employer's wife had said, but *not* what I said.

LANGS: So you interpose a different reality and the importance of reality. How do you think it influences the transference-countertransference sphere, or how would it influence the next session? Do you also follow the indirect material—the derivative response—and interpret them and accept some of these valid unconscious perceptions that they contain?

LITTLE: Well, there's a lot else to influence the next session, but this would certainly turn up, and more than once. With borderline psychotics you find one reality used as defense against another and have to break through it.

LANGS: You would expect it to turn up, and you'd expect to interpret something related to it, wouldn't you, having invoked something of this kind?

LITTLE: Yes. Certainly I did follow and interpret it as much as possible. I had intended not to speak of the car incident until she came again, but she was phoning each morning between sessions because there was a long gap that she was finding very difficult, and she was suicidal. I had insisted that she ring me at nine each morning, and we had twenty minutes on the phone. I found I simply could not refrain from saying this that morning, because I had heard of it the previous day and I was shocked that she could do this and not see the danger; I couldn't risk her repeating it—she might well have been killed.

LANGS: Again, you're talking about what you wrote about; the life-and-death issues that occur with these patients. And you feel that it calls for such measures on your part.

LITTLE: If she turned her car there, she couldn't swing it right around, she had to go halfway, reverse, and then round again, on a double bend. It was all sign-posted: "School, 30 mile an hour limit; Double-Bend, Danger," all this, but people just take no notice of it. I could have had her car and a couple of other cars piled up outside there, mangled corpses on my doorstep!

LANGS: If it were not a matter of life and death, would you have waited?

LITTLE: Yes, probably. I mean it wasn't a matter of life and death immediately, in the sense that she was not coming again for some days. But it would be when she came next, and in fact she did see then "for the first time" two trucks being driven just as I had described, and *she* was shocked. She told me much later that my definitely forbidding her to park or turn her car in this way had been helpful. It did not increase her guilt, but on the contrary relieved her, as I did not reproach her as her parents would have done. And it showed her the danger that she had been missing. But then I was giving her this other interpretation anyway, about the transference aspect of her situation with her employer and his wife.

LANGS: What prompted you to do that on the telephone, rather than in a session?

LITTLE: I think it came straight out of this same thing, because you see, she had just told me in the previous session the story of going home as a three-year-old without any idea of the danger. And I had only just realized that the situation at her work, with the risk of her losing the job, was really a matter of transferences on the part of all three people. And when I had said *this* to her, she had remembered her mother having said: "Everything would be all right if it weren't for you." She had suddenly been made the scapegoat. And I pointed out, you see, that it was not only her own transference but also her employer's and his wife's transferences to each other and to her, as in her childhood it had been her parents', which she could not then have understood. To some extent she was stirring the soup now, as she probably did then, without understanding. She had brought up the subject of the difficulty at work, in her phone call to me that morning.

LANGS: She was also stirring the soup up with you with that.

LITTLE: I interpreted *that* in showing her the mixed-up transferences in the situation, and anyway *my* soup is permanently stirred! Analysis does that. Countertransference and real relationship are both always there. And there is so much immediacy in the analysis of borderline patients. And of course I had stirred her soup. But with regard to the life-and-death issues, I am not only speaking of incidents of this kind, or where suicide or other dangers can arise. I am also speaking of times when it is important *not* to intervene in any way, *not* to "interpret" or even, perhaps, to speak or move. Times when it is all-important for the patient to make his or her *own* move—important for his *psychic* life that he makes some self-affirmation, however slight that may appear. If it is missed out, or goes unrecognized, it may not turn up again for a long while, or even not at all, and a failure that is unnecessary and harmful happens. We fail enough, without that.

This, too, comes out of my own experiences, but with Winnicott (mostly in the early stages of the analysis), rather than Ella Sharpe. I once said that I wished I could have got to him sooner, but he answered that he could not have done my analysis sooner—he would not have known enough.

But short of matters of life and death, I have intervened to protect patients from the possible consequences of their failure to use imagination realistically. More than once I have taken into my garage a patient's car where the driver's license was out of date, which invalidates all insurance, and consequently he could have been involved in enormous expense, as well as legal proceedings. Masud Khan (1960) reports a comparable action when he restored to a shop some books which a patient of his had stolen. Such interventions have to be looked at, of course, in relation to both transference and countertransference. They are usually resented quite bitterly at first, but appreciated later, when they are understood on a more mature level. And they must come from the analyst's mature levels.

LANGS: Do you have some thoughts about analysis today? What you think about it?

LITTLE: I can't really, because I've been so out of touch. When I came to live here [in Kent] in 1971, colleagues were saying: "Can we refer patients to you?" And I was having to say no for health reasons. I had expected to be able to get to scientific meetings in the Society, and I had to accept that it was virtually impossible physically: I mean, a journey to London for me is really quite something. I've only been there about six times since I've lived here. I have had both hip joints replaced, and stairs are difficult. And getting into a London taxi is extremely difficult, and public transport impossible. So I don't undertake it very lightly. When I first moved, colleagues used to come and see me fairly often. But they think I live at the end of the world! Of course, they are busy, and it takes time and energy to come.

LANGS: What about your own work? What are you working on now yourself?

LITTLE: Well, I've got one patient, and there's my book and an occasional consultation. But the work on the book got cut across last January. There was a program on B.B.C. television on bereavement, called "The Long Valley." Dr. Colin Murray Parkes, who has been researching bereavement at the Tavistock and at St. Christopher's Hospice, introduced people that he had interviewed and kept in touch with over a long time; and there had been two or three other programs concerned with bereavement. They all took the same line: "Time heals." "Mourning is for a 'twelvemonth and a day.'"

There was a critique of this particular program in Radio Times by the actress Fay Weldon, who said that the whole of this could have been condensed into a ten-minute talk on the radio, which I felt was true, and I took this up. I said I entirely agreed with what she had said, but I wanted to raise one specific point which I had never come across in any of the programs, which is that, yes, you work through anger, self-pity, and remorse, and so on, until you arrive eventually at a relatively peaceful state of pure grief. But, I said, mourning is *for life*, and every now and then the original thing just jumps up and hits you again and knocks you flat, and for the time being everything else is knocked out.

My letter was published by B.B.C, and I had ten letters in response to it, all thanking me and saying: "I have felt alone, and peculiar, having this happen. Other people have reproached me." And at the same time I had an almost similar thing from two quite separate friends of mine: neither of them having seen or heard any of these programs. Both said that they had suddenly found themselves with the original pain of the loss as bad as it had ever been.

Of course, I had to answer every one of these letters, separately, and individually, and personally. And I found it had hit *me* emotionally, very considerably. Then having done that, I had to write to Dr. Parkes and tell him this, and say that for every *one* who wrote to me—(and they were all very different: from all parts of the country, Inverness in the north of Scotland, and another from Deal in the far southeast; all completely different, in every way, socially, educationally, psychologically, you couldn't imagine a more widely differing group of people)—for everyone who wrote there would have been many more who did *not* write. I had to write this to him and say: "Look, this you left out, and you've got to put it in!" He replied that it is difficult to select what to put in and what to leave out, but I wrote again, saying that when the *same* thing is *always* left out it is not "selected"; it is *overlooked.*

LANGS: Oh, I see; it's that recent. Anything else?

LITTLE: Well, I've had one other patient in therapy. A girl—well, I say a girl, but she is thirty-one—having classical anxiety attacks if she saw a pregnant cow, or a hen lay an egg! I had her once a week for about ten months, I suppose, but for the time being at least I think we have finished. She had tried to deal with her phobia by having a baby, but because she was *so* afraid, she couldn't even tell the hospital people she was frightened. So the experience simply fulfilled her worst fears. It was exactly what she dreaded. She was very good fun to work with, and a creative person. Apart from that, I've been keeping up with several former patients, and I would very much like to get the work with one, in particular, published as a monograph if possible. She came to me for 542 sessions in all, spread over twenty years, with quite long gaps, and has kept in touch with me through the fifteen years since we finished.

The special interest about her is in the paintings which she brought, spontaneously—they are unlike any others that I have seen published in case reports. She turned up suddenly with the first one. In it everything is controlled and fixed, with firm outlines, except for an angry small girl, a "gollywog" (which had been her favorite toy), and a little man with a flying scarf that she "saw" in a picture in my office. (It wasn't there, but she had found it.)

The next one, a month later, scared me stiff. Everything was coming loose at once, and I really didn't know what was happening. I wondered if I was dealing with a full-blown psychosis. And some years later, after about another twenty-five paintings had appeared, she did have a short psychotic episode, during which she painted in her sessions, very much more freely, using her hands instead of a brush, and expressing emotion which had never been reached before.

I have altogether forty of her paintings, mostly done at home, and to me almost every one of them is a dream. It's very rare to see unconscious material laid out directly like that, and one so seldom has a chance to show it. I've shown slides of them several times, here and in the States, and people have found them interesting. For publication I would have to explain the content of each one, with an account of our discussion of them, and if they could not be reproduced I'd have to give a detailed description of each one as well. It means a lot of work!

The kind of painting that she did in her psychotic state is exactly the way that I had found of dealing with my own states of frenzy. The *movement* is the important thing that brings discharge at the climax, and relief follows, as it did with her.

I sometimes do fifteen or twenty wild scribbles in a couple of hours and find perhaps a dozen that seem worth keeping, that other people find interesting. That is, the frenzy is resolved into something creative.

With some patients I use plasticine, or newspaper to tear. Each one has to find his own medium and his own way. I'm just there, through it, and holding—not intervening—but ready to talk about it afterward.

LANGS: I would like to close off the dialogue by asking you one final question. What is your overall perspective on your work? Where does it belong in the historical sense, and what do you feel you have accomplished?

LITTLE: I'd really left the historical side to Dr. Ramana to define in my book because he knew the literature in a way that I don't, and Dr. Flarsheim has taken over from him. I don't think I can really say very much about it beyond what I have said very clearly and distinctly in my papers.

It comes straight out of the classical psychoanalytic tradition, from Freud himself. He was empirical in his work, and I have been empirical. I believe in so being, and I don't think it's off the mainstream at all, though that stream may have branched, and sometimes the branches have converged again, and sometimes not.

LANGS: It's clear to me at least, just focusing on your writings on technique, that your work is an extension of classical analytic thinking. It may be controversial, but that is its wellspring. Your papers on countertransference are not simply confined to that topic; in a way they are on the analytic unity. They offer a very basic approach.

LITTLE: Yes, but if you ask Masud Khan, for instance, about me, he will tell you: "Oh, of course she doesn't know *anything* about theory or metapsychology," and he wouldn't be very far out!

LANGS: Well, yes, you write clinically.

LITTLE: Yes. As for what I have accomplished, the most important thing from my personal angle is having used analysis to become more of my "real self." In the words of an old friend from my G.P. days, "You're not recognizable for the same person," and "You used to wear missionary hats!" Beyond that I've analyzed a number of people, some of whom are now my colleagues; I have done work for our Society and Institute, done some teaching both here and abroad, and writing.

Of course, putting forward something unfamiliar, as I did in 1950 and have done since, is liable to arouse anxiety, and so to be misunderstood and distorted. This need not be due to either resistance, or personal rivalry, or dislike, though they may all come in (and why not?). It may be a difficult concept, or it may be put badly, or in unfamiliar idiom. In any case there is plenty of room for people to find other ways of working. I can talk only about my own way, with my own particular patients. So we're back again to where we started!

What has been most misunderstood has been my reference to expressing my own feelings directly. This is in fact something I very rarely do—not *at all* T. S. Eliot's "undisciplined squads of emotion!" That would be subjective and entirely self-defeating—countertransference in its true sense, coming straight out of childhood.

LANGS: One of the things though that again we didn't mention was your appreciation for the patient's therapeutic intentions toward the analyst.

LITTLE: Yes.

LANGS: Which I think is a very important and neglected topic. Searles (1975) has written a paper recently . . .

LITTLE: Searles has written on that and I found all his papers stimulating and enormously valuable. I tried to stress that in my review of his book in the *International Journal*. I found one particularly valuable in fact not only as far as therapy is concerned, but in everyday life. "Phases of Patient-Therapist Interaction in the Psychotherapy of Chronic Schizophrenia" (1968). One finds these same phases in the formation of ordinary relationships—right now, yours and mine, I expect. People are so apt to think that relationships "just happen," and no doubt sometimes they do, but they usually need to be built up. Whether friendship, marriage, or whatever. And there will be these "confluences" and withdrawals, and ambivalences and resolutions.

LANGS: It is odd that you put it in terms of Searles' work being of so much value to you, since really in a sense you yourself had written much of this before him.

LITTLE: This seems to me to illustrate the rhythm of fusing and separating and fusing again. Being one, *and* separate.

I pointed out in the review the importance of Searles having taken it up. But in the early chapters he was still talking about symbiosis, and symbiosis and basic unity are not the same thing. Symbiosis comes later in development, basic unity being the primary state of total undifferentiatedness—a one-body relationship, whereas symbiosis must be a two-body relationship that is apparently denied. Just toward the end of his book he is beginning to get away from symbiosis, and to move on to basic unity.

LANGS: Something more basic, yes. Of course, that's another area to which you've contributed so much in terms of the study of the borderline patient—and I think even the psychotic patient and delusional transference. Your work in those areas is truly pioneering.

LITTLE: Yes. But to go back to your question about Searles and me and the patient's therapeutic intentions toward the analyst, I spoke a while back about another, still unfinished paper of mine, which belongs in the sequence.

When I was going to Washington, D.C., in 1964, I sent two papers, for the Society to choose which they would like: "Transference in Borderline States" and this other which I called "Transference/ Countertransference in Post-therapeutic Self-Analysis," which I said was experimental, and I felt it in some way incomplete, but couldn't find what it lacked. They chose that, and Searles was the discussant.

He reproached me for having stressed only the importance of one's former analyst, and leaving out the importance of one's patients, quoting the "Basic Unity" paper to me (Little 1960b). At the time I felt he *had* filled the gap for me. But on rereading both the paper and his discussion and my notes of the rest of the discussion (both there and, later, in the British Society) I came to the conclusion that the patients are in fact *very much* there in the "Basic Unity" paper, implicitly at least, as it follows on from the original "Countertransference" paper. For me, any analysis that ends without having brought about or at least started some growth (or healing) in the analyst has by so much failed both people.

And I feel that both the analyst's wish to heal the analysand and the analysand's wish to heal his therapist contain not only the transference and countertransference elements of the old parent/ child situations, but also the present-day one, of two ordinary people, ordinarily wanting to help each other, on a more mature level. In fact, *every* level of *each* partner is in play, *all* the time, in a living analysis, but ebbing and flowing. Something like counterpoint, or an orchestra playing a symphony or concerto, bringing order out of chaos, as Jelly d'Aranyi wrote of music (Macleod 1969). Beethoven's Triple Concerto comes to my mind.

The patient can be wanting to heal his therapist as he wanted to heal his parents. But he has come primarily for healing for himself, his parents are parts of his sum-total self. In the countertransference the therapist wants to heal *his* parents, who are parts of his sum-total self. So we're back to basic unity again, and every psychic restoration of *that* is healing, reaching to the still center.

These things come into self-analysis, but I think what I'm trying to say is that in self-analysis transference and countertransference both fuse and separate out again repeatedly, and they are then concerned chiefly with two things, which are so linked and yet so separate, that *they* become one, and all.

These two things are, first, the problems of ambivalence and paradox; and second, that of the shifting relations between inner, psychic and outer, factual reality. Neither can be the whole of reality—nor perhaps can both together—which is where creativity comes in, for both have to do with creativity.

I can't explain it any further. I have to leave it there, and someone else may take it further—you, perhaps?

But I would like to give you two of my "snippet" quotations. The first is a translation by James Michie (1969) of Catullus' "Odi et amo":

> I hate and love; if you ask me to explain
> The contradiction
> I can't, but I can feel the pain.
> It's crucifixion.

And the other is D.W.W. in a personal letter: "Forgive us our ambivalences, as we forgive. . . ."

LANGS: Any other final thoughts?

LITTLE: I don't think so. I think that's it.

LANGS: I thank you; thank you very much. It has been a most fascinating and stimulating—and warm—experience for me.

LITTLE: And *I* thank you for your interest and encouragement. I'm afraid I've talked too much about my own views and not taken the opportunity of finding yours!

REFERENCES

Aeschylus. *The Oresteian Trilogy.* Transl. Philip Villacott. The Penguin Classics: Theban Plays. New York: Penguin (1959).

Alexander, F. (1954). Some quantitative aspects of psychoanalytic technique. *Journal of the American Psychoanalytic Association* 2:685–701.

Arendt, H. (1963). *Eichmann in Jerusalem.* London: Faber.

Ayrton, M. (1965). *Fabrications.* London: Secker and Warburg.

Balint, A., and Balint, M. (1939). On transference and counter-transference. *International Journal of Psycho-Analysis* 20: 223–230.

Balint, M. (1955). The doctor, his patient and the illness. *Lancet,* No. 1, 2 April 1955, pp. 683–688.

——— (1957). *The Doctor, His Patient, and the Illness.* London: Pitman.

——— (1958). The three areas of the mind. *International Journal of Psycho-Analysis* 39:328–340.

——— (1960). The regressed patient and his analyst. *Psychiatry* 23:231–243.

——— (1968). *The Basic Fault: Therapeutic Aspects of Regression.* London: Tavistock.

Baranger, M., and Baranger, W. (1966). Insight into the analytic situation. In *Psychoanalysis in the Americas,* ed. R. Litman. New York: International Universities Press.

Bibring, E. (1954). Psychoanalysis and the dynamic psychotherapies. *Journal of the American Psychoanalytic Association* 2:745–770.

Bion, W. R. (1958). On arrogance. *International Journal of Psycho-Analysis* 39:144–146.

—— (1959). Attacks on linking. *International Journal of Psycho-Analysis* 40:308–315.

Bradbrook, M. C. (1946). *Ibsen the Norwegian: A Revaluation.* London: Chatto and Windus.

Bronowski, J. (1965). *The Identity of Man.* London: Heinemann, 1966.

—— (1973). *The Ascent of Man.* London: British Broadcasting Corp.

Bukovsky, V. (1978). *To Build a Castle.* London: Deutsch.

Burnet, F. Macfarlane (1962). *The Integrity of the Body.* Cambridge, Mass.: Harvard University Press.

Carroll, Lewis [C. L. Dodgson] (1871). *Through the Looking Glass.* London: Macmillan.

Catullus, Gaius Valerius (1969). *Poems.* Transl. James Michie. London: R. Hart-Davis.

Conolly, C. (Palinurus) (1945). *The Unquiet Grave.* London:Hamish Hamilton.

Dicks, H. V. (1972). *Licensed Mass Murder.* London: Chatto and Heinemann for Sussex University Press.

Dostoevsky, Fyodor (1958). *The House of the Dead.* London: William Heinemann.

Ferenczi, S. (1919). On the technique of psycho-analysis. In *Further Contributions to the Theory and Technique of Psycho-Analysis.* London: Hogarth, 1950.

—— (1928). The elasticity of psycho-analytic technique. In *Final Contributions to the Problems and Methods of Psychoanalysis,* pp. 87–101. New York: Basic Books, 1955.

—— (1929). The unwelcome child and his death instinct. *International Journal of Psycho-Analysis* 10:125–129.

—— (1930). The principle of relaxation and neocatharsis. *International Journal of Psycho-Analysis* 11:428–443.

—— (1930–1932). Notes and Fragments. Trans. M. Little and M. Balint. *International Journal of Psycho-Analysis* 30:231–242, 1949.

—— (1931a). Trauma-analysis and sympathy. In *Final Contributions to the Problems and Methods of Psychoanalysis,* pp. 249–250. New York: Basic Books, 1955.

—— (1931b). Child analysis in the analysis of adults. *International Journal of Psycho-Analysis 12:468–482.*

—— (1933). Confusion of tongues between adults and the child. In *Final Contributions to the Problems and Methods of Psycho-Analysis.* London: Hogarth, 1955.

—— (1955). *Final Contributions to the Problems and Methods of Psycho-Analysis.* London: Hogarth Press.

ffrench-Beytagh, G. (1973). *Encountering Darkness*. London: Collins.

Fordham, M. (1960). Counter-transference. *British Journal of Medical Psychology* 33:1–8.

——— (1977). Analyst-patient interaction. *Journal of Analytical Psychology*.

Freud, A. (1947). *Psycho-Analytic Treatment of Children*. London: Imago.

——— (1954). The widening scope of indications for psychoanalysis. *Journal of the American Psychoanalytic Association* 2:607–620.

Freud, S. (1900). The interpretation of dreams. *Standard Edition* 4, 5.

——— (1905). Fragment of an analysis of a case of hysteria. *Standard Edition* 7:3–123.

——— (1906). Delusions and dreams in Jensen's *Gradiva*. *Standard Edition* 9:3–97.

——— (1910a). Observations on "wild" psycho-analysis. *Standard Edition* 11:219–230.

——— (1910b). Future prospects of psycho-analytic therapy. *Standard Edition* 11:139–151.

——— (1912a). The dynamics of the transference. *Standard Edition* 12:97–108.

——— (1912b). Recommendations to physicians practicing psycho-analysis. *Standard Edition* 12:109–120.

——— (1913). On beginning the treatment. *Standard Edition* 12:121–143.

——— (1914). On narcissism. *Standard Edition* 14:67–102.

——— (1915a). Observations on transference love. *Standard Edition* 12:157–173.

——— (1915b). Instincts and their vicissitudes. *Standard Edition* 14:109–140.

——— (1919a). A child is being beaten. A contribution to the study of the origin of sexual perversions. *Standard Edition* 17:175–203.

——— (1919b). Lines of advance in psycho-analytic therapy. *Standard Edition* 17:157–167.

——— (1920). Beyond the pleasure principle. *Standard Edition* 18:7–64.

——— (1921). Group psychology and the analysis of the ego. *Standard Edition* 18:67–143.

——— (1923). The ego and the id. *Standard Edition* 19:3–66.

——— (1925). An autobiographical study. *Standard Edition* 20:7–75.

——— (1926). Inhibitions, symptoms, and anxiety. *Standard Edition* 20:77–175.

——— (1930). Civilization and its discontents. *Standard Edition* 21:59–145.

——— (1933). New introductory lectures on psycho-analysis. *Standard Edition* 22:3–182.

——— (1937). Analysis terminable and interminable. *Standard Edition* 23:209–253.

——— (1938). An outline of psycho-analysis. *Standard Edition* 23:141–207.

Galatzer-Levy, R. M. (1978). Qualitative change from quantitative change: mathematical catastrophe theory in relation to psychoanalysis. *Journal of the American Psychoanalytic Association* 26:921–935.

Gilbert, W. S. (1882). *The Bab Ballads.* London: George Routledge & Sons.

Gill, M. (1954). Psychoanalysis and exploratory psychotherapy. *Journal of the American Psychoanalytic Association* 2:771–797.

Gitelson, M. (1952). The emotional position of the analyst in the psychoanalytic situation. *International Journal of Psycho-Analysis* 33:1–10.

Goetz (1975). That is all I have to say about Freud. *International Review of Psycho-Analysis* 2:139–143.

Gordon, Seton (1936). *Highways and Byways in the West Highlands.* London: Macmillan.

Greenacre, P. (1953). Certain relationships between fetishism and faulty development of the body image. *Psychoanalytic Study of the Child* 8:79–98.

——— (1954). The role of transference. *Journal of the American Psychoanalytic Association* 2:671–884.

Greenson, R. (1967). *Technique and Practice of Psychoanalysis.* New York: International Universities Press.

Heimann, P. (1950). Dynamics of transference interpretation. *International Journal of Psycho-Analysis* 37:303–310.

——— (1960). Counter-transference. *British Journal of Medical Psychology* 33:9–15.

Hill, L. B. (1955). *Psychotherapeutic Intervention in Schizophrenia.* Chicago: University of Chicago Press.

Hillaby, J. (1973). *Journey through Europe.* London: Constable.

Hoffer, W. (1956). Transference and transference neurosis. *International Journal of Psycho-Analysis* 37:377–379.

Ibsen, Bergliot (1951). *The Three Ibsens.* London: Hutchinson.

Ibsen, Henrik (1866). *Brand.* Transl. F. E. Garrett, 1894. London: Everyman's Library, J. M. Dent.

——— (1867). *Peer Gynt.* Transl. Norman Ginsbury, 1945. London: Hammond, Hammond, and Co.

——— (1899). *When We Dead Awaken.* Transl. Michael Meyer, 1960. London: Rupert Hart-Davis.

——— (1905). *Correspondence,* ed. M. Morison. London: Hodder and Stoughton.

——— (1910). *Speeches and New Letters,* ed. A. Kildal. Boston: Frank Palmer.

——— (1964). *Letters and Speeches,* ed. E. Sprinchorn. New York: Hill and Wang.

Jacobson, E. (1954a). Contributions to the metapsychology of psychotic identifications. *Journal of the American Psychoanalytic Association* 2:239–262.

—— (1954b). Transference problems in the psychoanalytic treatment of severely depressive patients. *Journal of the American Psychoanalytic Association* 2:595–606.

Jones, E. (1953–1957). *Life and Work of Sigmund Freud.* 3 vols. New York: Basic Books.

—— (1957). Pain. *International Journal of Psycho-Analysis* 38:255.

Keats, J. (1816). "On First Looking into Chapman's Homer." In *Poetical Works of John Keats.* Oxford: Clarendon Press.

Khan, M. M. R. (1960). Regression and integration in the analytic setting. *International Journal of Psycho-Analysis* 41:130–146.

King, P. (1978). Affective response of the analyst to the patient's communication. *International Journal of Psycho-Analysis* 59:329–334.

Kipling, Rudyard (1908). *Captains Courageous.* London: Macmillan.

Klee, P. (1898–1918). *Diaries 1898–1918.* London: Peter Owen, 1965.

Klein, M. (1932). *Psycho-Analysis of Children.* London: Hogarth Press.

—— (1934). Contribution to the psychogenesis of manic depressive states. In *Contributions to Psycho-Analysis, 1921–1945.* London: Hogarth Press, 1948.

—— (1935). A contribution to the psychogenesis of manic-depressive states. In *Contributions to Psycho-Analysis, 1921–1945.* London: Hogarth Press, 1948.

—— (1940). Mourning and its relation to manic depressive states. In *Contributions to Psycho-Analysis, 1921–1945.* London: Hogarth Press, 1948.

—— (1945). The oedipus complex in the light of early anxieties. In *Contributions to Psycho-Analysis, 1921–1945.* London: Hogarth Press, 1948.

—— (1952). The origins of transference. *International Journal of Psycho-Analysis* 33:433–438.

—— (1957) *Envy and Gratitude.* New York: Basic Books.

Koht, Halvdan (1904). *The Life of Ibsen.* 2 vols. Transl. Ruth McMahon and Hanna Larsen, 1931. London: Allen and Unwin.

Kramer, M. K. (1959). On the continuation of the analytic process after psycho-analysis. (A self-observation.) *International Journal of Psycho-Analysis* 40:17–25.

Lang, A. (1884). *Ballads & Verses Vain,* New York: C. Scribner's Sons.

Langs, R. (1973). *The Technique of Psychoanalytic Psychotherapy.* Volume I. New York: Jason Aronson.

—— (1974). *The Technique of Psychoanalytic Psychotherapy.* Volume II. New York: Jason Aronson.

—— (1976). *The Therapeutic Interaction.* New York: Jason Aronson.

Leach, D. (1958). Panel report on "Technical aspects of transference." *Journal of the American Psychoanalytic Association* 6:560–566.

Leboyer, F. (1975). *Birth Without Violence.* London: Wildwood House.

Leeuw, P. J. van der (1977). The impact of the Freud-Jung correspondence on the history of ideas. *International Journal of Psycho-Analysis* 58.

Little, M. I. (1951). Counter-transference and the patient's response to it. *International Journal of Psycho-Analysis* 32:32–40. [chapter 2, this volume]

—— (1957). "R"—the analyst's total response to his patient's needs. *International Journal of Psycho-Analysis* 38:240–254. [chapter 3, this volume]

—— (1958). On delusional transference (transference psychosis). *International Journal of Psycho-Analysis* 39:134–138. [chapter 4, this volume]

—— (1960a). Countertransference symposium. *British Journal of Medical Psychology* 33:29–31.

—— (1960b). On basic unity. *International Journal of Psycho-Analysis* 41:377–384. [chapter 6, this volume]

—— (1966). Transference in borderline states. *International Journal of Psycho-Analysis* 47:476–485.

—— (1967). Review of: Searles, H. F. *Collected Papers on Schizophrenia and Related Subjects. International Journal of Psycho-Analysis* 48:112–117.

Macleod, J. (1969). *The Sisters D'Aranyi.* London: Allen and Unwin.

Mahler, M. S. (1968). *On Human Symbiosis and the Vicissitudes of Individuation.* New York: International Universities Press.

Mahler, M. S. et al. (1975). *The Psychological Birth of the Human Infant: Symbiosis and Individuation.* New York: Basic Books.

McFarlane, James, ed. (1970). *Henrik Ibsen, A Critical Anthology.* Harmondsworth, Middlesex: Penguin.

McGuire, W., ed. (1974). *The Freud/Jung Letters.* London: Hogarth Press.

Medawar, P. B. (1957). *The Uniqueness of the Individual.* London: Methuen.

Medawar, P. B., and Medawar, J. S. (1977). *The Life Science.* London: Wildwood House.

Melville, H. (1851). *Moby Dick, or the White Whale.* London: Collins, 1953.

Menninger, W. W. (1968). Introduction to "The psychiatrist's identity crisis: alumni association workshop." *Bulletin of the Menninger Clinic* 32:135–137.

Meyer, M. (1967). *Henrik Ibsen,* 3 vols. London: Hart-Davis.

Milner, M. (1952). Aspects of symbolism in comprehension of the not-self. *International Journal of Psycho-Analysis* 33:181–195.

———— (1977). *Chevauchement des Cercles.* Paris: L'Arc. No. 69.

———— (1978). Mysticism. *Festschrift for Dr. Paula Heimann.* New York: Jason Aronson, in press.

Nacht, S., and Viderman, S. (1960). The pre-object universe in the transference situation. *International Journal of Psycho-Analysis* 41:385–388.

Nunberg, H. (1951). Transference and reality. *International Journal of Psycho-Analysis* 32:1–9.

Orr, D. W. (1954). Transference and Counter-transference: a historical survey. *Journal of the American Psychoanalytic Association* 2:621–670.

Pasternak, B. (1968). *Letters to Georgian Friends,* London: Secker and Warburg.

Pickering, Sir George (1974). *Creative Malady.* London: Allen and Unwin.

Priestly, M. (1975). *Music Therapy in Action.* London: Constable.

Rado, S. (1926, 1928). The psychic effects of intoxication. *International Journal of Psycho-Analysis* 7:396–413, and 9:301–317.

Rangell, L. (1954). Similarities and differences between psychoanalysis and dynamic psychotherapy. *Journal of the American Psychoanalytic Association* 2:734–744.

Reich, Annie (1951). On countertransference. *International Journal of Psycho-Analysis* 32:25–31.

———— (1960). Further remarks on countertransference. *International Journal of Psycho-Analysis* 41:389–395.

Renoir, J. (1974). *My Life and My Films.* London: Collins.

Rosen, J. (1953). Direct analysis. New York: Grune & Stratton.

Rycroft, C. (1962). Beyond the reality principle. *International Journal of Psycho-Analysis* 43:388–394.

Sandler, J., Dare, C., and Holder, A. (1973). *The Patient and the Analyst.* New York: International Universities Press.

Santagana, G. (1920). *Little Essays,* New York: Arno.

Schur, M. (1972). *Freud—Living and Dying.* New York: International Universities Press.

Searles, H. F. (1961). Phases of patient-therapist interaction in the psychotherapy of chronic schizophrenia. *British Journal of Medical Psychology* 34:169–193.

———— (1965). *Collected Papers on Schizophrenia and Related Subjects.* New York: International Universities Press.

Séchehaye, Marguerite A. (1951). *Symbolic Realization.* New York: International Universities Press.

———— (1956). The transference in symbolic realization. *International Journal of Psycho-Analysis* 37:270–277.

le Shan, Lawrence (1976). *How to Meditate. A Guide to Self-Knowledge.* London: Wildwood House.

Sharpe, E. F. (1947). The psychoanalyst. *International Journal of Psycho-Analysis* 28:201–213. Also in *Collected Papers on Psycho-Analysis.* London: Hogarth Press, 1950.

——— (1949). *Dream Analysis.* London: Hogarth Press.

——— (1950). *Collected Papers on Psycho-Analysis.* London: Hogarth Press.

Smith, W. Robertson (1885). *Kinship and Marriage in Early Arabia.* Cambridge: Cambridge University Press.

Solzhenitzyn, A. (1972). The Nobel lecture on literature. Transl. T. Whitney. New York: Harper & Row.

Sophocles (n.d.). *Antigone.* Trans. E. F. Watling. New York: Penguin, (1947).

Spitz, R. (1956). Transference; the analytical setting and its prototype. *International Journal of Psycho-Analysis* 37:380–385.

Stark, F. (1934). *The Valleys of the Assassins.* London: Macmillan.

Stone, L. (1954). The widening scope of indications for psychoanalysis. *Journal of the American Psychoanalytic Association* 2:567–594.

Strachey, J. (1934). On the nature of the therapeutic action of psychoanalysis. *International Journal of Psycho-Analysis* 15:127–159.

——— (1961). Editor's introduction to *Civilization and Its Discontents. Standard Edition* 21:59–63.

Strindberg, August (c. 1887). Prose items from the 1880s. *Samlade Skriften,* vol. 22, 1914.

Tarachow, S. (1962). Interpretation and reality in psychotherapy. *International Journal of Psycho-Analysis* 43:377–387.

Thomas, Dylan. To his father. In *Collected Poems.* London: J. M. Dent, 1952.

Ticho, G. R. (1967). On self-analysis. *International Journal of Psycho-Analysis* 48:308–318.

Traherne, T. (n.d.). The salutation. In *The Oxford Book of Seventeenth Century Verse.* Oxford: Clarendon Press, 1943.

Underhill, E. (1912). *Mysticism.* London: Methuen.

Weigert, E. (1960). Loneliness and trust. *Psychiatry* 23:121–131.

Winnicott, D. W. (1949). Hate in the counter-transference. *International Journal of Psycho-Analysis* 30:69–74.

——— (1950). Aggression in relation to emotional development. In *Collected Papers: Through Paediatrics to Psychoanalysis.* New York: Basic Books, 1958.

——— (1951). Transitional objects and phenomena. In *Collected Papers.* New York: Basic Books, 1958.

——— (1952). Psychoses and child care. In *Collected Papers.* New York: Basic Books, 1958.

———— (1953). Symptom tolerance in paediatrics. In *Collected Papers*. New York: Basic Books, 1958.

———— (1954a). Mind and its relation to psyche-soma. In *Collected Papers*. New York: Basic Books, 1958.

———— (1954b). Primitive emotional development. In *Collected Papers*. New York: Basic Books, 1958.

———— (1955a). The depressive position in normal emotional development. *British Journal of Medical Psychology* 28:89–100.

———— (1955b). Metapsychological and clinical aspects of regression within the psycho-analytical set-up. *International Journal of Psycho-Analysis* 36:16–26. Reprinted in *Collected Papers*. New York: Basic Books, 1958.

———— (1955–1956). Clinical varieties of transference. In *Collected Papers*. New York: Basic Books, 1958.

———— (1956a). On transference. *International Journal of Psycho-Analysis* 37:386–388.

———— (1956b). Primary maternal preoccupation. In *Collected Papers*. New York: Basic Books, 1958.

———— (1958). *Collected Papers: Through Paediatrics to Psycho-Analysis* London: Tavistock.

———— (1960a). Ego Distortion in Terms of the True and False Self. In *The Maturational Processes and the Facilitating Environment*. London: Hogarth Press, 1965.

———— (1960b). Counter-transference. *British Journal of Medical Psychology* 33:17–21.

———— (1960c). The family and emotional maturity. In *The Family and Individual Development*. London: Tavistock, 1965.

———— (1965). *The Maturational Processes and the Facilitating Environment*. London: Hogarth Press.

———— (1969). The use of an object. *International Journal of Psycho-Analysis* 50:711–716. Reprinted in *Playing and Reality,* London: Tavistock, 1971.

———— (1971a). *Playing and Reality*. London: Tavistock.

———— (1971b). *Therapeutic Consultations in Child Psychiatry*. London: Hogarth.

———— (1974). Fear of breakdown. *International Review of Psycho-Analysis* 1.

Zetzel, E. (1956). Current concepts of transference. *International Journal of Psycho-Analysis* 37:369–376.

INDEX

identification
  with patient, 37-42
  psychic and actual views of, 156-
    157
  projective and introjective, 97-98
illness
  addiction to, 238-239
  as attempt at cure, 153
  recovery from, 233-234
  and sex, 12-16
inborn envy, 274-275
incompatibility, 242-243
"Independent Group" (in British
    Psychoanalytical Society)
    275
infant, normal, 172
integrity, 106, 153
interactional view of analysis, 133,
    269, 282-283, 296
interpretation
  of countertransference, 44
  nonverbal, 118, 285-286
  patient's inability to use 75-78, 81
intervention
  contraindicated, 299
  to protect patient, 300
intrauterine state, 115-116

James, M., 275
James, W., 174
jargon, use of, 271, 279
Jensen, W., 88, 96, 119
Jones, E., 87-88, 187
Jung, C.G., 281

Khan, M., 275, 300, 303
King, P., 275
King, T., 98
Kipling, R., 107
Klauber, J., 275
Klee, P., 248, 263

Klein, M., 28, 80, 167, 266-267, 270,
    273-278, 295-296
Kramer, M.K., 132

Lang, A., 258-259
Langs, R., 269-306 *passim*
limits, 60-61
love
  fire and, 19-22
  money and, 17-19

MacLeod, J., 306
magical thought, 139
Mahler, G., 202
Mahler, M., 293
maintenance therapy, 241
de la Mare, W., 121
Medawar, P., 262
Meltzer, D., 155, 295
memory
  body, 85-86, 98, 109
  from prenatal life, 258
Menninger, W., 174
mental health, 167-168
Michelangelo, 200
Michie, J., 306
Milner, M., 167, 275, 284, 290
Milton, J., 209
de Monchy, R., 289
money, and love, 17-19
monism, and dualism, 283
mother
  failure in during oral primacy,
    189
  loss of, 200
mourning, 300-301
movement of infant, 172-175
mutuality, reciprocity and, 163
mysticism, 124
  state of union in, 260-261